# Garden Tools & Gadgets You Can Make

## by Percy W. Blandford

TAB BOOKS Inc.
Blue Ridge Summit, PA

FIRST EDITION
FIRST PRINTING

Copyright © 1989 by TAB BOOKS Inc.
Printed in the United States of America

Library of Congress Cataloging in Publication Data

Blandford, Percy W.
    Garden tools and gadgets you can make.

    Includes index.
    1. Garden tools.   2. Gardening—Equipment and
supplies.   I. Title.
SB454.8.B56   1989         631.3        88-35935
ISBN 0-8306-1494-X
ISBN 0-8306-3194-1 (pbk.)

TAB BOOKS Inc. offers software for sale. For information and a catalog, please contact TAB Software Department, Blue Ridge Summit, PA 17294-0850.

Questions regarding the content of this book should be addressed to:

    Reader Inquiry Branch
    TAB BOOKS Inc.
    Blue Ridge Summit, PA 17294-0214

Acquisitions Editor: Kimberly Tabor
Book Editor: Nina E. Barr

# Contents

**Introduction**                                                                                                    **v**

**1  Craftsmanship**                                                                                                **1**

**2  Wood**                                                                                                          **4**
Nails—Screws—Joints—Edge Joints

**3  Metal**                                                                                                        **15**
Iron and Steel—Nonferrous Metals—Brass—Spelter—Tin and Lead
—Solder—Aluminum—Rivets—Other Metal Fasteners—Conical
Developments

**4  Tool Handles**                                                                                                 **28**
Cutting Wood Handles—Square to Round Handles—Fitting Handles
to a Tool—Metal Handles—Short Handles

**5  Small Hand Tools**                                                                                             **42**
Trowel—Socketed Trowel—Flat Hand Fork—Twisted Tine Fork—
Weeder—Hoe—Onion Hoe—Rake—One-Hand Dutch Hoe—
Dutch Hoe—Push-Pull Hoe—Weeding Hoe—Other Hoe Blade
Shapes—Seed Drill Hoe

**6  Simple Equipment**                                                                                             **70**
Line Winder—Metal Line Winder—Sectional Compost Box—Square
Line—Tool Box—Stacking Seed Boxes—Kneeler—Kneeler/Tool
Carrier—Row Markers—Edges—Bird Protectors

**7   Special Hand Tools**                                                93

Turf Edger—Adaptable Hoe—Simple Tools—Bulb Planter—Ridger
—Thistle Hook—Wood and Nails Rake

**8   Boxes and Bins**                                                    110

Basic Box Variations—Window Box—Plant Pot Container—Nailed
Plant Pot Container—Wall Box—Rod Hanging Pot Holder—Natural
Wood Hanging Pot Holder—Plywood Hanging Pot Holder—Board
Tool Box—Plywood Tool Box—Vertical Tool Locker—Sectional
Compost Cage—Stacking Compost Bin—Permanent Compost Bin

**9   Display Equipment**                                                 147

Wall Shelves—Shelf End Supports—Freestanding Wall Shelves—
Step Support—Slatted Plant Stand—Raised Rustic Trough—Formal
Raised Trough—Paling Pot Container—Take-Down Trough Stand

**10  Climbing Supports**                                                 171

Expanding Wood Trellis—Trellis Supports—Large Arbor—Rose
Arbor—Center Poles Arbor—Supported Arbor—Pergola—Bean
Poles—Tomato Poles—Wire Supports

**11  Carts**                                                             202

Garden Trolley—Cycle Wheels Cart—Tipping Cycle Wheels
Trailer—Wheelbarrow

**12  Buildings**                                                         218

Simple Shed—Playhouse/Shed—Greenhouse

**Glossary**                                                              239

**Index**                                                                 243

# Introduction

**A** GARDEN IS PRIMARILY A PLACE WHERE YOU HOPE THINGS WILL GROW. YOU MIGHT be mainly interested in producing vegetables and fruit. Your inclinations might be more toward flowers and shrubs. You might have enough land to divide into vegetable plots, formal gardens, and informal areas. There could be a large expanse of lawn with borders of flowers, bushes, and trees. At the other extreme, you might have little more than a few potted plants and a window box.

Whatever your form of gardening, you will need tools and equipment, although you might only need just a few tools. Even if your property is so extensive that you must have powered tools to work it, there are many gardening jobs that can only be done with hand tools. The equipment you need will range from such things as handles and boxes, through carts and bins, to a shed and a greenhouse.

Even if you are only an average handyman, you can make many of the items of equipment and tools you need. Although you might not think you have much ability in working with wood or metal, you can complete a large number of useful projects with a minimum of skill and very few hand tools.

If you are more of a workshop enthusiast with extensive equipment, you can make almost all the items you need to be a successful gardener. Besides saving money with everything you make, you can fashion tools to suit your particular needs, as well as get the double satisfaction of combining gardening and craftsmanship. Obviously, there are a few things that cannot be made with the usual home-shop facilities, but you can satisfy nearly all your gardening needs with things you make yourself.

And that is what this book is all about. May you enjoy the combination of successful gardening and satisfaction in your craftsmanship.

**Note:** Unless otherwise indicated, sizes are in inches and they are quoted in descending order of dimensions: length, width, and thickness. It is common to allow a little extra on lengths when obtaining wood.

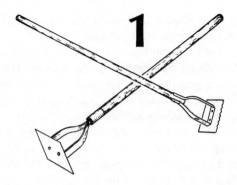

# Craftmanship

**T**HE COMBINATION OF CRAFTS ENTHUSIAST AND GARDENER IN ONE PERSON OPENS UP so many interesting possibilities that you might be carried away with the idea of making your own tools instead of buying them. You could spend all your time in the shop making things and have no time left to go outside and use them. That could happen if you tried to make all the projects in this book, so you have to be selective.

Few of the products require a high degree of skill or very elaborate facilities. What you choose to make depends on your needs, inclinations, shop equipment, and ability to make the best use of what you have. Most beginner craftsmen can tackle basic woodworking. Because many outdoor wood projects are made without cut joints, construction is very easy and can be done with few hand tools. Power tools will help by lessening labor and sometimes increasing accuracy.

It is the working of metal that will worry some readers. A few enthusiastic woodworkers have a prejudice against working in metal. If you have some skill at woodworking, basic metalwork should come naturally. For most projects involving metal, you only have to saw, file, drill, and bend. A substantial metal vise is valuable, but the other tools needed are simple and you might have them already.

Whether or not you should tackle some of the more advanced projects involving metal depends on your facilities for joining parts. If you have welding equipment, almost anything is possible. Without it, you can still make strong joints by *brazing*—using the flame of a propane torch. Easier, although weaker, is soldering. A combination of rivets with brazing can provide good tool strength.

You also must consider if you can work steel in larger sizes. If you are an expert blacksmith, with the facilities that go with the job, you might do such work, but most of us will use only strips and rods. This fact means that using steel for any tools bigger than a hoe are beyond the scope of most of us. Spades, shovels, digging forks, and similar tools should be purchased. You should purchase most mechanical tools, whether hand or power operated.

You can make things that pivot on bolts or rivets and have only a simple action, but if the device has rotating parts as well, you almost certainly will need a metalworking lathe. This fact, and the fact that most machines need special parts that are not always easy to obtain, makes the production of garden machines unsuitable for the majority of metalworking gardeners.

Although most readers will not have a metalworking lathe, more will be able to turn wood. Wood turning is not essential—you can produce acceptable parts without a lathe—but turned parts, where appropriate, give the tool or equipment a better appearance. This fact is particularly true for handles. An attraction for the user of a woodturning lathe is that handles and other parts can be made to exactly fit their needs. This fact is not always true with some manufacturers that use stock handles for a variety of the tools they sell.

An attraction of making your own tools and outdoor equipment is that you are dealing with one-shot projects, made to exactly fit a need. A deck will be exactly the size you want it. A tool shed can fit a space exactly. It can accommodate equipment measured to fit. If you are tall or short, tool lengths can be made to suit.

Overall, you have the satisfaction of knowing that the complete concept is under your control. When laying out the whole or a part of your property, you can make things to suit you, and you suddenly will not find that a purchased seat, shed, gate, or other item will not fit. You make it and it will fit.

You also will have the satisfaction of being able to make things that cannot be bought. For many of the tools described here, there is no store-bought equivalent. You can make tools to suit a particular purpose and need. Those tools offered in a store suit average needs. In many cases, purchased tools are satisfactory, but when you make a tool, it should be right for you every time.

Very low on the list of priorities for a craftsman gardener is economy. The advantages of making things to exactly suit their purpose and the sheer satisfaction of saying, "I made that," outweigh considerations of cost. Usually, of course, the homemade tool is less expensive than the purchased equivalent (if there is one). That is, assuming you are not allowing yourself a wage.

Making individual tools for sale would involve a high-selling price if the scheme is to be viable. With larger projects, there might be no mass-produced item with which to compare. You might find a prefabricated tool shed or seat to compare, but a fence, gate, arch, or other item fitted to its surroundings will not be like anything you could buy. Economically, you will have a very good deal compared with paying someone else to do the job.

Planning is important. Do not rush into making things, particularly large projects, and then find they will not fit or do not match their surroundings. It is helpful to draw a plan of the garden and yard—with the house and other fixtures shown on it—even if your property has a simple, square outline. If the drawing is to scale and you draw additions to scale or cut their outlines to shape on loose paper to move around, you will avoid most mistakes. Even things like widths of paths or gates in relation to wheel tracks of carts to be used need advanced planning. If you are making a shed or tool locker, measure the contents first or you will feel silly having to shorten a handle to get it in.

You already might have some garden tools and equipment. Do these things function as they should? Before rushing into making new tools, you might be able to think of ways of altering or improving existing tools. Even if you decide to make replacements, there might be old parts you can recycle. You can use handles of discarded tools. Also, you often will find a new use for any old, mild, steel strip or rod. Pieces of tool steel are worth saving even if they have not been tools. Springs are tool steel. You can cut sheet mild steel from many discarded domestic appliances.

An advantage of wood that has already been used is that you can assume it is well seasoned. Obviously, if there are signs of rot or worm holes, you will not want to use the wood again, but you can obtain much useful wood from old furniture, crates, and similar things.

In a garden you will probably want to make bins and containers to hold soil or store crops. Although you can use new wood, an assembly of recycled wood can be just as effective. Even plywood with nonwaterproof glue might last several months in dry weather. Another advantage of old wood is that its appearance probably will blend into its surroundings.

If you are an enthusiastic gardener but you live in an area where, for many months of the winter, you cannot work outside, making tools and equipment—prefabricating parts of sheds, seats, fences, and other large projects—can keep your gardening interest alive. When you can work outside again, it will not take long to install your new work and then get on with the serious business of sowing, planting, and all the activities your garden will demand of you.

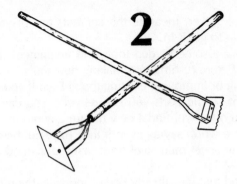

# 2

# Wood

MOST AMATEUR CRAFTSMEN MAKE THINGS FROM WOOD. IT IS ASSUMED THAT YOU have some familiarity with wood and the basic techniques of working it with hand and power tools. Wood is a good choice for making a great many things. It has many applications in tools and equipment for the garden and yard.

Almost any wood has possibilities. You can buy lumber, you can recycle wood that has been used in some other construction, or you can cut and convert wood growing on your own land.

Woods are divided into hardwoods and softwoods. The names are not strictly true definitions because the differences are botanical, rather than descriptions of relative hardness. The majority of hardwoods are harder than most softwoods. The available softwoods are mostly firs, spruces, and pines. Some softwoods are not durable, but if they are resinous, they have a longer life. You can assume that most hardwoods, such as oak, last longer than softwoods. Hardwoods tend to be heavy. For tools where lightness is important, it would be advisable to choose softwood and accept the fact that it will not last as long. You can protect softwood by using paint and preservative on it and by storing it inside when not in use.

Wood straight from the tree contains a considerable amount of moisture in the form of sap. There is less sap if the tree is felled in the winter, but there is still more than is acceptable for anything except rough construction. If you are planning rustic work where stability of the wood is not important, you can start your project immediately. For anything else, dry the wood to a small moisture content by the process called *seasoning*. If wood is not seasoned, it will shrink and warp after being built into something, and it might develop lengthwise shakes (cracks).

Natural seasoning is done by stacking boards in a sheltered place, where air can circulate, and then leaving them for some time (1 year for each 1 inch of thickness is appropriate). Commercially, faster methods of seasoning exist. Lumber bought from a regular supplier should be seasoned correctly. Even then, it is a good idea to buy well ahead of your needs and keep the wood for perhaps 2 months before using it. Then you can see if the wood will retain its shape and size.

Softwoods are sold in standard sections so it is advisable to plan projects to suit them. Everyone knows about 2 × 4s, but there are many other sizes. With hardwoods, it is advisable to check what sections your supplier has, rather than present him with a cutting list of different sections. Otherwise, he will charge you extra. Of course, if you have your own power saw of sufficient capacity, you could buy economical larger sections and cut them down yourself.

Wood typically is sold in the quoted sawn size. Although 2 inches × 4 inches might be the true sawn size, a planed 2 × 4 will actually be 1⅞ inch × 3⅞ inch (or less). You should allow for that difference in your projects. Several outdoor projects can be made with wood that has not been planed. An advantage of buying planed wood is that you are able to see better any flaws quickly, rather than discover them later.

Natural wood, either round as it comes from the tree or just split down the middle, has many uses in the garden for making fences, arches, and similar items. You can make even smaller plant containers or other more compact constructions with small pieces of poles or branches.

You must decide first whether to use the wood with its bark on or to strip the bark off. Most fir, spruce, and similar softwoods tend to shed their bark as they dry and shrink. What might look attractive when first constructed eventually could take on an untidy appearance where some bark is retained and some has fallen off. That type of wood is better stripped of its bark before making it into a project.

Some woods have bark that is held very securely. You can leave it, but in general, it is better to remove bark. Insects and other pests tend to gather between bark and wood. It is better for the life of the wood, and possibly for things growing nearby, to strip the poles or branches down to the wood.

Plywood has many uses in outdoor construction. Make sure you get the type bonded with a waterproof glue, which is described as *exterior* or *marine* grade. The latter is more expensive and not usually necessary.

Veneers mainly affect appearance. For something like a compost container, the lowest veneer category might be just as useful as the more costly, higher-quality plywood. If your project is a piece of patio furniture, the better-looking, high-grade plywood is preferable.

Hardboard is not suitable for outdoor use. Even the oil-tempered kind will not stand up to weather for long. Particleboard and some of the other manufactured boards might have exterior uses, but check what the manufacturer says about specific grades. In general, you are more likely to be satisfied with solid wood and the appropriate plywood for exterior work.

Not so long ago, joints in exterior woodwork required mechanical fasteners because there were no glues that would stand up to moist conditions indefinitely. Otherwise, there had to be wedges or interlocking joints. All of these techniques are still used, but there are modern, fully waterproof glues that will make secure joints unaided or to complement mechanical fasteners. Some of these glues require two parts to be mixed together before use or applied separately to the surfaces before bringing them together. Others are one-part glues. Unfortunately, trade names do not always give you a clue to the chemical content. If the glue is a two-part product or described as suitable for boats, it should be fully waterproof and strong enough.

## NAILS

Many wooden items for use in the garden or yard are nailed together, which is quite satisfactory for most assemblies. Usually, there is not much to worry about, providing you use sufficient nails of sufficient length.

Common nails are made from round wire. These nails and the similar "box" nails are suitable for most garden carpentry. They are made of mild steel which will rust, so it is advisable to buy them protected with zinc or other coating. Available lengths are from 1 inch to 6 inches, with increases in diameter to suit. They are sold by penny(d) sizes, from 2d for a 1-inch nail through 6d for a 2-inch nail, and 20d for a 4-inch nail to 60d for a 6-inch nail.

If you are joining two pieces of wood, it is the amount of nail in the lower piece that provides strength. Therefore, you must choose a nail that will penetrate sufficiently. How much penetration is needed is more a matter of experience than a matter of rule, but you need a greater length in softwood than in hardwood and more in end grain than in side grain.

For many assemblies, you can drive nails without drilling, but it might help you to drill the top piece to the same size as the nail diameter. Drilling makes it easier to drive the nail into the wood and reduces any tendency for the top piece to split. It also is advisable near an edge—even if you drive without drilling further along.

You can increase the strength of a nailed joint by dovetail nailing (Fig. 2-1A), with alternate nails sloping opposite ways. You can increase strength in the joint by placing end nails closer together (Fig. 2-1B).

With thin wood, you might only be able to get sufficient strength by taking a nail through and clenching its point. This procedure also will provide a pivot if two parts have to move on each other. An example is a trellis that will fold when not required to be opened out. The best way to clench is to drive the nail through, with enough point projecting (Fig. 2-1C), and then curve the point over a spike while supporting the other side on an iron block (Fig. 2-1D). While still supporting the other side, bury the point diagonal to the grain (Fig. 2-1E), rather than along the grain (which might start a split).

## SCREWS

You can describe screws as *wood screws* to distinguish them from *metal-thread* screws, which are used with nuts. Screws provide a more positive fastening than nails, with joints that are pulled closer and stronger. It is also easier to withdraw a screw with less risk of damage to the wood. Screwed construction is considered superior to nailing and is preferred for better work.

Several types of screws are available, but for most purposes, flat-headed ones are appropriate (Fig. 2-2A). Round-head screws are the only other kind you might

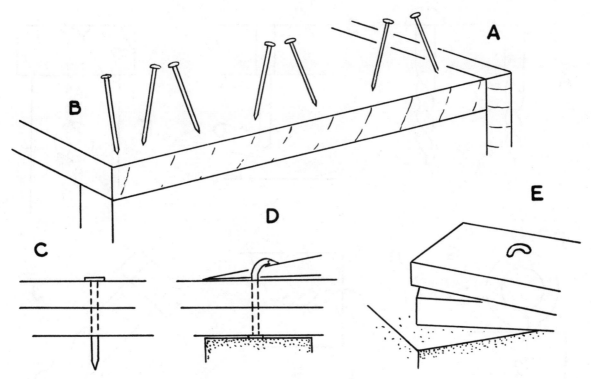

Fig. 2-1. *You can increase the strength of a nailed joint if you drive the nails in a dovetail fashion. With thin wood, a nail will go through and you can clench it.*

need (Fig. 2-2B). The kinds with slotted heads for a common screwdriver are all you need. Other types with socket heads really are intended for quantity production and require special screwdrivers.

Screws are described by their length from the surface of the wood and are obtainable in several gauge thicknesses for each length. In small sizes, there are single-gauge number differences, but in lengths from about 1½ inches up, your supplier will probably only have even-numbered gauge sizes. Table 2-1 shows the most-used screw sizes.

Common screws made from mild steel can be bought protected from rust by various platings. They might be made of brass, which has a good resistance to moisture, or one of several other metals that usually are more costly but also have a good resistance to corrosion.

The threaded part of a screw is about two-thirds of its length. It is the pull of this thread in the lower piece of wood that draws the top piece tightly down. Nothing is gained by having the screw fit tightly in the top piece.

There should be a clearance hole for the shank of the screw in the top piece (Fig. 2-2C). If that wood is thin and part of the parallel shank enters the lower piece, you could also take the clearance-size drill a little way into that. Otherwise, the plain shank forcing its way there might lift fibers on the surface and interfere with the joint pulling tight. With a small-diameter screw in softwood, you can start

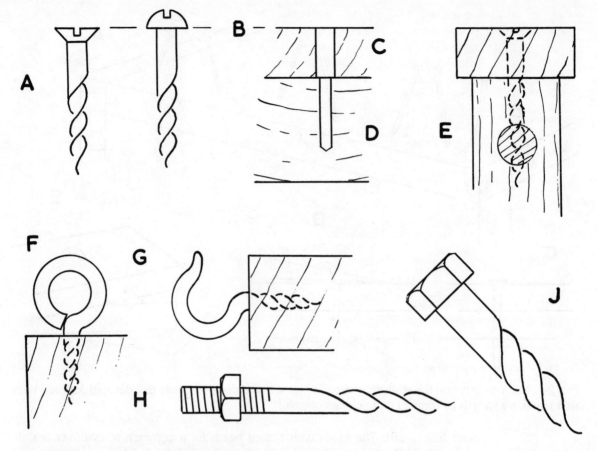

Fig. 2-2. Wooden screws need holes (A-D) and you can use a dowel to strengthen them in end grain (E). Other parts can have screw ends (F-J).

Table 2-1. Common Screw Sizes.

| Length (inches) | Gauge sizes available |
|---|---|
| 1 | 6, 8, 10 |
| 1¼ | 8, 10, 12 |
| 1½ | 8, 10, 12 |
| 2 | 8, 10, 12, 14 |
| 2½ | 10, 12, 14 |
| 3 | 14, 16, 18 |
| 4 | 16, 18, 20 |

the screw in the lower piece with a tap from a hammer and let it cut its own way in as you turn it. In most cases, it is better to drill an undersized hole in the lower piece (Fig. 2-2D). In softwood, it need not be as large nor go as far as a hole in hardwood.

With many woods, a flat head will pull itself in flush with the surface. With harder wood, you can use a countersink bit to prepare the hole. Even then, it is advisable to only partly countersink to allow for some pulling in. Round heads are used more often to hold metal to wood, but otherwise, it is worthwhile to put a washer under the head to spread the load and increase pressure.

Screws generally are stronger than nails so they can be spaced more widely, but there still should be a good penetration of the lower wood and a greater length allowed in end grain. You can install screws closer to an edge. For an assembly like a box corner, you could use a screw for strength near the open top, and still use nails in the joint further down.

The grip in end grain is much less than in cross grain, particularly in some softwoods. You can improve the grip by putting a dowel across so that the screw goes through its cross grain (Fig. 2-2E).

Wood screw ends are provided in some other applications. Screw eyes (Fig. 2-2F) have uses in many outdoor projects, such as hanging containers. Several sizes and forms of screw hooks are available (Fig. 2-2G) that have obvious applications. Less obvious is the hanger screw or bolt (Fig. 2-2H). You would use this screw or bolt where you want to drive a wood screw—usually because you cannot take a bolt right through—and then attach a metal part. To drive a hanger bolt, tighten two nuts on it against each other, and then use a wrench on the top nut to turn the screw into a hole in the wood. Release the nuts by using two wrenches.

Very large, thick screws would be very difficult to turn tight with an ordinary screwdriver. Therefore, lag screws or coach screws (Fig. 2-2J) have heads to take wrenches. You must start them by hammering into the top of an undersized hole.

## JOINTS

For much exterior woodwork, it will be sufficient to put one piece of wood over another and either nail or screw them together. In some constructions, such as seats and tables, you will have to make the joints more like those for interior furniture. Even then, some variations are advisable to suit the exterior situation.

If you want to positively locate one part over another, even if the fastening is to be a nail or screw, it is helpful to notch one of the pieces (Fig. 2-3A). Notch both pieces if accuracy of location is needed both ways. Notching is helpful to retain symmetry even with rustic poles. The notches can be quite shallow.

If parts have to cross at the same level, whether square to each other or not, you must cut a halving joint (Fig. 2-3B). This cut weakens the wood. If you can cross without bringing surfaces to the same level, the notches can be shallower and the wood stronger.

Dowel construction is possible for some things, but you are then dependent upon only glue. It is better to build in some mechanical strength, which is done more easily with mortise-and-tenon joints. If the ordinary mortise-and-tenon joint

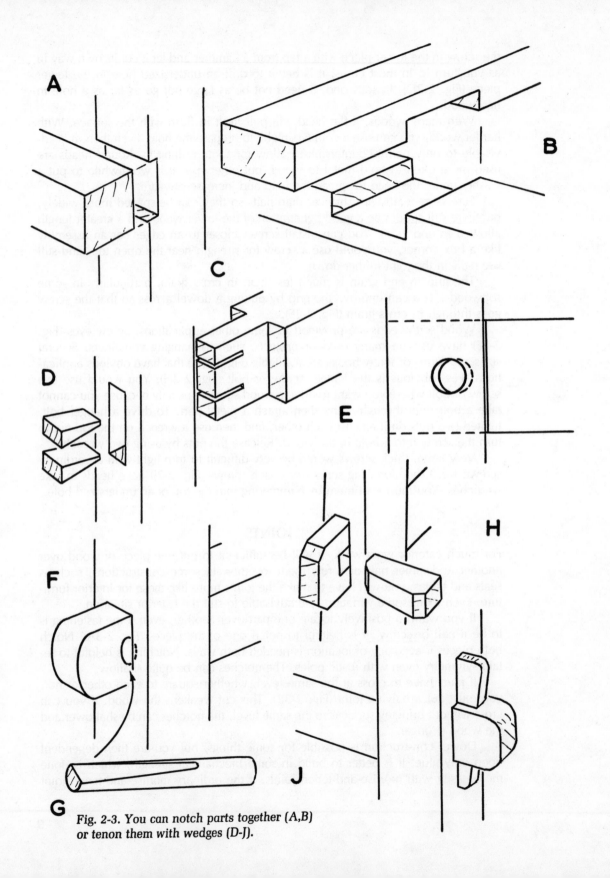

Fig. 2-3. You can notch parts together (A,B)
or tenon them with wedges (D-J).

has the tenon right through (Fig. 2-3C), you can make one or two saw cuts across the tenon end and drive wedges into this end (Fig. 2-3D). Do so with the wedges in the direction that expands the wood of the tenon toward the end grain of the mortised part.

A good way of coupling mechanical and glued strength is to draw-pin a mortise-and-tenon joint. For large seats and similar items, where it would be difficult to use clamps, draw-pinning pulls joints together. Cut a mortise-and-tenon joint and then drill across the mortised part, either central or toward the side where the tenon shoulder will come. In the tenon, mark and drill a similar hole, but slightly toward the shoulder (Fig. 2-3E). How far you move this hole depends on the wood, but 1/8 inch is probably right for a 1/2-inch hole. Taper the end of a dowel rod longer than the thickness of the wood. Glue the parts and fit them together. Drive in the tapered dowel to pull the joint tight, and then cut off the extending tapered and top parts.

Another way to tighten a mortise-and-tenon joint is with external wedges through what are called *tusk tenons*. These external wedges can also serve as decorations. In its simplest form, let the end of the tenon extend, and drill a hole across the piece that will have its edge below the surface of the other part (Fig. 2-3F). Plane a taper on the side of a dowel that fits the hole in order to make a wedge (Fig. 2-3G), and drive the wedge through the hole with the flat surfaces together. This procedure pulls the tenon tighter into its mortise. You can shape the end of the tenon and cut the dowel so it projects evenly after driving.

A wedge with a rectangular section might look better than a tapered dowel. The important thing is to cut the slot for the wedge so its inner edge is below the surface of the mortised part. This way, the wedge forces outward against the wood of the tenon. The slot should taper to match the wedge (Fig. 2-3H), which can have decorated ends.

It might be better in some constructions to have the wedge the other way through the tenon (Fig. 2-3J). In all of these wedged tenons, there is a considerable thrust on the end grain. It is advisable to only use the method on compact hardwoods and then to allow adequate wood outside the slot.

Variations on these and other joints are described in this book with the particular projects to which they apply. For most exterior woodwork, simpler joints are preferable to some of the more complicated ones appropriate to indoor construction.

## EDGE JOINTS

For some outdoor projects it is necessary to join pieces of wood to make up a sufficient width. Where a wide board is available, it is usually preferable to use it, but there might be a risk of warping and that is often counteracted by different grain patterns in several boards joined to make up a comparable width. If you are buying wood, the wide pieces might be disproportionately more costly because of their rarity.

Gluing is the obvious way to join boards edge to edge. Modern waterproof glues should be as successful outdoors as indoors, providing the wood has been

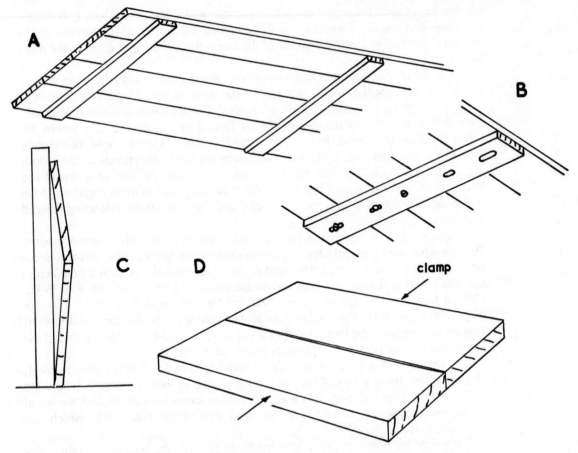

Fig. 2-4. A wide top can have the boards held with strips across (A,B). Check edges for gluing to be sure they are square (C), and a slight hollow helps in clamping tightly (D).

seasoned to only a small moisture content. No glue can be very effective on wood containing an excess of water. If the wood is unsuitable for gluing, it is still possible to make a mechanical joint that will be satisfactory in many outdoor situations. Even with simple glued joints, there might be a problem in an assembly that has to stand up to all the rigors of year-round exposure. The glue line might hold, but wood fibers nearby might fail. Therefore, it would be advisable to do more than merely glue surface to surface.

For many assemblies, you can join strips with cleats or battens across at the back or underneath (Fig. 2-4A). You can nail or screw these pieces. If you are putting together wide objects that might have to withstand rain and sunlight, allow for expansion and contraction. This allowance will apply to a door or tabletop, possibly 30 inches wide, when a ¼-inch alteration in total width is expected at different seasons.

You can take care of the variations by slot screwing. If you must allow for equal expansion, use round holes for central screws. Place them farther out in slots

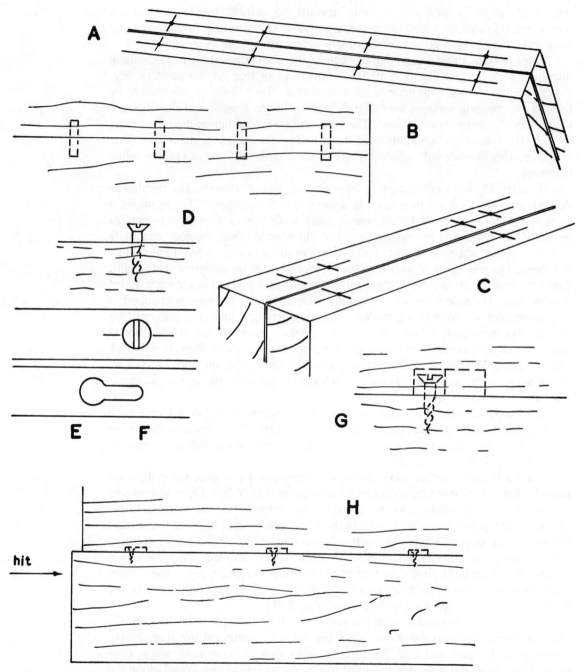

Fig. 2-5. You can dowel edge joints (A,B) or hold them together with secret slot screws (D-H).

(Fig. 2-4B) up to ¼ inch long or more, toward the outside. If it is an assembly where one side should remain unaltered, put screws at that side in round holes and have the others in slots getting progressively longer toward the other side.

If dry wood is to be glued edge to edge, plane both edges straight. Place them together to make sure that they will not finish out of true on the surfaces (Fig. 2-4C). Trouble comes with ends of joints opening. You can avoid this trouble by making the meeting surfaces very slightly hollow in the length, and then using a central bar clamp to close the joint. The ends will be forced tighter than the center (Fig. 2-4D). If several edge joints make up a width you are using, make them one at a time. This practice will reduce the risk of the boards buckling out of true while clamping.

If you want increased strength in an end joint, include dowels. The number of dowels you will need and their spacing depends on circumstances. For example, a joint in a tabletop made of 1-inch boards might have ⅜-inch dowels at 6-inch intervals. Care is needed in marking out. Put the planed edges together and mark across, and then gauge from what will be the top surfaces (Fig. 2-5A). Drill slightly too deep. Dowels going 1 inch into each piece should be sufficient (Fig. 2-5B). Taper the ends of the dowels so they will enter easily. A saw cut along each dowel is worthwhile because it lets air and surplus glue escape as the joint is clamped.

Secret slot screwing is a good way of strengthening a joint and pulling it together. This procedure is just as suitable for outdoor as indoor woodwork. Secret slot screwing is intended for use with glue, but even without glue, it will lock edges together in addition to battens or in place of them. This method uses screws in one edge, with their heads projecting into slots in the other piece. Careful marking out is essential.

For boards about 1 inch thick, suitable fasteners are steel screws 1 inch by 8 or 10 gauge. If you are using hardwood, choose thicker screws because they have to resist bending. Space the screws according to the strength needed, but 6-inch intervals will probably be satisfactory.

Put the boards together and mark hole positions as if you were using them for dowels. Then mark more hole centers ½ inch away (Fig. 2-5C). Drive screws into the board with single-hole positions, going far enough in to bury the threads. Leave about ¼ inch projecting (Fig. 2-5D). In the other board, drill holes at the second position, large enough to clear the screw heads (Fig. 2-5E). At the points opposite the screws in the other board, drill holes large enough to clear the neck of the screws. All of the holes should be slightly deeper than the projection of the screws. Make slots from the small holes into the larger ones. You can drill some of the waste away and true the slots with a chisel (Fig. 2-5F).

Bring the boards together with the screw heads in the large holes (Fig. 2-5G). Hit one board along so the screw head cuts its way along the slot (Fig. 2-5H). Knock it back again and coat the surfaces with glue. Tighten each screw one-quarter of a turn and assemble the joint again. As you drive one board along the other, the joint should pull very tight.

Brass screws might seem more suited to outdoor use, but they might bend during tightening, except in very soft wood. The screws are buried and protected with glue, so there is little risk of steel rusting.

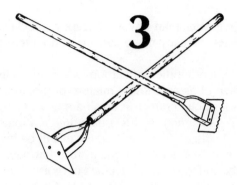

# 3

# Metal

**B**ASIC METALWORK IS AS INTERESTING AND LESS DIFFICULT THAN WOODWORKING.
You can do a considerable amount of metalwork with hand tools. For most of
the projects described in this book, you will not need power tools, other than an
electric drill.

Many tools and equipment for the garden and yard combine wood and metal.
This combination offers some interesting work, and probably a greater satisfaction
to the maker than something in wood or metal alone. A knowledge of metals and
alloys helps in selecting suitable material, and knowing about the effects of heat
treatments gives you scope for interesting constructions. This chapter describes
some general metalworking techniques. More specific techniques are described
where they apply to particular projects.

## IRON AND STEEL

Most tools for garden and farm have their principal parts made of what is loosely
termed "iron." Iron is a convenient general term, but it is not strictly correct any
more than talking of a "tin" roof. Tin is a fairly valuable metal, and a roof made of
it would be very expensive. The roofing material is really iron coated with zinc.
This combination has a good resistance to corrosion. Tin is used as a very thin protective coating on iron for cans and other items because it is safe in contact with
foodstuffs. Tin is not used on roofs.

Pure—or almost pure—iron is rare today. Blacksmiths search for it because of
the ease with which they can work it. Now they have to be satisfied, usually, with
mild steel. Cast iron is a form of iron, often with many impurities, that you can
melt and pour into a mold. It is of use when you must cast a part. It is unsuitable
for working in bar and strip and cannot be made into sheets. Since the heat needed

to melt iron to be cast is greater than anyone except a specialist worker would want to use, cast iron (except as ready-made parts) is of no interest to the maker of land tools.

Steel is iron containing a proportion of carbon (which alters iron's characteristics). It is sometimes spoken of as an *alloy*, a mixture of metals, but, as carbon is not a metal, the term is not strictly correct. A small amount of carbon in iron does not have much effect on it. Such *mild steel* is usually inferred today when "iron" is used. Mild steel is not as ductile as pure iron, but it can still be bent and shaped or forged to a sufficient degree. Steel is more prone to rust that pure iron.

Rust is oxidation of the surface due to the effect of moisture in the atmosphere. The corrosion is a layer of ferrous (meaning iron) oxide. On pure iron, the first corrosion is slight. This first corrosion forms a skin that restricts further corrosion. On steel, corrosion will go on progressively if unchecked by protective coatings. This protective coating could be a coating of other metal with a good resistance to corrosion, painting, or wiping occasionally with oil or grease (which is the most usual treatment for outdoor tools).

Anything that does not have to be cut can be made satisfactorily with mild steel, sometimes termed *low-carbon steel*. With an increased amount of carbon, the steel will accept heat treatment so that it can be hardened and tempered (the dual treatment for giving it the required hardness) or *annealed* (which brings it to its softest state). This steel is *high-carbon* or *tool steel*. You can heat treat straight-forward-tool steel, which is made into many tools, satisfactorily with the facilities available to most craftsmen or the operators of small shops. There might not be the precision that is available for heat treating at a large manufacturing plant, but simple methods and approximate temperatures should give a satisfactory result.

Today, a large number of steels with other metals alloyed are available to give special characteristics, including stainless and nonmagnetic. Unfortunately, these steels require careful temperature control when heat treating and, therefore, are unsuitable for most makers of individual tools. When you require something harder than mild steel, the choice should be straight-tool steel.

For practical purposes, nothing you do to mild steel will affect the characteristics noticeably. You can hammer it, bend it, drill it, machine and forge it to different shapes, and its characteristics will still be the same.

## Hardening

If you heat tool steel to redness and cool it rapidly in water, it will be hardened. It is then as hard as it can be. Unfortunately, it is also brittle. If it is given a cutting edge, it will crack or splinter if you try to use it. If you drop the tool, it might break. Metal-cutting files are left fully hard, or almost so, but this state would be unsuitable for other tools.

## Annealing

If you heat tool steel to redness and let it cool extremely slowly, it will be annealed to the softest state. New tool steel might be annealed fully and described so by the makers. If you want to anneal tool steel yourself, the best way is to heat it in a fire and leave it to cool overnight with the fire. If you heat it with a blow-lamp flame, surround it with coke or other fuel, so that you heat it as well, and then leave it all to cool. Annealing is important if you want to machine or drill the steel. In any state, but not fully annealed, you would blunt the drill and probably not make a hole. The drill is also tool steel; you cannot expect it to cut through something as hard as itself. Today, drills are usually alloyed with other metals to give increased toughness, but they still cannot cut through unannealed tool steel.

## Tempering

For most of the things we want, the final hardness of the steel has to come between the fully-hardened and fully-annealed states. By reducing some of the hardness, the tendency to brittleness is also reduced. The required hardness for a particular tool is found by tempering, which is done after hardening. You must heat the steel to redness and then quench it to harden it. Again heat it to a certain temperature, which varies according to the intended use, then quench it again.

If we had to measure the temperature, most of us with limited equipment would have difficulty. Fortunately, colored oxides form on the smooth, bright surface of tool steel at definite temperatures. By watching the formation of these oxides and quenching at the right moment, you can get the correct temper without special equipment. The oxides will still be there after quenching; you can check results. Remember, the oxides are only a clue to temperature. You can get the same colors on mild steel, but that does not mean you have done anything to the hardness of the metal. When you are dealing with tool steel, it is only the part that was previously brought to redness in hardening that will be tempered. Nevertheless, you will see the oxide colors on other parts.

The oxide colors come in rainbow formation in a definite sequence. You can see them on a clean, polished surface. Heating to harden takes away the polished effect. If you start with a bright surface, you can rub it bright again, after heating and quenching, by using emery cloth or a piece of sandstone.

To familiarize yourself with the colors, have a length of flat steel available, perhaps 12 inches long, with one surface rubbed bright. Hold it by one end and heat it near the middle with a flame. Once colors begin to appear, withdraw the steel from the flame and only return it briefly, if necessary, until the whole set of colors spread from the heated part. If you keep the heat to the minimum necessary, each band of color will widen as it spreads so you get a better idea of the color sequence and the way the colors blend into each other. Overheating, or quick heating, will produce much narrower bands of color. The sequence of colors and their shades, with examples of tools that are tempered to those colors, is shown in Table 3-1.

Annealing should be done before working on the steel. Then you usually completely make the tool before hardening and tempering it.

As a practical example of hardening and tempering, make a screwdriver from a piece of ¼-inch round tool steel. If it is newly-annealed steel, file the taper at the end (Fig. 3-1A). If you prefer an awl, you could make a point. At the other end, file a square point for driving into a handle. Brighten the working end with abrasive. If

## Table 3-1. Tempering Colors.

| Color of oxide | Tools |
|---|---|
| Light yellow | Files |
| Yellow | — |
| Dark yellow | Chisels |
| Brown | Shears, scissors |
| Dark brown | Knives, punches |
| Brown/purple | Axes |
| Light purple | Hoes, spades |
| Dark purple | Saws |
| Blue | Screwdrivers, springs |

you do not know if the steel has been annealed, your first attempts at filing will show you. If you cannot file, do not continue, because that would ruin the tool. Anneal the steel before going further.

Heat the screwdriver end to redness for a distance of up to 1 inch and quench it in water. Lower it vertically into the water (Fig. 3-1B). If the tool goes in sideways, the slight unevenness of quenching might cause cracking. The end is now hardened and brittle; treat it gently. Brighten all of that end with emery cloth or other abrasive.

Use a blow-lamp flame to heat the rod a few inches back from the end (Fig.

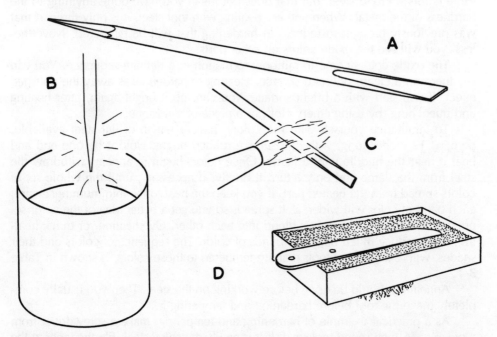

Fig. 3-1. A screwdriver end is hardened and tempered with a flame (A-C). You can heat a blade on sand (D).

3-1C). Watch the oxide colors form. They will spread outward. The colors that go away from the working end are of no consequence. Keep the heating to a minimum once the colors form so that they spread in wide bands. When the blue color reaches the end, again quench the steel vertically in water. If you are satisfied that you have the right color at the end, clean off the colors and the whole tool with emery cloth, and fit a handle.

If you make a mistake and quench too late or too early, you must go back to hardening again before making another attempt at tempering. This method works with any pointed tool or even one with a broad end, like a chisel. You can harden and temper a chisel for cutting rock or metal or deal with the end of a pick ax or other end-cutting tool.

If you work quickly, it is possible to harden and temper such a tool end with one heating. Heat the end to harden it, as just described, but when you quench the red hot end, do not plunge the whole tool into water. Immerse enough to cool the red end and a little further, leaving plenty of heat still in the bar a few inches from the end. Quickly rub the end, and a few inches back, bright with abrasive and watch for the oxide colors coming along from the hot part. When you get the correct color on the end, immerse the whole tool endwise, and it will be correctly tempered.

If you want to harden and temper a larger area—as would be necessary for the cutting edge of a knife, hoe, or other tool with a long or broad edge—you have to adopt a different method because local heating would give a patchy result. It might be possible to fan a blow-lamp flame over an area to get the degree of temper, but that is a chancy method.

For a piece of plate steel or other tool, such as a knife blade that is broad and not very thick, clean it bright, and then heat it just to redness as evenly as possible over the part that includes the cutting edge, to harden it. Quench it quickly and clean it bright again.

Have a tray of sand ready. It should be a metal container which is larger than the metal to be heated for tempering, and the sand should be about ½ inch thick. Put this container over a flame to drive out moisture in the sand. Put the steel on the sand (Fig. 3-1D) and heat from below. The sand will spread the heat fairly evenly. At first you could immerse the steel in the sand to quicken its heating, but once the sand and steel get warm, have the steel on top and watch as oxides form. Once they begin to appear, they will change quickly. Be prepared to act as soon as you see the color you want. Use pliers or tongs to lift the steel and drop it in the water. If you get it wrong, you must go back to hardening again before trying tempering a second time.

There is obviously a limit to the size of the tool that you can harden and temper by these methods. Many garden and farm cutting tools are within the practical range. If a tool part needs to be stronger than could be expected with mild steel, it is possible to use tool steel satisfactorily without hardening and tempering it. When you need a cutting edge that will last, hardening and tempering are essential. Tools that have to cut wood and metal as well as tools to cut hay and other crops are obvious examples. For a tool such as a garden hoe that only has to cut soil, you can expect a reasonable life from an untreated blade. You can revive its edge by filing.

# NONFERROUS METALS

Most metals used in garden and yard tools are varieties of steel. Others (described as nonferrous, because they lack iron) have different uses. The term *metal* is applied loosely to alloys as well as pure metals. None of the other common metals are as strong as steel, but most of them are easier to work and have better resistance to corrosion.

Copper is a soft, reddish metal that is now rarely used without being alloyed to other metals. Many people have used copper for pipes because it suits their manufacture, and copper pipes are easily bent. The only way that copper can become hard is by work hardening. If it is hammered, rolled, or otherwise worked, it could reach a stage where it gets hard. If nothing is done about it, it will crumble and crack. You can anneal it by heating to redness, and then by either cooling quickly or slowly. To a certain extent, it will age harden if left as is, but in the annealed state, it is very ductile.

You can hammer sheet copper into deep bowl shapes, but you will have to anneal it many times in the process. If something made of sheet copper is to be brought to maximum hardness after you have reached the desired shape, you must *planish* it (hammer all over), while supporting it on a stake or anvil, so you squeeze the metal at each blow between the hammer and the supporting steel surface.

Zinc is a metal that seldom is used alone today. It is a drab, grey color and difficult to polish. At one time, it was used for kitchen utensils because of its considerable resistance to corrosion and the ease with which you could solder it. You can still obtain perforated zinc sheets. They had much use in pioneer days for food storage cabinets, before the days of refrigeration, as they let cooling draughts through but kept flies out.

## BRASS

Zinc is alloyed with copper to make brass. The quality and characteristics of the resulting alloy depend on the proportions of the two base metals. In any case, the result is yellow: paler if the zinc proportion is high and more golden if there is more copper. Sheet brass is made with a fairly high copper content, and you can work and anneal it in the same way as copper (although it is never as soft or ductile). Brass takes a good polish to produce an attractive appearance. Brass parts on wooden objects or another metal always gives a high-quality appearance.

Brass for machining contains more zinc. You can machine rods cleanly, but this quality brass will break if an attempt is made to bend it. Where bending rather than machining is intended, rods and strips are made with copper and zinc proportions more like sheet material. Brass tubes will take slight bends, but they will also machine; pieces of brass tube make attractive ferrules on handles.

## SPELTER

The melting point of an alloy is always lower than the melting points of its individual metals. This fact is used advantageously in the making of *hard solder* or *spelter* for use in brazing joints using a flame. Copper and zinc in the correct proportions for a low melting point will form the spelter used in these joints. It is possible to vary the proportions so a spelter with a low melting point can be used near a joint made with a spelter having a higher melting point, and without the first joint separating. You can lower the melting point by adding silver. The resulting *silver solder* is obviously expensive and unlikely to be used on garden tools. However, there are low-melting-point hard solders obtainable with less expensive alloyed metals.

Brass and copper will corrode, but not to the same extent as iron and steel. Polishing gives a resistance to corrosion. When corrosion occurs, it is a greenish powder that rarely goes very deep. The initial corrosion provides a barrier to further corrosion. This fact can be seen in the green roofs of some old buildings where the copper sheathing has turned green, but will then last a very long time.

## TIN AND LEAD

You can alloy tin with copper to make bronze; the sheet alloy is sometimes called *gilding metal*. Bronze has a better resistance to salt water corrosion than brass, so it is used on boats. In an extreme case, saltwater will take the zinc out of brass so that screws and other parts crumble. Bronze has characteristics and appearance otherwise very similar to brass. You can use the alloy in similar situations on garden tools, if available, although it is not an alloy to choose specially.

Lead is a dull grey, heavy metal. Its concentrated weight governs most of its uses. If you want the most compact weight, it must be lead. Its melting point is low enough for it to be melted with an ordinary flame. Therefore, it is possible to make a mold and pour in molten lead while using quite simple equipment.

Lead is obtainable as sheets that are very easily bent and formed. It has uses in gutters and as a valley between parts of a roof where it can be bent and cut to shape in position. Water pipes were once made of lead, but it is now known to be unsafe for carrying drinking water. In making tools, lead is more likely to be used to provide weight. There is no way of hardening or softening lead, but it has almost complete resistance to corrosion.

## SOLDER

Lead and tin are alloyed together to make common or "tinman's" solder. The melting point is such that you can make the solder flow with a soldering iron (actually a copper bit) or a flame. The proportions of the two metals affect the melting point and characteristics of the solder. At one time, a solder with a high lead content was used to make joints in lead pipes by *wiping*. This solder remained ductile enough before fully cooling for it to be wiped to shape with a suitable cloth or moleskin.

When most pots and pans were made of tinplate, soldering played a big part in construction and repairs. A tinsmith or tinman was a busy craftsman, while the travelling tinker made his living from repairs.

In making garden and yard tools and equipment, soldered tinplate can be the best way to make special containers, measures, planters, and similar things. For a one-off item, soldered tinplate can provide better and easier results than fabricating from other materials.

# ALUMINUM

Aluminum is well known as a lightweight, silvery metal with a good resistance to corrosion but not much strength. Pure aluminum is very soft. Most material loosely described as aluminum has other metals alloyed, in very small quantities, for hardening and strengthening. Most aluminum tubes are of this type.

You might use sheet aluminum for making special containers and similar things, but it cannot be soldered by normal methods. Therefore, you must screw joints, rivet joints, or you must join the joints in some mechanical way or by specialized welding.

Corrosion of aluminum is usually slight. It takes the form of a fine powder that can be brushed off. Many structures of aluminum used outdoors are left untreated. Iron and most other metals require paint or other protection from the weather. There is no way to anneal or harden aluminum to any appreciable extent.

# RIVETS

Rivets are used to make more permanent joints in metal than screws or bolts and nuts. They can provide all the strength needed. In many garden tools, one or more rivets are used to keep the parts in the correct relation to each other while they are brazed or welded. In that case, the rivet is not expected to provide much strength in the finished tool. Therefore, it can be thinner. Because most parts being joined are steel, the rivets should normally be iron or steel. For purely locating purposes, copper rivets are easy to work. Aluminum is not compatible with brazing. If the rivets have to provide strength without the assistance of brazing or welding, they should be iron or steel.

In most small tools, the rivets can be ⅛ inch, ³⁄₁₆ inch, or ¼ inch diameter. You can make them from rod or you can buy rivets with prepared heads on one end. The common head is round (Fig. 3-2A) and sometimes called a *snap rivet*. It can be countersunk (Fig. 3-2B). Several others are also available. You can shape heads in position with a ball-pane hammer (Fig. 3-2C), although a crosspane (Fig. 3-2D) has uses in getting a head edge close to the surface.

A tool called a *snap* or *set* has a hollow to match a particular rivet head and might have a hole to match the diameter of the rivet (Fig. 3-2E). You would use the hole over the end of the rivet to set down tightly the metal parts the rivet end projects through (Fig. 3-2F). You would use the hollow to support a prepared head, with the tool held in a vise, while you form the other head. If you hammer a round head to a reasonable shape, use the snap over it to finish its surface. Without the support of a snap, a prepared head resting on an iron block will flatten, but that might not matter. Without a snap, you can support a prepared head on a lead block to avoid damage to it.

A hole for a rivet should be a close fit to avoid bending the shank when you hammer the end. If you want the head to finish level, countersink the hole properly to make a head that will have sufficient strength. Estimate the amount of rivet end left standing to be enough to fill the countersink (Fig. 3-2H).

If you have to make a rivet from rod, cut it to sufficient length to make two heads. Support one end on an iron block or with a snap, and start forming one

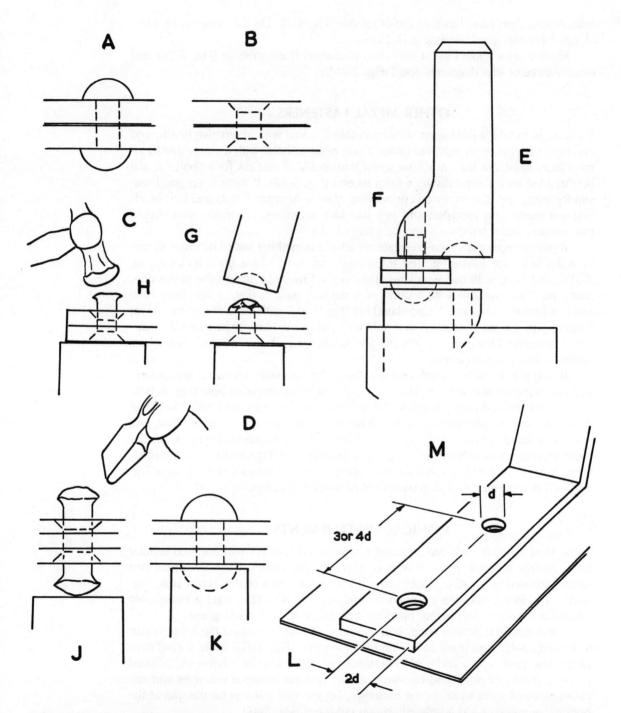

Fig. 3-2. Rivets can have round or countersunk heads and you can close them with a hammer and set.

side. After a short time, work on the other side (Fig. 3-2J). Do this progressively until you have two good heads (Fig. 3-2K).

Rivet centers should be at least two diameters from an edge (Fig. 3-2L) and usually three or four diameters apart (Fig. 3-2M).

## OTHER METAL FASTENERS

If you want to take a joint apart, as when making a tool with alternative heads, you can hold the parts with nuts and bolts. If you need a "bolt" with a screw thread almost to its head, ask for a machine screw (Fig. 3-3A). If you ask for a "bolt," it will be threaded only a short distance from its end (Fig. 3-3B). If there is no good reason for using any other screwed connection, choose hexagonal nuts and bolt heads that are made with precision and suit standard wrenches. Normally, you should put washers under bolt heads and nuts (Fig. 3-3C).

If one or more parts have to rotate on a bolt, something has to be done to prevent the nut from loosening. The traditional way is to add a plain locknut (Fig. 3-3D), and then, with two wrenches, tighten the lower nut against the upper one. Many nuts are available with friction of some sort built in (Fig. 3-3E). They hold without further assistance. A castellated nut (Fig. 3-3F), with the bolt end drilled for a cotter pin, is used more often in machinery and is less likely to be needed in garden equipment. However, a cotter pin and washer (Fig. 3-3G) is a good way of retaining a loose part on a rod.

If one part is thick enough and you have the necessary screwing equipment, you can dispense with a nut by driving a bolt end into a threaded hole (Fig. 3-3H).

A nut tightened with a wrench is most secure, if you want to be able to change a part or make an adjustment, but you have to find the wrench. To avoid that, you can use a hand-operated nut. For a small part, it can be knurled (Fig. 3-3J). For more leverage, it is better to use a wing or butterfly nut (Fig. 3-3K). In some situations, it might be better to cut a thread through a hole at the end of a flat strip (Fig. 3-3L). This procedure will give you more of a wrench action.

## CONICAL DEVELOPMENTS

Some long-handled tools are attached to the wood handles with tapered tubular parts, usually secured with one or two screws through holes. Cut the conical part square across (Fig. 3-4A) or it looks neat if you shape it to a central screw hole (Fig. 3-4B). The lower side can be open. Therefore, it is possible to get a reasonable shape for the sheet steel before bending it by doing special marking out.

For a simple truncated cone, you can draw the size you want the finished part to be (Fig. 3-4C) and mark each side of it the same (Fig. 3-4D) using a card template. That gives you a width of three times the diameter. For a full-width, closed cone, it should be three and one-seventh (the relation between diameter and circumference of a circle) times the diameter. Let the odd fraction be the gap at the bottom, or you can add a little when you cut it out (Fig. 3-4E).

Round the ends and you have a shape that you can roll to the final cone (as nearly accurate as it needs to be on most tools). If you are shaping the top, you can

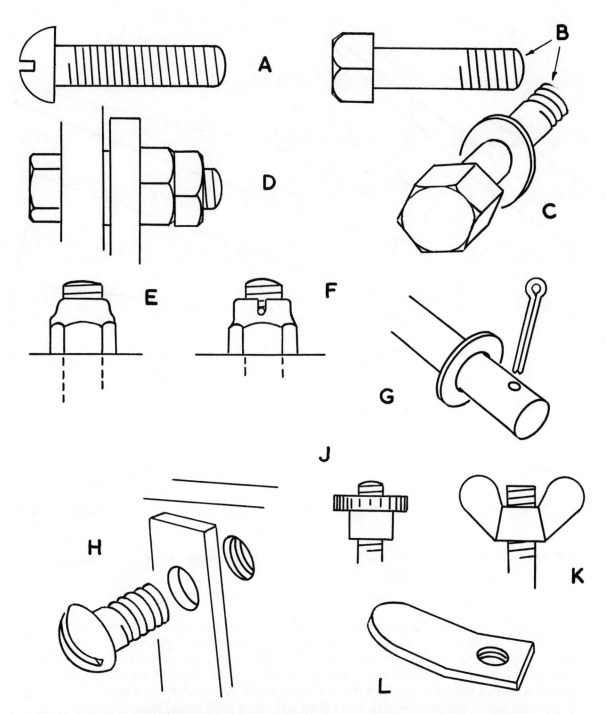

Fig. 3-3. Use screws and bolts with several types of nuts (A-F). A cotter pin (G) holds parts on a rod. A thread in a part can take the place of a nut (H). You can turn nuts without a wrench (J-L).

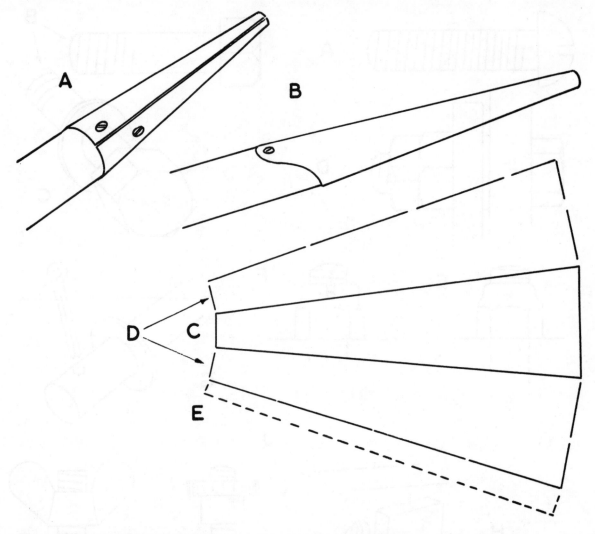

*Fig. 3-4. Sheet metal for a tapered socket can have its developed shape set out approximately.*

draw in the outline freehand on half of the development, and then reverse it on the other side.

For a more exact truncated cone, particularly if you want to curve the large end, set the shape out geometrically. Draw a side view (Fig. 3-5A). If you want a shaped top, continue to where the point would be if cut square (Fig. 3-5B). At the small end, extend the lines until they meet (Fig. 3-5C). With that point as center, draw curves that will be the ends of the developed shape. Draw a line from one edge to the center (Fig. 3-5D) and measure three and one-seventh times the diameter around the outer curve for a line to mark the other side of the development (Fig. 3-5E). That gives you the shape to cut the metal to roll into a square-ended conical object, if that is what you need.

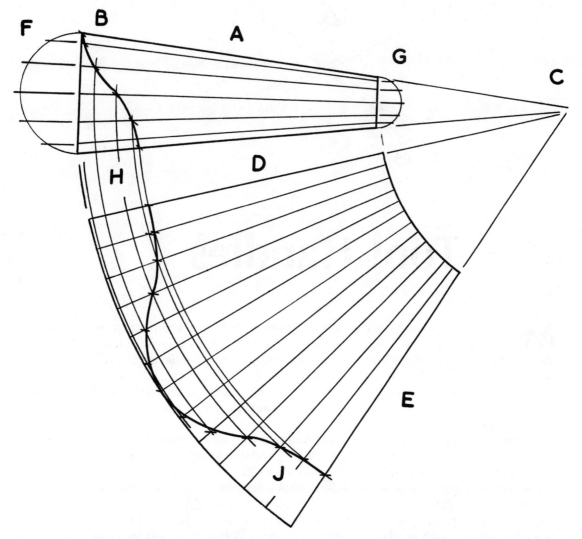

Fig. 3-5. *A more accurate development of a tapered socket has ordinates transferred from a side view to the open shape.*

If there is to be a curved end, or there is any other shaping to be done, you have to draw lines (ordinates) on the side view and repeat them in appropriate places on the development. You can then mark points on the curve and join them. Draw semicircles on the ends (Figs. 3-5F, G) and divide them into equal divisions, six should do (making 12 in a full circle). Project the points to the ends and join them. Divide the outer curve of the development into 12, and draw lines toward the center. Working around the center, project crossings on the side-view lines to the matching lines on the development (Fig. 3-5H). Draw through these points to get the developed shape of the end curve (Fig. 3-5J).

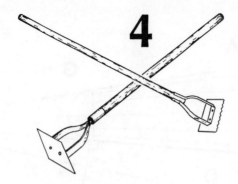

# 4

# Tool Handles

**M**OST TOOL HANDLES ARE MADE OF WOOD. THERE IS A RESILIENCE AND SPRING IN wooden handles, as well as comfort, not found in other materials. It has a pleasing feel that is difficult to define, but a tool with a wood handle usually will be considered superior to one with a handle made of metal or plastic. For anyone making tools away from quantity production facilities or an elaborately equipped shop, wood is easier to work with when using simpler equipment, than are the possible alternatives.

If you must make a long handle for a tool that is to have a chopping action (such as a hoe) or if you must lever it (as a spade), use springy wood or it will soon crack or break. The best woods for this purpose are ash and hickory. If the handle is not to receive the shock of blows, make it from a light wood. Straight-grained fir or pine provide lightness in a tool you will be using for a long period. This lightness allows you to continue working for a greater time without fatigue. Old-time hay rakes are examples of ultimate lightness in tools. Willow was used for rakes even though it does not possess much strength or durability.

For short handles, such as those for trowels, hardwood is preferable. There might not be much load on the wood handle and weight is not of much importance, but a nicely-shaped hardwood handle, finished with varnish, is attractive and pleasant to use. Certainly a wood handle is much better than plastic or the metal extension sometimes seen on small tools.

You can make the handles of some tools from metal tubes. Aluminum alloy is usually chosen because of its lightness. For a tool such as a fruit picker, where lightness with length is important, this would be preferable to wood. There is little resilience or spring in aluminum tubing, so it would be a bad choice for a hoe or other chopping tool, but for a more gentle action, such as that of a rake, aluminum tube might be a good alternative to wood. Metal tubing does not provide a com-

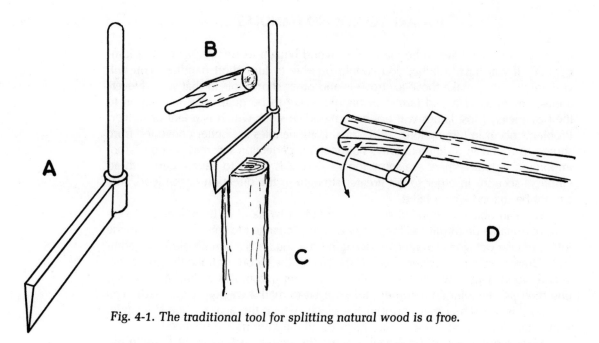

Fig. 4-1. The traditional tool for splitting natural wood is a froe.

fortable or firm grip. Something must be done to improve the grip where it is held. For some tool handles, you can use aluminum tubing with wood. The tube provides the length and wood makes the gripping handle at one end and, possibly, the tool attachment at the other end.

## CUTTING WOOD HANDLES

One way of cutting wood for handles, particularly where the strength of continuous grain is more important than perfect straightness, is to split or *rive* the wood. The traditional tool for doing this is a froe (Fig. 4-1A), which is a long, thick knife with a wedge section and a handle projecting square to the cutting edge at one end. This handle is driven into the end grain, usually with a crude mallet made from a log (Fig. 4-1B). Once it has started a split (Fig. 4-1C), move the handle from side to side to open, and continue the cut (Fig. 4-1D). The split will follow the grain; therefore, its lines are parallel to the cut.

You finish with a piece of wood of an even thickness. If the grain lines wander, so does the shape of the piece of wood. If you have chosen a piece of wood with reasonably straight grain lines, the handle you produce will be acceptable as it is. You know it has maximum strength because of the full-length grain. For some tools, it is advantageous to have a curved handle.

Another way to cut wood for a handle is to choose a young tree, or a branch from a larger one, of the right thickness, and peel the bark off it. It might not be exactly straight, but the grain lines follow the outside (as in a riven piece). Season round wood prepared like this in the same way as flat boards. In some cases, the wood will split as it dries. Season more than you need, to allow for some waste. When you season flat boards, the ends might open.

# SQUARE TO ROUND HANDLES

Many handles will have to be made from wood bought as square pieces at a lumberyard. If you have a lathe, you should be able to turn short handles. You will certainly want to make those for trowels and other short tools in that way. Nevertheless, many garden and farm-tool handles have to be quite long in relation to their diameter. Most lathes will not accommodate stock which is 6 feet or longer. Problems occur in turning long, thin strips. Long handles are better converted from square to round in a different way. Fortunately, perfection in cross section is not important. Actually, there are some tools where it is better to have a part with an elliptical section, in order to get greater strength in the direction of the load, that cannot be shaped with a lathe.

You can obtain a rounded section by planing by hand or by machine. To secure reasonable uniformity as the cross section is changed to round, it is first made into a regular octagon. Forming an octagon on a square is a simple piece of geometry. Draw a square on paper which is the size of the wood, or trace the end of the actual wood. Draw two diagonals (Fig. 4-2A). Set a compass to half a diagonal, and then put its point on a corner and swing it to mark two sides (Fig. 4-2B). You can do this at each corner and join the places where the arcs cut the sides (Fig. 4-2C), but doing it from one corner gives us all the information we need.

Mark the corners of the octagon along the wood, making eight lines in all. You can do this with a marking gauge. If you want to avoid scratches, cut a notched piece of wood and use a pencil (Fig. 4-2D).

Plane off the corners, and you should finish with eight surfaces of equal width. You can do further shaping by eye. Plane off the eight angles until you can see that you have sixteen surfaces of about the same width. It helps to have your light source, whether natural or artificial, on the other side of the bench so that you look across the wood and the plane marks are seen more easily. Usually you will have some unevenness to correct. A block plane in one hand, while you move the wood with the other hand, is useful at this stage.

From this point, complete final rounding with abrasive (perferably cloth-backed) paper. Use a strip that you can pull backward and forward around the wood (Fig. 4-2E). Place the wood in a vise and move it around as necessary. It is also possible to hold the wood on a trestle, by sitting on it. Then it is easy and quick to release pressure for the many times you have to turn and move the wood. Of course, for some tools you might not need the fully-sanded finish, and you do not need to plane the handle.

If you are going to oil or varnish the handle, you should give the wood a good surface by doing a final sanding along the grain to remove the scratches made by the abrasive around the wood.

You must taper some round handles. If it is a straight taper, you can mark out the octagons at opposite ends and join them with lines drawn with a straightedge. You cannot use a simple gauge because of the diminishing width. Some handles are complicated further by being thicker at some point, then tapering toward the ends, and probably by different amounts. There is no basic way to mark this. You can estimate the shape; but, there is a fairly simple method borrowed from boat

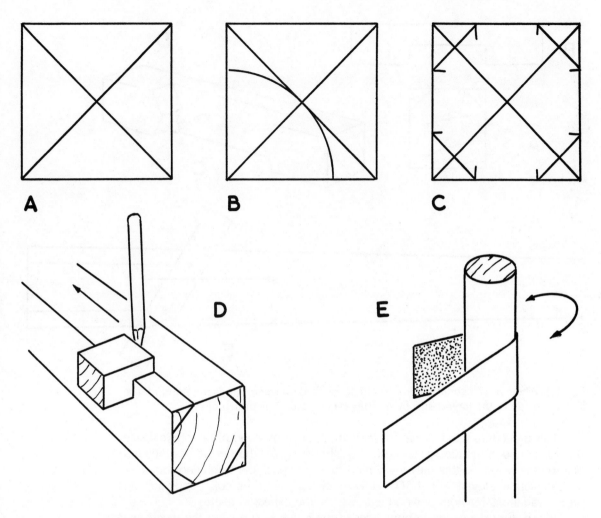

Fig. 4-2. To convert a square piece of wood to round, first mark it and plane it to a regular octagon. Remove the angles before sanding round.

spar makers who use a special gauge. Cut the wood to the intended lengthwise shape, tapered straight or curved, or with one or more thicker parts.

If it is a one-off job, work to a square the same size as the largest section. If you expect to have to deal with other squares, work to a square of the largest section you expect to have when making the special gauge (which can then be used on any square-sectioned wood smaller than that). Draw the square, and mark the points on one edge for the corners of an octagon (Fig. 4-3A). Make a block of hardwood to fit over the square. Exact size is not important, but for a 2-inch-square maximum handle, it could be 1 inch square and 5 inches long, with a notch ½ inch deep (Fig. 4-3B). There must be two points to scratch lines along the wood. Mark on the gauge where the corners of the octagon come, and drive in two nails. Cut them off ¼ inch or less from the wood, and file points on them (Fig. 4-3C).

31

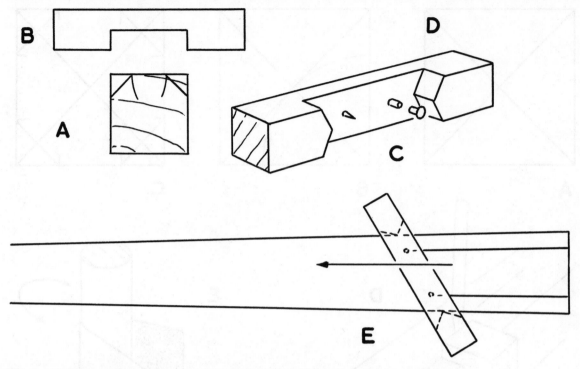

*Fig. 4-3. When an octagonal section has to be marked on wood that is not parallel, use a gauge made to the largest size by altering its angle as it is drawn along.*

This procedure would serve for marking a piece of wood of the original size, but for narrower and tapered pieces, angle the gauge for the sides of the notch to bear on the wood. So that only the centers bear, cut back the notch ends but leave their centers unaltered (Fig. 4-3D). How much you taper the notch ends depends on the variations in width of wood with which you expect to deal.

In use, turn the gauge so both sides of the notch bear against the wood, and keep them there while you pull it along (Fig. 4-3E). If there are variations in the width of the wood, the angle of the gauge will alter, but the proportions of the widths marked will remain the same so long as you keep the side surfaces in contact.

When the octagonal sections are marked even when the wood tapers or when they are irregular in the length, finishing is similar to that of a parallel piece of wood: plane off the corners to get regular octagonal sections, plane off the sharpness of the eight angles, and then remove any high spots. Sand with strip abrasive around the wood to finalize the shape, and sand lengthwise to get a good finish.

## FITTING HANDLES TO A TOOL

Usually the top end of a long handle has to be rounded. If you are to wrap your hand over the end, it is important that this is an even shape and smooth (if you are to avoid blisters). The common shape to aim for is half a sphere, but perfection is

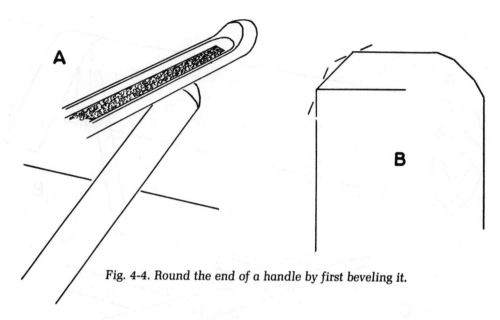

Fig. 4-4. Round the end of a handle by first beveling it.

unlikely. Nevertheless, that is what you should be aiming to produce. Have the end cut square across, and then go around cutting at about 45 degrees to the wood. You can use a plane or chisel, but a Surform tool is particularly suitable. You can hold the wood over the edge of a bench and rotate it with one hand, while cutting with the other (Fig. 4-4A). If you make a bevel all round, comparable with the width left on the end, you will be working similarly to the way an octagonal section is achieved in the length. Then it is easy to take off the angles (Fig. 4-4B) and finish rounding with more Surform work and some abrasive paper.

At the other end, you might have to taper the wood to fit a socket in a tool head. With practice, you can do this by eye. If you taper too much, you can cut off the end so more of the wood goes into the socket, or even cut right back and try again (assuming there is some wood to spare in the total length).

If you want to work with precision, mark out for the taper. Draw a circle where the small end is to be on the wood (Fig. 4-5A). At the limit of the taper, you need a line around the cylindrical wood. A freehand line is sufficient, but mark it accurately with the straight edge of a piece of paper wrapped around as a guide for the pencil (Fig. 4-5B).

You can put the wood in a vise and plane the taper a little at a time. You could use a belt or disc sander and rotate the handle against it to remove surplus wood. Another way is to use a plane light enough to hold in one hand. Rest the wood over the edge of the bench and plane the taper while rotating the wood with the other hand (Fig. 4-5C).

Some tool heads have a spike to drive into the end of a handle. It is unwise to attempt this procedure without strengthening the end. The usual way to resist splitting is to fit a *ferrule*, (a tight-fitting piece of metal tube). You can purchase special ferrules, cupped to close over the wood end. For most tools, you can use a piece of metal tube. For small hand tools, the ferrule can be brass, copper, or aluminum.

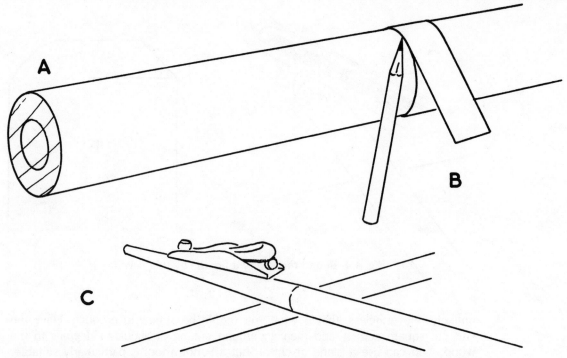

Fig. 4-5. To make a handle end to fit a socket, mark the size of the end and the length of the taper.

For such things as hoes and rakes which need larger ferrules, steel tubing is better. If you expect to make many tools, it is worthwhile to accumulate a stock of odds and ends of various sized tubes for use as ferrules.

As a general guide, a ferrule made from tubing can be about the same length as its diameter; but, you might want to vary this to suit a particular tool or just for the sake of appearance. On thicker wood, the tube length can be less than the diameter.

You will have to taper the wood slightly so the ferrule is a drive fit (Fig. 4-6A). For many tools, a tube ferrule on the surface is all that you need. For neatness, you can reduce the end of the wood so the outside of the ferrule is flush with the main part of the handle (Fig. 4-6B). Cut in at the ferrule limit, and then reduce the wood carefully up to the cut. Try not to cut the shoulder too deep and do not reduce the end too much because either of these things will defeat the object, and the wood might split. It is usual to let the wood project a little through the ferrule (say ⅛ inch on a 1½-inch diameter).

Drill for the spike or tang of the tool. In nearly every case, it is unwise to attempt to drive the metal point in without making a hole first. Despite the ferrule, the risk of splitting is too great. How much you should drill depends on the wood. You can make holes smaller in softwood than hardwood. You can let the tang point penetrate the last of the depth without a hole going all the way in softwood. In hardwood, however, there should be a hole as far as the metal is expected to

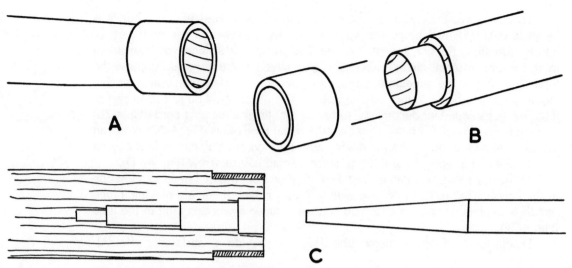

Fig. 4-6. A metal ferrule prevents wood splitting when a tang is driven into a hole.

go. You should drill holes in steps (Fig. 4-6C). For a short distance, the hole might be almost the full size of the metal, and then you should reduce it two or three times. In wood that tends to clog the drill, start large. If you can drill the wood cleanly, go all the way with a small drill first, because that guides the other drills. It is easier also to keep the final drilled hole straight. A depth gauge on the drill, or careful measuring, will prevent drilling too much or too large.

You must estimate how undersized you want to make the hole. If the tang is square, work to the sizes across the flats; the corners will provide grip as they penetrate the wood. Measure the length of the tang, before you drive it in, so you know when it has gone in the required amount. Usually, the tightness of the fit is all that is needed to keep the handle and the tool head together. You could smear epoxy glue inside the hole to bond the wood and metal. If you are unfortunate enough to drill too much, so a tang would not grip, all is not lost. Mix sawdust with epoxy glue and put it in the hole around the metal. The mixture will set and fill any gaps.

## METAL HANDLES

Solid metal rod would be too heavy on most tools, but for some long handles, metal tubing is an alternative to wood. In particular, aluminum alloys make lightweight, stiff handles. They are unsuitable for tools that have to deliver blows because spring in the tubing is minimal and a jarring action would be transmitted to a hand, or a tube might break or buckle. For example, a long handle made of aluminum tube for a rake should be at least as good, and probably lighter, than a wooden rod.

A common fault with aluminum handles is that they are often too small in diameter to be comfortable for long use. An outside diameter of 1 to 1¼ inches is needed for a comfortable grip.

You can leave the end of a tube open, with any sharpness filed off, but, it is better to plug it. Plastic plugs are available that are intended for use with parts of tubular furniture. Rubber and plastic feet also are available and you can adapt them for tubular metal chairs. Obviously, you have to match these. Purchase the tubes and plugs at the same time. Quite often diameters are less than you want. For larger tubes, it is better to turn wooden plugs. The plugs could be just short pieces (Fig. 4-7A), extended for decoration, to permit a hole for a hanging cord (Fig. 4-7B) or even longer to make a better grip than the metal tube offers (Fig. 4-7C). You can just drive in a plug, but shrinkage might cause it to loosen. You can hold it in with epoxy adhesive or you can drill the tube for a small nail or screw (Fig. 4-7D).

At the other end, you can extend a rod or tube from the tool head to telescope in the handle (Fig. 4-7E), to be held with a screw or rivet. If you are making a tube handle to replace a wooden one, you can use a tapered wooden plug in the tube (Fig. 4-7F).

Except for brief use, a metal tube does not provide a satisfactory grip. Al-

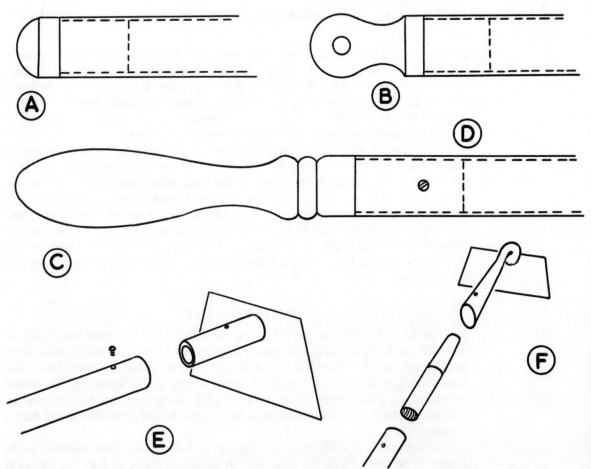

Fig. 4-7. A metal tube can have wooden ends to make handles or a means of attaching to a tool.

though it might be clean, your hands will turn black, and it is slippery. Even if it does not look very attractive, binding it with electrician's tape will produce a good grip. Flexible plastic sleeves are available which you can soften in hot water and stretch over the metal tube to provide a grip. If the size is right, you can use bicycle handlebar grips.

Metal tubing is useful if you want to make a long handle which you can take apart. You would want this type handle for a fruit picker (which is easier to store if reduced to half-length). If you want to put a long tool in the car trunk, it might be easier if it is in two parts.

Some aluminum tubing is available in telescopic sizes; each diameter fits easily into the next size above it. If you can get those tubes, it is easy to make a takedown joint. You can push one tube into the other as far as a bolt or rivet stop (Fig. 4-8A). If you want both parts to be the same size, place a tube, held with screws, in one piece so the other pushes on it (Fig. 4-8B). An overlap of each part of about 4 inches would be about right. If the parts ought to be locked together, you could use a self-tapping screw (Fig. 4-8C). For that, you need a screwdriver, but for a safe joint without tools for assembly, the end of the outside tube can have L-shaped slots to engage with a screw on one or both sides (Fig. 4-8D) or there could be a rod through it (Fig. 4-8E).

Both parts do not need to be metal tubes. The tool could have a wooden handle, and then you could use a tube when it has to be extended. In that case, the wood end goes inside the tube (Fig. 4-8F) in the same way as an inner-metal tube. The only problem with using a wood-plug piece is the probable expansion and contraction of the wood, which would cause variations in the fit. An improvement is a metal sleeve on the end of the wood part (Fig. 4-8G). Both parts could be wood with short pieces of tube to make the joint (Fig. 4-8H).

## SHORT HANDLES

You should fit trowels and many other small tools that a gardener uses with hardwood handles. A varnished handle, possibly with a brass ferrule where appropriate, is a pleasant thing to use and much better than a plastic or metal extension of the working end of the implement. You can make a great variety of wooden handles. Anyone with a lathe can produce many attractive handles that are often of better design than some on manufactured tools. Certainly, they are more individual. Short handles, as described in this section, are those up to about 20 inches long.

Without a lathe, the handle shapes you can make are straight types or those you can carve. A simple square, with the corners taken off, can be practical but rather unattractive (Fig. 4-9A). If it is tapered and given a regular octagonal section, it immediately looks more attractive (Fig. 4-9B). It might need a tapered end to fit a socket (Fig. 4-9C), or for a tang on the tool, it should have a ferrule (Fig. 4-9D).

You can make a carved handle to fit your hand, with an enlarged part for the fingers and an extension at the end to prevent your hand from sliding off (Fig. 4-9E). On a square piece of wood, cut and mark the view from the side (Fig. 4-9F), and then draw the outline of the top view (Fig. 4-9G). If there is to be a tubular fer-

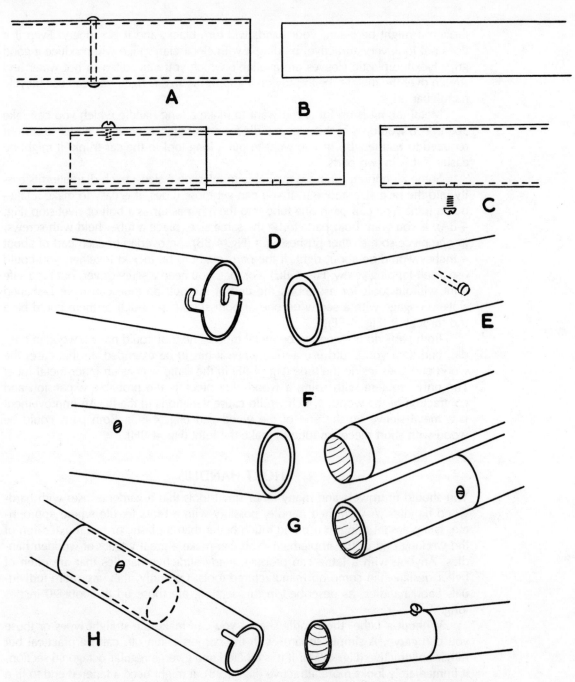

Fig. 4-8. Joints in tubes are made with one tube inside another. You can use tubes for joints between wooden rods.

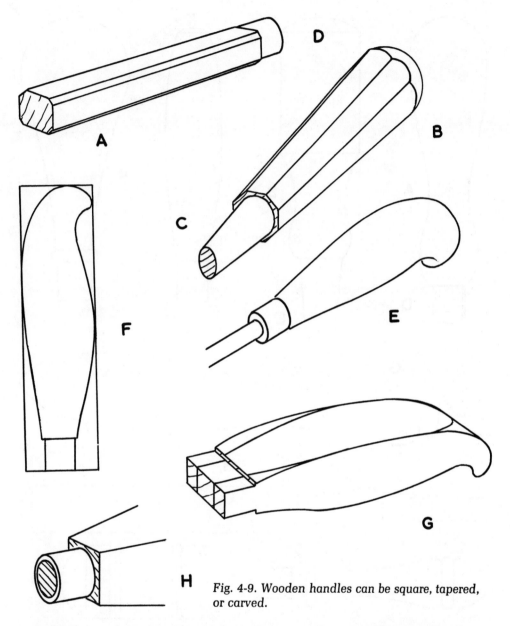

Fig. 4-9. Wooden handles can be square, tapered, or carved.

rule, fit that at this stage (Fig. 4-9H), and then carve or whittle the handle shape. When it is finished, there should be none of the flat cross-sectional surfaces remaining.

For turned handles, there are some basic shapes to use as guides. Most common is what can be called a file-handle shape (Fig. 4-10A). A variation on this has a parallel part for the grip (Fig. 4-10B). The barrel-shaped chisel handle pattern (Fig. 4-10C) has some uses on garden tools, but it is not so good for end thrusts. Any of these, about 5 inches long and with a 1-inch or 1⅛-inch maximum diame-

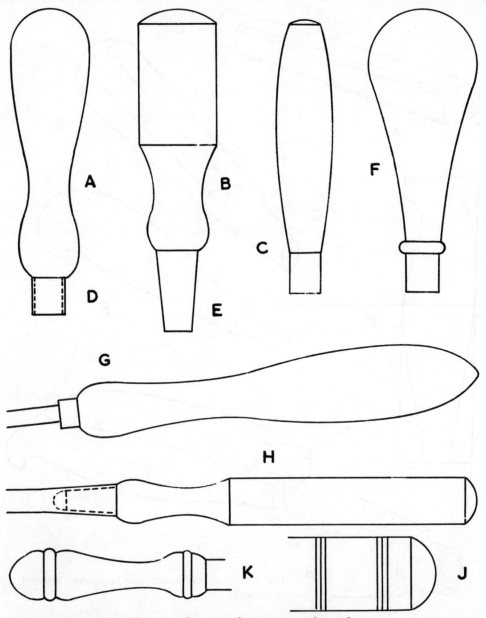

Fig. 4-10. Turned handles can take many forms to suit the tool.

ter, will provide a good one-hand grip. There could be a tubular ferrule to take a tang (Fig. 4-10D) or a tapered end to go in a socket (Fig. 4-10E). Make the taper so that it binds against the socket to get a tight fit before its end reaches the limit inside. Testing before completion of turning will show where the wood is rubbing and what you have to take off.

If the tool is one where most of the work is pushing, turn more of a knob on the end (Fig. 4-10F) for the palm of the hand to push against. If you want a longer reach, you can stretch the file handle shape (Fig. 4-10G) or give the design with the parallel part whatever length is needed (Fig. 4-10H). In both cases, there is enough space for two hands. Rings (Fig. 4-10J) or beads (Fig. 4-10K) will decorate a handle and strengthen your grip. Beads for the whole length of a parallel handle are useful and attractive.

On any handle that will require a thrusting action, make sure the end is well rounded in order to reduce the risk of sore hands. A hole, drilled through near the end of a handle, can take a cord for hanging the tool on the wall or on your belt. Countersink the hole on each side to remove roughness.

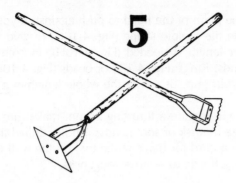

# 5

# Small Hand Tools

**M**UCH GARDENING AROUND THE HOME HAS TO BE DONE WITH SMALL TOOLS, MANY of which you can control with one hand. Sometimes the tool has a long handle, for use when standing, but when the work is done kneeling or the soil is in a raised bed, a tub or a window box, the tools are better with short handles.

An advantage of making your own tools is that they can be the size and shape you prefer or which suit the particular circumstances. Someone in an urban situation, with a "garden" consisting of window boxes, can have light, narrow tools that are smaller than those obtainable in a tool store. Someone with extensive flower beds might want tools bigger than usual to complete the tasks quicker.

Small tools have the attraction of not needing much material. In most cases you can do the work with simple equipment. Although some more ambitious tools really require the use of a well-equipped shop, hand gardening tools usually can be made with hand woodworking and metalworking tools only—which seems appropriate.

The tools described in this chapter involve several methods of construction and the sizes given are average. Even if you only want to make one of the tools described, at least look through the instructions for the others. You can then select an alternative detail to incorporate. An example could be a tang instead of a socket to connect to the wood handle or rivets to join parts without the help of brazing or welding.

If you are doubtful about your ability to work in wood and metal, you will find it worthwhile tackling some of the small hand tools first. When you are more certain of your skills, move on to larger and more complicated things. In many cases, you will find that a larger project only requires a greater quantity of simple work and not necessarily anything more difficult.

# TROWEL

One advantage of making your own trowels is that you can choose your own sizes instead of accepting what the manufacturers provide. You also can make several trowels of different sizes for less than the cost of one manufactured tool. If you are going to use the tool only for small plants or seedlings in a box or greenhouse, make it smaller and more slender. For dealing with heavier work in the garden, make the tool larger.

The method of construction suggested includes a tang on the tool to fit into a handle. The handle could be a plain piece of wood, but it is better to have a turned handle with a ferrule to resist any tendency to split. The handle can be any length.

For one-handed use when working with the hand close to the ground, the handle need be no more than 6 inches long. If you prefer not to bend as much, the handle could be 18 inches or longer. For use in a standing position, you could have a handle 48 inches or longer. In any case, a ferrule at the end is advisable. With longer handles, there is a greater inclination to apply more leverage, and that puts a strain on the joint. For longer handles, it is better to make a trowel with a socket handle.

1. The trowel is shown with a blade of moderate curve (Fig. 5-1A). Besides giving a useful shape, the curve provides stiffness.

2. Cut the blade with a slightly tapered outline (Fig. 5-1B). At the narrow end, the metal can be semicircular or taken to a slight point (as drawn). Do not make a slender point that would be weak and soon bend or wear away.

3. Curve the blade over an iron rod, extending from the side of a vise, or over the beak of an anvil. The rod should be a smaller diameter than the curve of the blade (Fig. 5-1C). It should be possible to bend the blade by a combination of pressure and hammering; you can hammer one side while you hold the other side with pliers or tongs. Carry the curve along the blade, as close as possible to the point, to ensure stiffness there. It should be possible to shape the blade without heating.

4. If you are making the shaft without the use of heat, flatten the end that will be attached to the blade by hammering and filing. Use a vise to make the double bend. You can hammer over the rod or you can lever it to shape with a tube slipped over it. Cut off to length and file the square tang to go into the handle (Fig. 5-1D).

5. If you are using heat, flatten the end that will take the rivet, by hammering to about half thickness. Then hammer the double bend over an anvil or iron block. Cut off the rod and hammer the square-pointed tang end.

6. Drill the shaft and blade for the rivet; a $\frac{1}{8}$-inch or $\frac{3}{16}$-inch diameter will be suitable. Countersink the hole in the blade underneath (Fig. 5-1E).

7. File or scrape the meeting surfaces bright, and then rivet the parts together. Braze or hard solder the joint. If you do not have facilities for doing this, or for welding, you could flatten the rod far enough to allow two rivets in line (Fig. 5-1F). Allow for raised heads on the rivets underneath. This procedure gives more strength than countersinking heads in thin metal.

8. Do not paint the working part of the blade, but the tool looks best if you paint the shaft and the blade to just ahead of the joint.

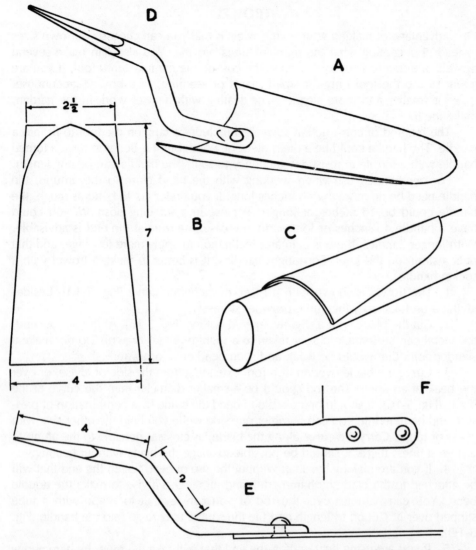

Fig. 5-1. The trowel blade is cut and shaped (A-C). Its tang is riveted (E,F) and can be brazed.

**Table 5-1. Materials List for Trowel.**

| | |
|---|---|
| All mild steel | |
| 1 blade | 7 × 4 × 16 gauge |
| 1 shaft | 10 × ⅜ diameter |
| 1 or 2 | ³⁄₁₆ rivets |

# SOCKETED TROWEL

The alternative to giving the metal part of a trowel a tang to go into a hole in a wood handle is to provide it with a socket into which you can thrust the tapered wood handle. You can provide this socket with a handle of any length, but it is particularly suitable for longer handles because the socket joint is stronger. Even when there is a ferrule, levering the tool will make a tang try to split the wood. With a socket, the wood is compressed and less likely to break.

You can make the trowel and its socket of one piece of sheet mild steel. Heat is necessary to get a good shape. You also need some sort of tapered steel former no bigger than the desired taper. You might use the beak of an anvil or a sheet-metalwork bick iron. You can file a piece of round rod or turn one on a lathe and hold it in a vise.

1. Cut a piece of sheet mild steel to shape (Fig. 5-2A). This figure gives a blade of average size, but you could increase or decrease it without affecting the method of construction. The socket tapers down from about ⅞-inch diameter, to go on a handle of any length (Fig. 5-2B).

2. The socket tubular taper continue into a hollow in the blade to provide stiffness between the socket and the blade (Fig. 5-2C). To form this hollow, have the vise jaws open slightly more than the thickness of the metal and the tapered rod end. Heat the steel to redness, hold it over the vise jaws, and hammer the tapered rod into the socket end of the blade between the jaws for a distance that overlaps the blade by about 2 inches (Fig. 5-2D). In preparation for uniformly curving the metal, flatten the blade on each side of the hollow.

3. Heat the metal again and curve the blade to a suitable shape (Fig. 5-2E), taking the curve the full length to provide stiffness toward the point.

4. On the end of a bick iron or the tapered rod held in the vise, hammer the hot metal to shape for the socket (Fig. 5-2F).

5. Check that the shapes are symmetrical. Drill for a screw to secure the handle in its socket.

6. Leave the working end of the blade untreated. Paint the socket and perhaps a short portion of the blade.

7. To get a good bearing inside the metal for as far as possible, use the socket as a guide when tapering the end of the wood handle.

# FLAT HAND FORK

You can make a hand fork as part of a set with a trowel. It can have its tines flat if it is intended to lift soil as well as loosen it. Such a fork is useful for lifting small plants for potting or setting them out in the garden. The fork shown in Fig. 5-3A has three tines, but it could have four. They could be tapered or splayed out. The parallel form is simple to make and quite effective.

Because the fork does not get any stiffness from curves, the part forming the blade should be stiff in itself. It could be mild steel, ⅛ inch thick. If you use tool steel, use 3/32 inch thick (preferably then hardened and tempered). Because thicker material is not easy to form into a socket with ordinary hand tools, a sepa-

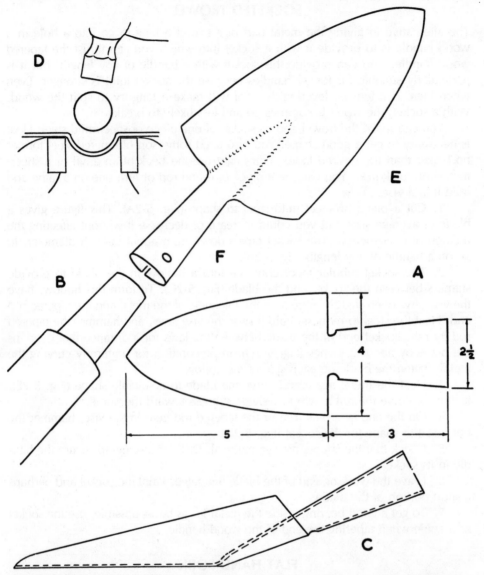

Fig. 5-2. The developed shape of the trowel (A) has its end curved to fit the handle (B-F) and the blade is shaped.

rate tang handle is recommended. The wooden handle could be any length. It might even be long enough for use at a standing position.

1. Cut the steel for the blade to the overall size and mark it out (Fig. 5-3B).

2. Saw and file the spaces, and shape their bottoms by drilling ⅜-inch holes (Fig. 5-3C) so you can saw into them to remove the waste.

3. Round the end of the wide part and taper the tines to rounded ends (Fig. 5-3D). If you shape them to very fine ends, they will wear quickly away. If you have used stout metal, you can taper and round the ends in thickness.

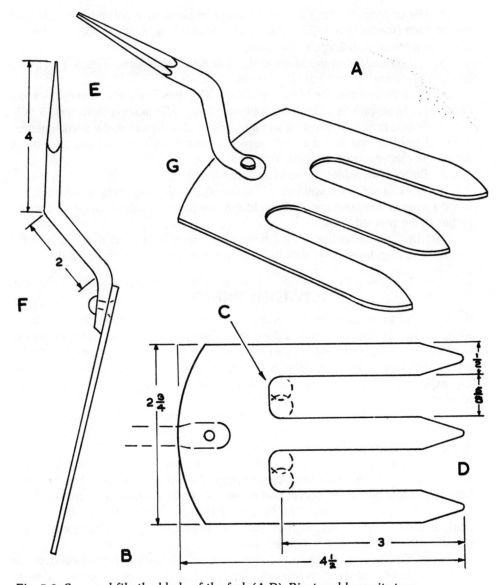

Fig. 5-3. Saw and file the blade of the fork (A-D). Rivet and braze its tang.

### Table 5-2. Materials List for
### Flat-Hand Fork.

| | |
|---|---|
| 1 blade | 5 × 3 × ⅛ (mild steel) or ³⁄₃₂ (tool steel) |
| 1 piece mild steel rod | 10 × ⅜ diameter |
| 1 | ³⁄₁₆ inch rivet to suit |

4. File or forge the tang handle to a square point so it will go into a hole in the wooden handle (Fig. 5-3E). Bend it in the vise (Fig. 5-3F) so that the handle slopes at a convenient angle to the blade.

5. Cut off the rod at the blade end. Heat it to redness and flatten it so that it can be drilled and rounded to take a rivet.

6. Drill the rod and the blade for a rivet. The rivet need not be very thick because its only purpose is to hold the parts together while brazing them (Fig. 5-3G).

7. Scrape or file the meeting surfaces bright, and then rivet the parts together. A round head on top and a countersunk one underneath will be suitable, but it would not matter if both heads were round.

8. Braze, hard solder, or weld the parts together.

9. Work in soil soon will rub any paint off the working ends of the tines, but you do improve the appearance of the tool if you paint the steel (except for about 2 inches of the pointed ends).

10. Drill a hole to the full diameter of the tang for a short distance into the handle, and then taper to smaller holes so you can drive the tang in tightly.

## TWISTED TINE FORK

If you intend to use a small fork mainly for loosening soil, rather than for lifting plants or soil, the thin direction of the tines should come square to the main area of the tool. This placement will enable the tines to slice through the soil. This tool is shown with four narrow tines (Fig. 5-4A) and a socket for the wooden handle. You can make the fork with a tang handle that is similar to that described for the flat-hand fork.

Use tool steel because mild steel tines tend to bend. Tool steel need not be thicker than $\frac{1}{16}$ inch or 16 gauge. This gauge will work easily, but after hardening and tempering, the tines should be quite stiff.

1. Cut the steel sheet to the overall size and mark out the shapes (Fig. 5-4B). Notice that the points of the tines curve toward the outsides in pairs. You need the hollowed edges where the socket part meets the blade to facilitate shaping.

2. Cut the steel to shape. The hollows at the roots of the tines are better elliptical, as shown (Fig. 5-4C), than semicircles. Ellipticals make twisting easier and provide some stiffness in the finished tines.

3. Shape the socket before twisting the tines. Shaping is best done over the beak of an anvil or a sheet-metalwork bick iron. It also can be done over a round rod held in a vise.

4. Continue the hollowing into the side part of the blade in order to provide stiffness (Fig. 5-4D). It will help in shaping this part if you hammer a rod into the metal over a partly open vise (Fig. 5-4E). Hammer the parts flat on each side of the hollow. This shaping probably can be done with the steel cold. If you have to heat the steel, do not cool it by dipping it in water because that will harden tool steel. Try to get a good conical shape to the socket. If the edges do not meet closely underneath, it does not matter (Fig. 5-4F).

5. When twisting the tines, two are dealt with each way (Fig. 5-4G). With the side part of the blade held in a vise, you can grip each tine with pliers (preferably

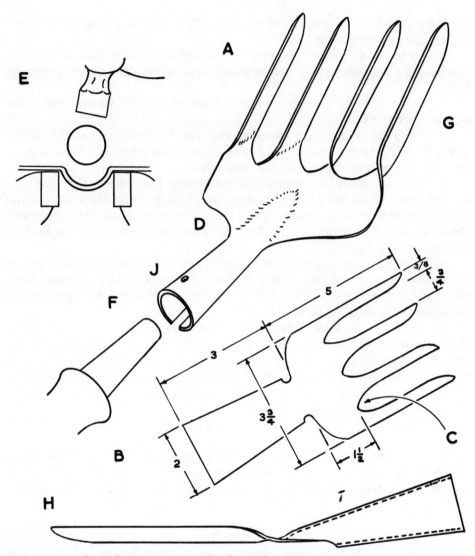

Fig. 5-4. Saw the fork tines (A-C), make the socket (D-F), and twist the tines (G,H). Drill a hole for a screw into the handle (J).

**Table 5-3. Materials List for Twisted-Tine Fork.**

| | |
|---|---|
| 1 piece tool steel | 8 × 4 × ¹⁄₁₆ or 16 gauge |
| If with tang: | |
| 1 piece tool steel | 5 × 4 × ¹⁄₁₆ gauge |
| 1 piece mild steel | |
| rod | 10 × ³⁄₈ diameter |
| 1 | ³⁄₁₆ rivet to suit |

the type that lock on) or with a hand vise. Grip at the same height each time so that you can get matching twists.

6. Try to make all twists the same amount and in the same plane so that, in a side view, the tines are parallel and the socket slopes up at a convenient angle (Fig. 5-4H).

7. Drill a hole for a screw through the socket into the tapered end of the wooden handle (Fig. 5-4J).

8. If you are going to use a tang handle, cut the sheet metal straight across where the metal for the socket would come. Then make a tang and braze it on in the same way as described for the flat-hand fork.

9. The blade might have enough stiffness without heat treatment, but the tines will hold their shape and be better able to spring back (if roughly treated) if you harden and temper them. The socket and upper part of the blade can remain soft. Clean the steel bright—so you will be able to see the oxide colors—at least on one side of each tine.

10. Use a propane torch to heat the broad part of the blade and the lengths of the tines to redness, and then quench the tool in water. Carefully rub bright those parts you had previously brightened. Be careful because the steel will be brittle and the narrow tines could be broken.

11. Reheat, with most of the flame directed at the broad, upper part of the blade, but watch for the oxide colors traveling along the tines. Try to spread the action of the flame so the oxides along the tines travel at about the same rate. Keep the heat gentle, once the colors have started traveling, so that the bands of color are as broad as possible. When the points turn purple, quench the steel in water. The tool is then correctly tempered.

12. You can paint the steel, but leave at least 2 inches of the ends of the tines bare.

13. Taper the wooden handle to fit the socket, then drive it in and secure it with a screw. The handle in the photograph extends about 5 inches above the socket, but it could be any length, to suit a standing or kneeling working position.

## WEEDER

A small weeder is useful for lifting individual weeds among flowers and plants, and particularly for removing weeds in a lawn, with the minimum disturbance to the surrounding grass. A tool with a forked end will get around deep roots and pull them without breaking off the tops. The tools described here are basically strips of flat mild steel, but some variations are suggested.

For most purposes, you can make a weeder from strip mild steel with a section about 1¼ inch × ³⁄₁₆ inch. For more delicate work in window boxes and hanging baskets, you can make the tool of light material. For larger weeds in a more extensive garden, you can make it larger. For many purposes, the tool need not be longer than 12 inches. If you want to use it without stooping too much, you can make a tool 24 inches long.

1. For the simplest weeder, (Fig. 5-5A), drill a ¼-inch hole for the bottom of

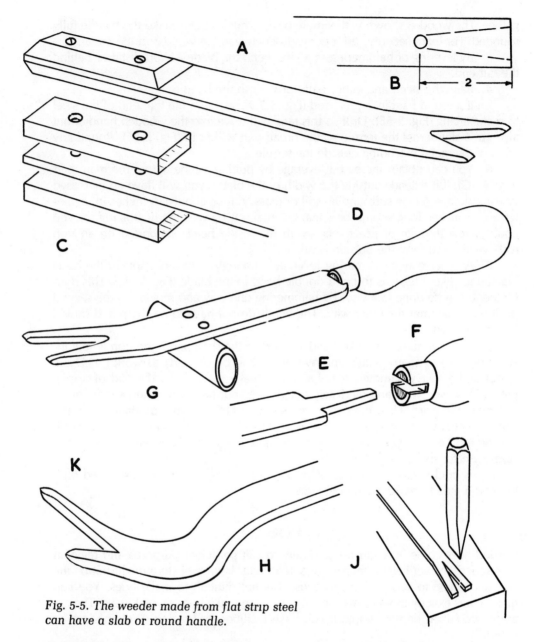

Fig. 5-5. The weeder made from flat strip steel
can have a slab or round handle.

the fork slot (Fig. 5-5B). Next, draw two lines from this hole and saw and file to
shape. File the ends to rounded points.

2. At the other end, cut two hardwood slabs about 5 inches long for the handle (Fig. 5-5C). Drill one of them and the steel with clearance holes for two screws.
Mark through on the other slab and drill undersized holes for the threaded parts of
the screws. You can shape the slabs before assembly or after screwing them to-

gether. The wood is shown with simple bevels, but you can make the handle fully rounded. For extra security, use epoxy glue between the wood and the metal.

3. By levering or hammering in a vise, bend the blade a short distance behind the cut end.

4. Paint the steel, and either paint or varnish the handle.

5. If a round handle is preferred (Fig. 5-5D), saw and file that end of the steel to make a tang (Fig. 5-5E). Drill so this tang will drive into the wooden handle, but also cut a slot across the ferrule so the broad part will fit in (Fig. 5-5F). Round any parts of the metal extending outside the ferrule.

6. You can obtain increased leverage by putting a tube across the main part (Fig. 5-5G). If it extends outside the width of the blade, you will have an increased bearing surface on the surrounding soil or grass. A tube about 1¼ inches in diameter and 3 inches long should be suitable. Attach it by welding or brazing, or you could screw through or use rivets—with the inside heads supported on an iron rod—while you form the outside heads.

7. Another way of increasing leverage, although it does not spread the bearing surface like a tube, is to put a double bend in the blade (Fig. 5-5H). This double bend can be done in a vise, by hammering one way and moving to the second position to hammer the other way. The bends do not have to be sharp and should be left rounded.

8. You can make the forked end wider than the shaft part if the iron is split instead of sawn to shape. Have an anvil or an iron block ready to work on. Use a chisel and a heavy hammer. It helps if you make the fork on the end of a long piece. This way, you can hold it without getting your hand hot. Then cut the piece to length afterward. Heat the end to redness in a fire or with a propane torch and split it centrally with the chisel (Fig. 5-5J). You can start with a central saw cut if you prefer. Because you have not removed any metal, the jaws will spread out to give a greater spread (Fig. 5-5K).

9. A mud scraper is a strip of metal, like a weeder without its forked end, thinned a little to make a scraping edge.

## HOE

Garden hoes come in a surprising variety to suit particular purposes and regional preferences. Nevertheless, those available in your local tool store might not be the size and shape to suit your own needs. It is not difficult to make hoes. You can make yours exactly to your own pattern. You can make hoes several ways. The example described here is simple if you have facilities for brazing. Welding is even better.

This hoe has a small blade, and it is arranged at a moderate angle not far from the end of the handle (Fig. 5-6A). For this size tool, you can make all the parts out of mild steel. The tool will stand up to reasonable use for a long time. The blade can be tool steel, which is stronger and needs sharpening less frequently, even if you leave it untempered. If hardened and tempered, it is the ultimate in durability.

1. Mark out and cut the steel for the blade (Fig. 5-6B). Mild steel should be 14

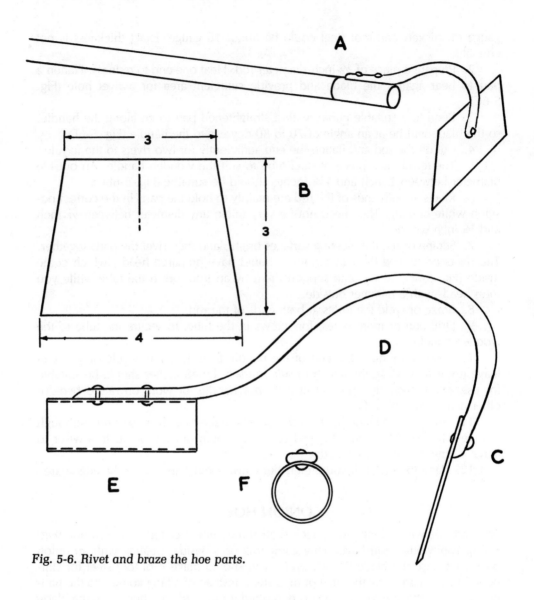

Fig. 5-6. Rivet and braze the hoe parts.

**Table 5-4. Materials List for Hoe.**

All steel except handle
1 blade          4 × 3   × 14 × or 18 gauge
1 rod           15 × ⅜ diameter
1 tube           3 × 1⅛ × 18 guage
rivets to suit
1 handle        58 × 1⅛

gauge or thicker, and tool steel could be about 18 gauge. Exact thickness is not crucial.

2. Prepare a piece of ⅜-inch-diameter rod. Heat one end to redness. Flatten a part to bear against the blade and provide sufficient area for a rivet hole (Fig. 5-6C).

3. Bend to a suitable curve, with a straightened part to go along the handle, so the blade will be at an angle of 70 to 80 degrees to the handle (Fig. 5-6D).

4. Cut off the rod and flatten the end sufficiently for two rivets to the ferrule.

5. The ferrule is a piece of steel tube to suit the wooden handle. An outside diameter between 1 inch and 1¼ inches should be suitable (Fig. 5-6E).

6. Rivets at both ends of the rod are mainly to hold the parts in the correct position while brazing. They need not be very thick; any diameter between ⅛ inch and ¼ inch will do.

7. Scrape or file the meeting surfaces bright, and then rivet the parts together. The rivets positioned through the tube should have prepared heads, which come inside (Fig. 5-6F), so you can support them by an iron rod in the tube while you form heads with a hammer outside.

8. Braze or weld the joints at both ends of the rod.

9. Drill one or more holes, for screws in the tube, to secure the tube to the wooden handle.

10. You can reduce the end of the handle to fit into the ferrule or you can leave it full size. Make the length to suit yourself, by 48 inches should be suitable for use when standing. You can fit a shorter handle for work on raised beds or other nearer-the-soil surfaces.

11. Sharpen the blade by filing the outer surface to a chisel section. Although a knife edge would cut into the soil easily, it would quickly blunt. It is wiser to leave a little thickness on the edge.

12. Paint the metal, if you prefer, but leave about 1 inch from the edge bare.


## ONION HOE

A broad hoe with a long, swan-neck shaft sometimes is called an onion hoe (Fig. 5-7A). It obviously can have many gardening uses besides dealing with an onion patch. Because the blade is fairly wide, you should make it of tool steel for stiffness, but you can make the shaft of mild steel. Instead of a tang going into the handle, you can attach it to a ferrule (as described for the ordinary hoe). Join the blade and shaft by brazing or welding.

The amount of curve given to the shaft depends on personal preference, but the blade should be 10 inches or more from the end of the handle. This length allows you to get a clear view of where the blade is cutting, then you do not cut off the young shoots that you are supposed to be working around.

1. Mark out the steel for the blade (Fig. 5-7B). If you receive the tool steel in a hard state, you will have to anneal it first (by heating to redness and allowing to cool slowly). If you are going to harden and temper the tool, you can do it after joining it on the shaft.

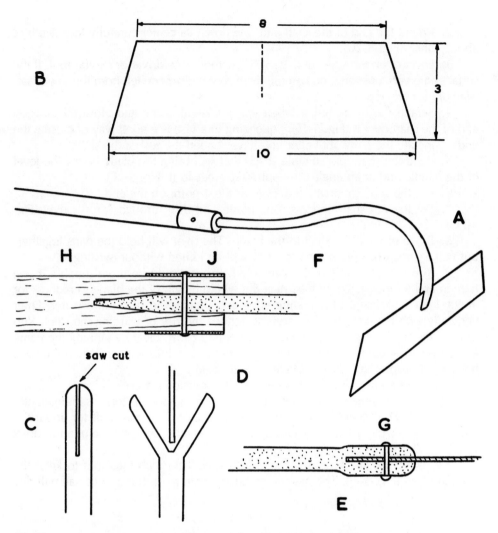

Fig. 5-7. *The onion-hoe blade fits into a slot in the shaft. The tang is held with a rivet through the ferrule.*

**Table 5-5. Materials List for Onion Hoe.**

| | |
|---|---|
| All steel except handle | |
| 1 blade | 10 × 4 × 16 guage |
| 1 shaft | 24 × ⅜ diameter |
| 1 | ferrule tube to suit handle |
| 1 handle | 48 × 1⅛ |

2. Round the end of the shaft and saw down its center carefully to a depth of about 1 inch (Fig. 5-7C).

3. Lever open the saw cut (Fig. 5-7D) with a screwdriver or similar tool. If the surfaces are very uneven, you can file them, but the surface left from the saw is satisfactory for brazing.

4. Scrape the blade bright where the joint will come and close the opened end of the shaft over it (Fig. 5-7E). Squeezing in a vise is a good way of closing the ends. Seperate the parts until after you have shaped the rest of the shaft.

5. Bend the shaft to a suitable shape that will bring the blade below the level of the handle and at an angle of about 70 degrees to it (Fig. 5-7F).

6. Cut the shaft to length and forge or file a point on the end.

7. Put the cut shaft end over the blade and drill through it for a rivet (Fig. 5-7G).

8. Braze or weld the shaft to the blade. The rivet will hold the parts together, but make sure you support them so they will be joined without twisting.

9. You can use the blade untempered, but it would be more durable if you harden and temper it. To do this, heat the whole length of the blade to redness for about 1 inch back from the cutting edge and plunge the blade into water. Enter vertically with the edge level in order to reduce the risk of warping the steel. Rub most of the blade bright with sandstone or emery cloth. Heat by fanning the flame along the top of the blade until you see the colored oxides appear. When the edge has turned purple, quench the blade in water again.

10. Sharpen the blade with a bevel on the outside surface.

11. Fit the wooden handle with a tubular ferrule about as long as the diameter of the wood. Drill centrally to almost the full diameter of the shaft for about the length of the ferrule. Make undersized holes of reducing sizes for the point to drive in (Fig. 5-7H).

12. Drive the shaft into the handle, then drill through for a pin to keep the shaft in place (Fig. 5-7J). The pin can be a long, thin rivet, but a stout nail will do.

## RAKE

Rakes of many sizes are useful in the garden. You can make rakes in various widths, but it is drawn as a narrow type (Fig. 5-8A) with five round prongs and two more formed with the ends of the frame. If it is made very wide, the single, centrally-attached shaft to the handle would not be stiff enough. The alternative then is to

**Table 5-6. Materials List for Rake.**

All mild steel except handle
| | |
|---|---|
| 1 frame | 11 × ¾ × ³⁄₁₆ or ⁵⁄₃₂ |
| 1 tang shaft | 6 × ³⁄₈ diameter or |
| 1 rod | 3 × ³⁄₈ diameter and |
| 1 socket | 5 × 4 × 18 guage |
| 1 handle | 48 × 1⅛ |

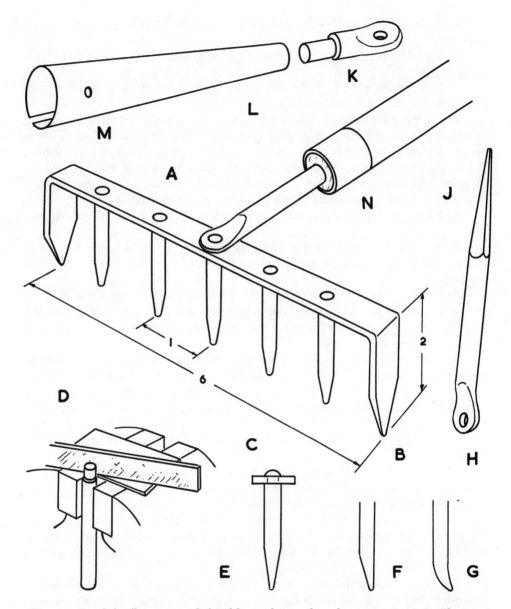

Fig. 5-8. Bend the flat strip and shoulder and rivet the rake tines to it (A-G). There can be a tang or socket to attach to the handle (H-N).

have double shafts, as described for the Dutch hoe, with the ends of the parts engaging with the tops of two prongs instead of just the central one.

If a lathe is available, you can turn the shoulder parts and the points of the prongs, but it is easy to make the prongs with hand tools. Great precision is unnecessary. A tang into a hole in the handle is the simplest attachment, but a socket also is shown. In either case, a handle long enough for you to use the tool when standing is the usual choice.

1. Mark out a 10-inch strip, for the frame, with the hole positions center-punched.

2. Taper the ends to rounded points (Fig. 5-8B). Fine points would soon wear away in use.

3. Drill for the prongs. If the prongs are made from ¼-inch rod, the holes should be ³⁄₁₆ inch. For ⁵⁄₁₆-inch rod, they should be ¼ inch.

4. Cut the pieces of rod slightly too long for the prongs. Shoulder the tops to fit into the holes with enough projecting to make rivet heads (Fig. 5-8C). Allow about ⅛ inch extra on the center prong to go through the shaft as well. With a lathe, turn the shoulders. Otherwise, use a file on a prong held in a vise, with a piece of scrap sheet metal to prevent the file coming into contact with the vise jaws (Fig. 5-8D). Test each shouldered end in a hole; it should make a push fit.

5. Bend the ends of the frame by hammering over in a vise. Check squareness.

6. Use the bent ends of the frame as a guide for marking the lengths of prongs. The prongs should project so that their ends come in line with the points at the ends.

7. Shape the prongs to rounded points. The ends can be central (Fig. 5-8E) or the points can be toward the rake side which you will pull (Fig. 5-8F). Carried a stage further, you can curve the points over (Fig. 5-8G) by hammering on the beak of an anvil or on a round rod.

8. Make a tang shaft. Its length will depend on how far you want the rake to project ahead of the handle; 4 or 5 inches should be suitable. Flatten one end to a wide enough palm to allow for you to drill a hole for the top of the central prong (Fig. 5-8H). Forge or file the other end to drive into a hole in a handle (Fig. 5-8J).

9. If you prefer a socket for a handle, make a similar palm on the end of a rod. A short distance behind that, cut the rod off and make a shouldered end (Fig. 5-8K).

10. Roll a sheet-metal cone so that its large end is the same as the handle diameter and the small end fits over the shouldered piece of rod (Fig. 5-8L). For the method of setting out the cone, see Chapter 3.

11. Arrange for the cut edges of the socket to be downward when you braze the cone to the shouldered rod. Drill holes on opposite sides of the socket for screws into the wooden handle (Fig. 5-8M), but stagger their positions so they come into different parts of the wood.

12. After cleaning the meeting surfaces for brazing or welding, fit the handle extension over the central prong top and rivet it there. Support the parts squarely while joining.

13. Drive the tang into stepped holes in the end of a handle with a ferrule (Fig. 5-8N) or taper the end of the handle to fit the socket.

14. Paint the metal parts and varnish the wood, if you wish.

## ONE-HAND DUTCH HOE

A small Dutch hoe, for use in one hand, can form part of a set with a trowel and a fork for work on small soil containers, in a greenhouse, or in a congested part of a flower bed where you must work on your hands and knees. Its particular uses are in freeing soil or surface weeds before they get an opportunity to develop and for breaking a hardened soil surface in order to aerate it.

The first hoe described is of simple construction. You can join it with rivets only, if you do not have brazing facilities, because not much strain ever is likely to be put on the joint. A file type of handle is suitable, but you can use a longer handle. It is not likely that this size of blade would be put on a handle for use when standing.

1. Mark out the blade (Fig. 5-9A) by working each side of a centerline. Cut to shape. Round the upper corners. Thin the cutting edge slightly, but do not take it down to a knife edge (which would soon blunt). Bend the blade on the marked line (Fig. 5-9B). The amount of bend is not very important, but between 10 and 15 degrees is suitable.

2. Flatten the end of a rod to make a palm long enough to take two rivets (Fig. 5-9C) and put a point on the other end to drive into a handle (Fig. 5-9D).

3. Drill the shaft and the blade for $\frac{1}{8}$-inch or $\frac{3}{16}$-inch rivets (Fig. 5-9E).

4. Join the parts with rivets, preferably forming shallow, round heads (Fig. 5-9F).

5. If you want to braze or weld the shaft to the blade, you need only one rivet to keep the parts in position during heat treatment.

6. Drill a suitable handle and drive in the tang. If you prefer, you can paint the shaft and upper part of the blade.

## DUTCH HOE

You can make a push hoe for use on a long handle like the one-hand Dutch hoe, but unless it is rather narrow, the single, central shaft might not be stiff enough to resist bending and twisting loads in use. The Dutch hoe is given a broader support with a double shaft. It could have a wider blade and still retain sufficient rigidity.

The blade can be mild steel, but if you use tool steel, it will be thinner and will be stronger and less liable to wear on the edge (even if you do not harden and temper it). The divided shaft parts can be mild steel in any case. The two parts of the shaft are intended to go into a hole in a wooden handle. Because the action of the hoe is thrust and tends to tighten the joint, this should provide adequate security. It would not be difficult to form a socket from sheet metal and braze shortened shafts into it, but that is not described here.

1. Mark out and cut the blade to shape (Fig. 5-10A). Round the upper corners and thin the cutting edge slightly.

2. The two sides of the shaft should make a pair. It is advisable to set out the blade shape and a centerline on scrap wood. Shape one side to that drawing and then make the other side the same.

3. Cut the two pieces for the shaft a little overlong and prepare the ends that will fit on the blade before doing any other shaping. Round the ends and saw centrally about $\frac{3}{4}$ of an inch deep (Fig. 5-10B). Open these ends by levering with a screwdriver (Fig. 5-10C), and then close them over the blade (Fig. 5-10D) by hammering and squeezing in a vise.

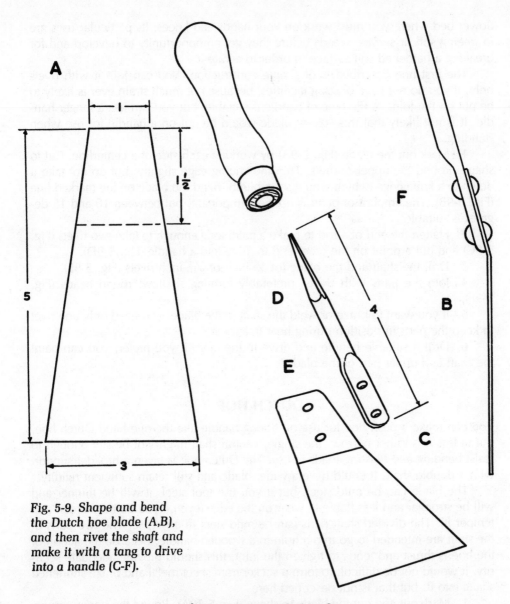

Fig. 5-9. Shape and bend
the Dutch hoe blade (A,B),
and then rivet the shaft and
make it with a tang to drive
into a handle (C-F).

**Table 5-7. Materials List for
One-Hand Dutch Hoe.**

All mild steel except the handle
1 blade      5 × 3 × 16 gauge
1 shaft      4 × ⅜ diameter

2 rivets to suit
1 file type of handle

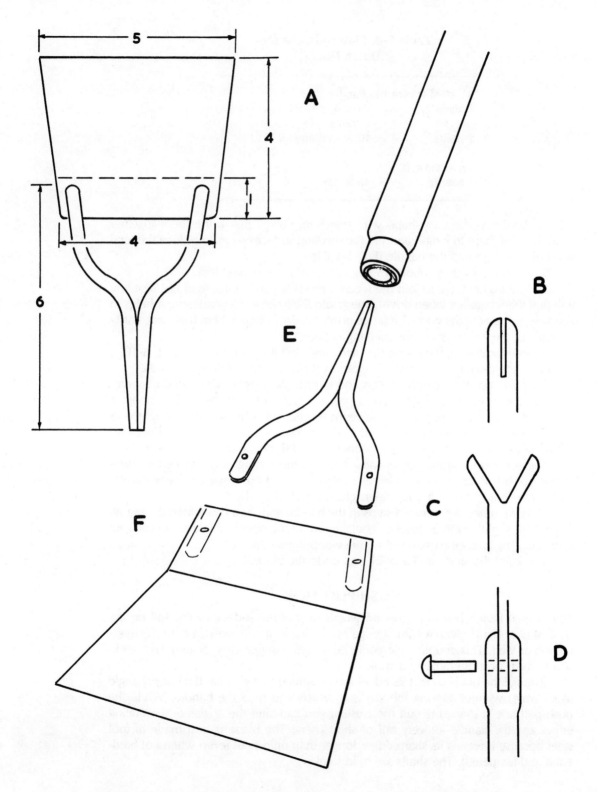

Fig. 5-10. *The double shaft fits over the blade and is tapered to fit into the handle.*

## Table 5-8. Materials List for
## Dutch Hoe.

---

All steel except the handle

| | |
|---|---|
| 1 blade | $5 \times 4 \times \frac{1}{8}$ mild steel or $\frac{3}{32}$ tool steel |
| 2 shafts | $10 \times \frac{3}{8}$ diameter |
| 2 rivets to suit | |
| 1 handle | $48 \times 1\frac{1}{8}$ |

---

4. Bend the shafts to shape with matching curves that bring them together centrally. Cut them to length and file the meeting surfaces so as to reduce the total width that will go into the handle (Fig. 5-10E).

5. Bend the blade to about 15 degrees across the marked line.

6. You do not have to join the tapered meeting parts of the shaft because you will pull them together when driving them into the handle. Nevertheless, it helps in keeping the parts in the correct relative positions if you braze them (not necessarily throughout the full length of the meeting surfaces).

7. Position the shaft ends on the blade and drill through for rivets (Fig. 5-10F). File or scrape the meeting surfaces before riveting, and then braze the joints.

8. If you do not have to harden and temper the blade, construction is complete. If it is to be heat treated, use a propane torch to heat the blade—about 1 inch back from the cutting edge—to redness, after rubbing its surface bright with abrasive paper. Then quench it in water. Rub the surface bright again and heat the blade by fanning the flame along its upper part until the oxide colors appear. Continue heating gently so the colors spread toward the cutting edge. Move the flame so the spread of colors is as even as possible. When the edge becomes purple, quench the blade again. If you prefer, clean the steel bright.

9. Drill holes in graduated steps in the handle end. You can widen the mouth of the hole slightly with a chisel or gouge to admit the double thickness of rod, but further in, the tapered parts should drive without difficulty.

10. Paint the shafts and a short way on to the blade.

## PUSH-PULL HOE

The normal Dutch hoe only cuts off weeds or stirs the surface of the soil on the push stroke. If it is given a cutting edge on the back, it will work in the reverse direction as well. This double edge could be an advanatage when dealing with awkward weeds or those close to a wall.

Arrange the blade so that its edges are presented to the soil at the correct angle (both ways) without altering the angle at which you hold the handle. While the push-pull hoe is shaped to suit most users, you can alter the angles of the cutting edges and the handle for very tall or short users. The blade is best made of tool steel because it retains its sharp edges longer than mild steel (even when not hardened and tempered). The shafts are mild steel.

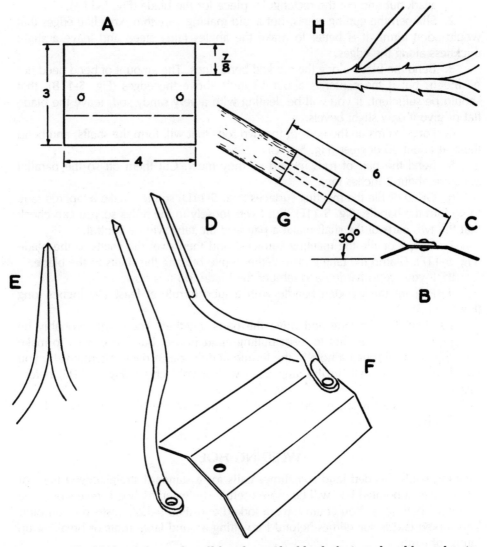

Fig. 5-11. The blade of the push-pull hoe has a double shaft riveted and brazed to it (A-G). Its tang end can have teeth cut in it to resist pulling out of the handle.

**Table 5-9. Materials List for a Push-Pull Hoe.**

| | |
|---|---|
| 1 blade | 4 × 3 × 16 gauge tool steel |
| 2 shafts | 10 × ⅜ diameter mild steel |
| | |
| 2 rivets to suit | |
| 1 wood handle | 48 × 1⅛ with tube ferrule |

1. Mark out and cut the rectangular piece for the blade (Fig. 5-11A).

2. Sharpen the cutting edges, but avoid making very thin, knifelike edges that would soon blunt. It is better to make the angles fairly steep and leave a slight thickness along the edges.

3. Bend the blade along the marked bend lines. The amount of bend need not be much, but if the center is about ¼ inch above the edges (Fig. 5-11B), that should be sufficient. If you will be dealing with a very sandy soil, leave the blade flat or give it only slight bevels.

4. Forge palms on the ends of the two rods that will form the shafts, and bend them at about 30 degrees (Fig. 5-11C).

5. Bend the pair of rods inward so they meet. Cut them off so the parallel parts are about 2 inches long.

6. Grind or file the meeting surfaces (Fig. 5-11D) so they make a tapered tang to go into the handle (Fig. 5-11E). Put rivets loosely in the holes so you can check that the two parts of the shaft make a pair and the tang will be central.

7. Scrape or file the meeting surfaces, and then rivet the shafts to the blade (Fig. 5-11F). Clamp the tang ends together while brazing the shafts to the blade.

8. If you are to harden and temper the blade, do this now.

9. Prepare the wooden handle with a tube ferrule at least 1½ inches long (Fig. 5-11G).

10. Drill for the tang and drive the parts together. There will probably be enough friction in the joint to resist pulling apart in use, but if you want to make sure, put a nail through a hole in the ferrule and tang as a rivet. Alternatively, you could raise a few teeth in the tang parts with a cold chisel (Fig. 5-11H) before assembly.

11. Paint the metal, except for the bent parts of the blade, and varnish the wooden handle.

## WEEDING HOE

Clearing badly weeded land sometimes calls for a standard straightedged hoe. At other times, a pointed hoe will be more useful. The weeding hoe is reversible; one tool does both jobs. You could have a forked end (Fig. 5-12A) instead of a point. This forked end is sometimes helpful for getting around large roots or breaking up lumps of earth.

Make the blade fairly stout and of tool steel; ⅛ inch is suggested. Braze or weld on the tube that forms the socket for the handle. Because this joint takes all the chopping strains, it needs to be as strong as you can make it. If you are brazing, use the hardest spelter that the available flame will melt.

1. Mark out the rectangle for the blade, and then curve to a central point at one end (Fig. 5-12B) or saw the forked end. You can get a symmetrical curved shape by drawing a freehand curve at one side of the centerline on a piece of paper. Then cut this out and reverse it on the metal to mark the other side.

2. Cut the blade to shape. You can give the straight-end edge a bevel, but you should round the other edges or let them square.

3. The tube should be mild steel. It should have walls about 1/16 inch

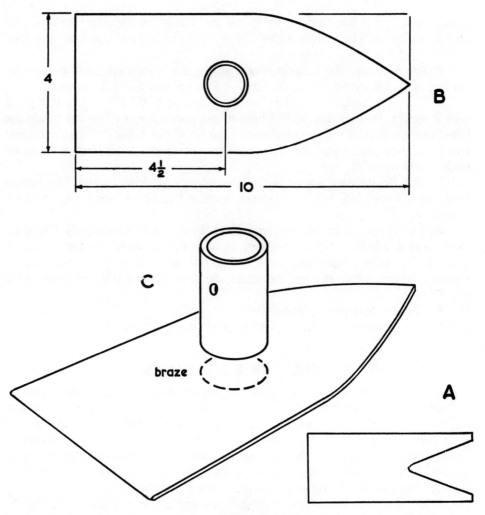

Fig. 5-12. The weeding hoe has a tube to take the handle brazed to the center of the blade.

**Table 5-10. Materials List for Weeding Hoe.**

| | |
|---|---|
| 1 blade | 10 × 4 × ⅛ or thicker tool steel |
| 1 tube | 3 × 1⅛ diameter mild steel |
| 1 handle | 40 × 1⅛ or 1¼ diameter hardwood |

thick, and it should have a diameter to suit the chosen handle. The handle should be 1⅛ inches or 1¼ inches. Either file or turn the ends of the tube true (Fig. 5-12C).

4. File or scrape the surfaces bright where the brazed joint will come—including the inside of the end of the tube—so spelter can build up inside.

5. Have the blade level and the tube standing on it. Wire it or hold it in place with a weight. Besides flux, it will help to put some pieces of spelter inside the tube. This spelter will augment the spelter fed on to the outside of the joint when you heat. Then you should get the maximum amount of spelter fillets built up on each side of the joint.

6. Drill the tube for one or two screws into the wooden handle. This handle could be a round rod, but you can use a natural piece of wood with the bark peeled off.

7. If you prefer to harden and temper, treat the two ends separately. Clean the steel bright to within 1 inch of each end. Heat an end to brightness and quench it. Brighten the surface again and fan the flame above it. Watch the oxide colors spread until the purple reaches the edge, and then quench. Do the same at the other end.

8. Drive in and secure the handle.

9. Paint the metal except for 1-inch bands at the cutting edges.

## OTHER HOE BLADE SHAPES

It might be thought that any hoe would suit any gardening purpose, and except for differences in size, there would be no need for many hoes. Regional preferences do exist, however, and those engaged in different branches of horticulture have their own preferences. This difference in preferences means that a tremendous range of hoes are in use, and anyone making their own can settle for the locally accepted shape. This acceptance of different shapes is true even if your neighbors have difficulty in explaining why they prefer the shape they use.

When making a hoe blade of special size and shape, you must consider the choice of steel and its thickness. Large hoes that get heavy use should be tool steel (preferably hardened and tempered). Tool steel would also be the better choice for small hoes, but it is possible to use the more easily-worked, mild steel if the blade is kept a little thicker. For normal use in the garden and yard, mild steel blades should have a reasonable life. You can resharpen them with a file, but you would have to grind a tempered tool steel blade.

A few special blade shapes are shown in Fig. 5-13. The warren hoe (Fig. 5-13A) would be about 6 inches deep and made of steel at least ⅛ inch thick in order to stand up to a chopping action in heavy soil. A narrow, triangular hoe with a long point downward might be 4 inches deep (Fig. 5-13B). It goes on a long handle and would be used for weeding and cultivating in places where there might be danger of a wider blade cutting off shoots or roots.

When you are using a hoe for long periods, anything that will lighten it and reduce strain on the arms is valuable, but there has to be weight at the cutting edge. A light handle is helpful, but it must be strong enough and of sufficient diameter to

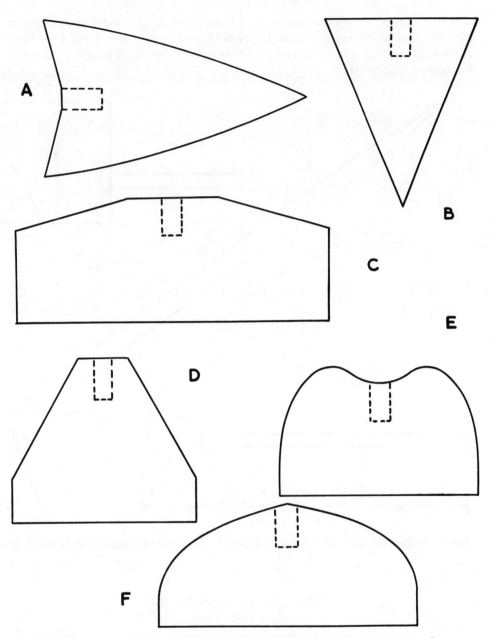

Fig. 5-13. You can make hoe blades in many shapes to suit requirements and preferences.

provide a comfortable grip. You can reduce weight, where it is not needed, by cutting off the top corners of a wide blade (Fig. 5-13C). This cut should not go so far down the sides as to reduce the effective blade area when hoeing deeply, but if the blade is deeper and narrower, the bevels can be steeper (Fig. 5-13D).

It might be the association with pretty and attractive-looking produce that

67

makes a worker in a flower garden favor curves instead of straight lines in his or her tools. The more severe straight lines would work just as well. Some hoes have curved, arched tops (Fig. 5-13E) or the whole upper edge might sweep in curves to the bottom (Fig. 5-13F).

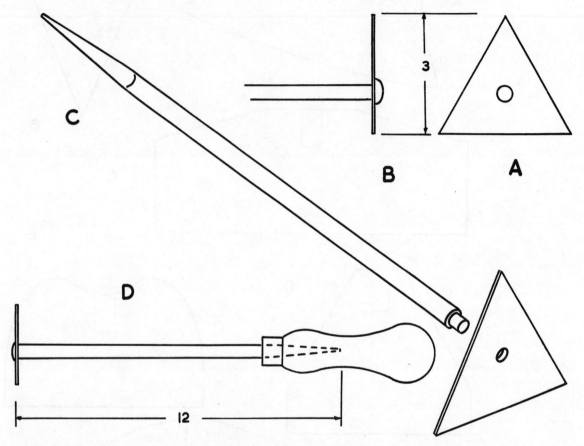

Fig. 5-14. Rivet the shaft of the seed drill tool to the blade and taper it to fit into a handle.

**Table 5-11. Materials List for Seed Drill Tool.**

| | |
|---|---|
| 1 blade | 3 × 3 × 14 or 16 gauge mild steel or tool steel |
| 1 shaft | 12 × ⅜ diameter mild steel |
| 1 file-type handle with ferrule | |

# SEED DRILL TOOL

The instructions on the packets of many seeds instruct you to plant them perhaps ¼ inch or ½ inch deep. Scraping a drill or trench as shallow as this with the corner of a hoe or other large tool is rather clumsy. The one-hand tool will scrape a seed drill at any depth you want. You could put in seeds as you progress and use the flat side of the tool to draw the soil back over them.

Exact sizes are unimportant and you could use oddments of available material, but those shown (Fig. 5-14) will produce a tool that should suit most gardeners. There is not much load on the tool so you can make all parts of mild steel. Tool steel for the blade would give maximum durability.

1. Cut the blade as an equilateral triangle with a ¼-inch hole at the center (Fig. 5-14A).

2. Shoulder the end of the shaft by filing or turning to go through the hole and project enough so you can rivet a good head (Fig. 5-14B).

3. At the other end of the shaft, file or forge a point to go into the handle (Fig. 5-14C). Make the shaft long enough to keep the handle well back from the blade (Fig. 5-14D) so that you can work comfortably and see how the blade is making a groove in the soil.

4. Attach the shaft to a file type of handle. Paint the shaft and varnish or paint the handle, but leave the blade untreated. You do not have to thin the edges of the blade unless you expect to use it like a small hoe to break up soil.

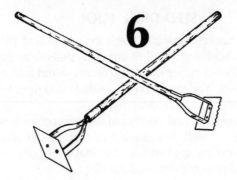

# 6

# Simple Equipment

A LL OF THE THINGS YOU USE TO PREPARE SOIL, PLANT SEEDS, AND ATTEND TO GROW-
ing crops can be called *tools*, but it is convenient to regard only those items
you have to handle regularly as tools (described in Chapter 5). You can describe
things that have a more static use as equipment. If you have to dig, cultivate, remove weeds, harvest crops, or generally handle an implement, you are using a
tool. If what you are using defines an area, provides storage, or has an otherwise
more passive purpose, it is equipment. You can make the equipment described in
this chapter mostly with simple woodworking and metalworking tools.

### LINE WINDER

To keep rows straight when planting seeds, a stretched cord is the usual guide. It is
much better to have a prepared line, with its winder and peg, than to use any odd
piece of string with sticks that you pick up. You can make a winder of wood. You
can vary from the suggested sizes to suit available material (Fig. 6-1A). Hardwood
should be more durable than softwood. For the spool around which the line is
wound, you could use solid wood, with the grain across, or ¼-inch exterior or marine plywood would be suitable. The other parts can be made from wood about 1
inch square.

For a line that will last and not kink in use, it is worthwhile getting braided,
synthetic cord not more than ³⁄₁₆ of an inch thick. You can seal cut ends by
heating with a flame from a match or cigarette lighter, and then rolling the semi-
molten ends between moistened finger and thumb.

1. Prepare the wood by planing to size, if necessary.
2. Mark out and cut the spool (Fig. 6-1B). Do not make the hollows too deep
or the turns of cord will be small, and you will take a long time winding it on.

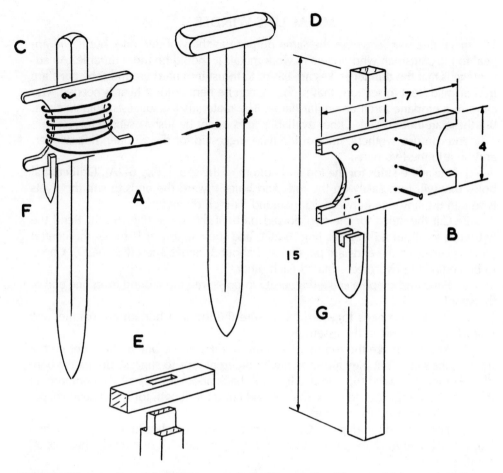

Fig. 6-1. You can have alternative tops to the line winder. The spool has a peg to press into the ground and prevent unwinding.

3. Make both sticks the same length and whittle points at their lower ends.

4. For the simplest tops, thoroughly round the wood (Fig. 6-1C).

5. For a better top, that makes it easier to thrust hard into stubborn ground, make T handles (Fig. 6-1D). You should make these handles with mortise and tenon joints (Fig. 6-1E). Make all the parts you will grip well rounded. You could round the lower parts that will penetrate the ground, but a square section is just as good.

6. The stick with the spool might try to turn in the ground when the line is strained. To prevent this, make a little spike at one side of the spool (Fig. 6-1F). It could be just a flat piece nailed on one side, but it is better made to notch into place, so you can glue it and screw it (Fig. 6-1G).

7. For the most durable results, assemble the parts with waterproof glue as well as screws or nails. You can then treat the wood with a preservative or paint.

# METAL LINE WINDER

The metal line winder serves the same purpose as the wooden one, but it will appeal to the craftsman who prefers to work metal. It should be more durable. An advantage is that the thinner spikes are easier to thrust into hard ground. The parts are iron or mild steel in sections that probably can be bent cold. If heat is needed, you can use a propane torch or similar flame. The materials list suggests suitable sizes, but these are not crucial. Other available sizes might be just as satisfactory.

You can use synthetic line, of the type suggested for the wooden line winder, and tie it to the two parts.

1. Make the strips for the top and bottom of the spool (Fig. 6-2A). Drill central holes that will turn easily on the rods and holes toward the ends to suit the rivets (you can use any size between ⅛-inch and ¼-inch diameter).

2. Cut the strips for the two bowed parts of the spool (Fig. 6-2B). Bend the two ends to about 45 degrees (Fig. 6-2C), and then spring or hammer the central parts to curves so the ends are parallel and about 3 inches apart (Fig. 6-2D). Check to be certain the two pieces match each other.

3. Bend and shape a spike (Fig. 6-2E) to press into the ground from one end of the spool.

4. Rivet these parts together. Make sure the top and bottom are parallel and that there is no twist in the assembly.

5. You can make the rod that takes the spool and the one at the other end of the line the same, but they are shown with different tops to suggest alternative handles. For the T-shaped top (Fig. 6-2F), bend back about 4 inches by hammering in the vise. Then fold over to make the top and cut off to length for a balanced shape. File the end rounded for comfort.

6. For a round top (Fig. 6-2G), bend back about 5 inches in the vise, and then hammer the eye to shape over a round rod held in the vise or over the beak of an anvil.

7. File the bottoms of the rods to rounded points (Fig. 6-2H) or file or forge square ends (Fig. 6-2J) which might cut into the earth better.

8. To keep the spool in place on its rod, use two washers that fit easily over the rod (Fig. 6-2K) and two cotter pins through holes in the rod (Fig. 6-2L) with the points turned over (Fig. 6-2M). Position the washers and pins so the spool will turn easily.

### Table 6-1. Materials List for
### Metal Line Winder.

All iron or mild steel

| | |
|---|---|
| 2 pieces | 18 × ⁵⁄₁₆ round rod |
| 2 pieces | 7 × ¾ × ⅛ flat strip |
| 2 pieces | 6 × ¾ × ⅛ flat strip |
| 1 piece | 4 × ¾ × ⅛ flat strip |

2 washers, 2 cotter pins, and 4 rivets to suit

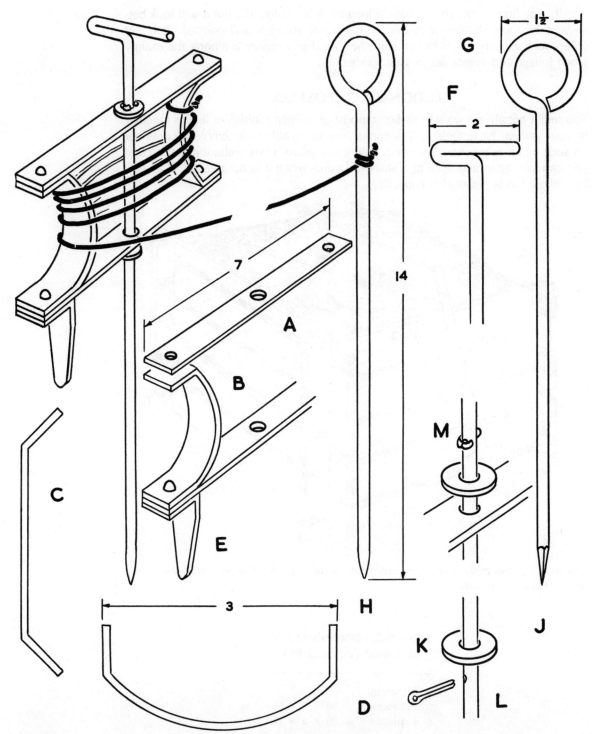

Fig. 6-2. The spool of the garden line winder is made from riveted strips. Alternative handle shapes are shown.

**9.** The line winder should have a long life if left untreated, but it will look better and be more durable if treated with antirust solution and painted. A bright color, such as red, will help you find the tool if you mislay it among the mainly green foliage and vegetables in your garden.

## SECTIONAL COMPOST BOX

You might not always want to make compost or to keep rubbish or leaves together in your garden. Nevertheless, it is convenient to be able to assemble a container for such things as you have the need. Figure 6-3 shows a box without a bottom that you can take apart and store as a stack of boards when it is not needed. It assembles into a bin of reasonable capacity.

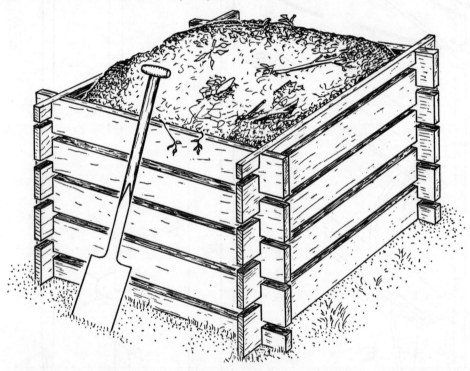

Fig. 6-3. You can make a sectional compost box in any size. The parts will store compactly when out of use.

**Table 6-2. Materials List for Sectional Compost Box.**

| | |
|---|---|
| All wood | |
| 16 pieces | 30 × 5 × ⅞ |
| 4 pieces | 30 × 2 × ⅞ |

As drawn, the capacity is about 24 inches square and deep, but you can vary the sizes to suit your needs or available wood. Except for four narrower pieces used to level the top and bottom, all of the parts are the same. Any number of parts can be put together to make an assembly of any depth. You can extend upward with more pieces or you can reduce the box after you have used some of the contents. You can use the removed parts to make a second container.

The wood should be a durable hardwood or you can use softwood treated with preservative. As shown, the pieces are 5 inches wide and 7/8 inch thick. Other sizes will be just as suitable, but it would be inadvisable to use thinner wood because the pressure from inside could cause the wood to bow outward. Gaps of 1 inch are allowed between the boards for ventilation (Fig. 6-4A).

1. Prepare all the wood. For the assembly shown, you have to make 16 pieces that match each other and 4 narrow pieces with notches to match them. It is best to have the wood prepared in long runs. You do not have to have the wood planed, but planed wood looks better and is more likely to have a consistent thickness. Consistency is important if the parts are to be suitable for assembly in any sequence.

2. Mark out the wide parts (Fig. 6-4B) together, with all notches the same at the ends (Fig. 6-4C). From these boards, mark the notches in the narrow pieces (Fig. 6-4D). Use the actual wood to get the widths of the notches; they should be cut to make an easy fit on the wood (Fig. 6-4E).

3. It will be helpful to prepare the end of a scrap piece of wood carefully with notches exactly as you want them to be. Then use these notches as a template to check marking out and cutting as well as the fit across the wood. Make a trial assembly of the parts and adjust any notches where necessary.

4. You can let the ends of the strips cut square across. Remove sharpness and roughness, but if you prefer, you can decorate the ends. You must trim many ends so select a simple pattern. You could cut the corners at 45 degrees (Fig. 6-4F), choose a flatter angle (Fig. 6-4G), or round the ends (Fig. 6-4H).

5. If you make sure the ground is reasonably level where you assemble the box, the parts will go together better and have a longer life because they will not get distorted. Make sure it is put together squarely when viewed from above.

## SQUARE LINE

If you want to lay out a formal garden, set out the ground corners "square" or 90 degrees; otherwise the plot will lack symmetry. Even when you are planting many rows of seeds across a plot, it is a help to start off squarely to avoid wandering lines. It is very easy to have rows getting progressively wider or narrower apart at one end or becoming increasingly out of true. If you mark the first row square and measure the other rows parallel to it, the pattern will be kept neat and you will not be annoyed with yourself every time you look at an unevenly arranged growing crop.

This technique also allows you to square your layouts for paths, patios, decks, and other comparatively large patterns when you plan the way you want to use the land around your home.

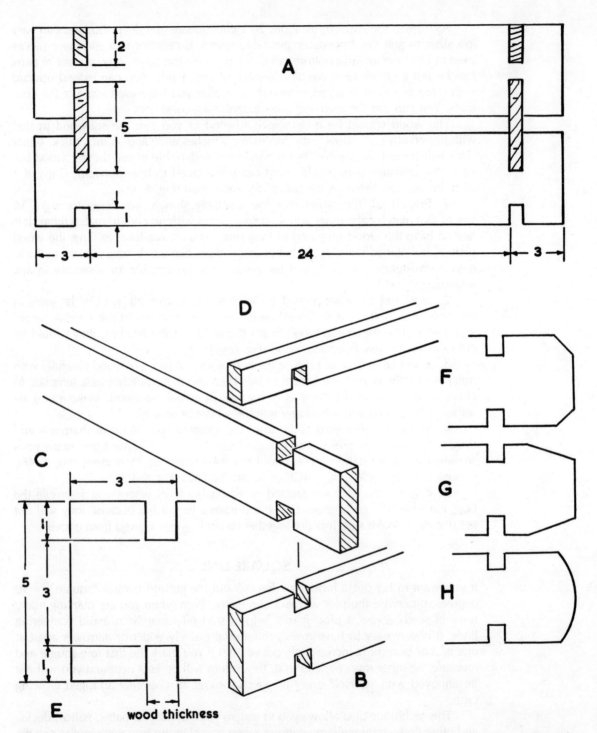

Fig. 6-4. The main parts of the compost box are all the same (A-C), with narrow strips (D) at top and bottom. Alternative end shapes are possible (E-H).

Fortunately, it is very easy to lay out one line square to another whatever the size involved. Suppose you have a straight path or border, you can mark a line at 90 degrees to it right across the plot and measure other lines you need parallel to it. The method is based on the fact that any triangle with its sides in the proportion 3:4:5 will have a 90-degree angle between the 3 and 4 sides (Fig. 6-5A).

To adapt this fact to your needs requires a length of cord—preferably a type with no stretch in it—and 4 metal rings about 1 inch in diameter. Decide on the greatest length you expect to have to set out on the ground and relate this to the "4" side of the triangle. Suppose this is 20 feet. Dividing it by 4 gives us a unit of 5

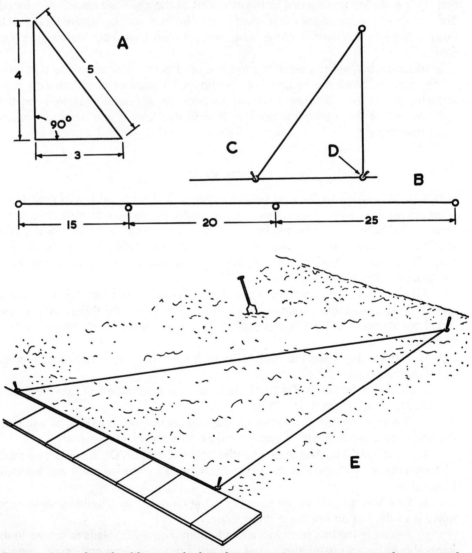

Fig. 6-5. Use a length of line marked in the proportions 3:4:5 to set out lines squarely on the ground.

feet. Therefore, the sides of the triangle will be 15 feet, 20 feet, and 25 feet. The length of cord needed will be the total of this (with a little over, for example 65 feet).

Tie a ring to one end of the cord, measure three units (15 feet in the example), and then tie in another ring. Go four units (20 feet) and tie in another, and then a further five units (25 feet) to tie on the last ring (Fig. 6-5B). Cut off any surplus cord.

Put the three-unit ring at the point where you want the end of the square line to be and push a peg through it. Pull the cord along the base, path edge, or border that you are working from and push a peg through the first ring (Fig. 6-5C). Lay out the cord loosely in a triangle and hook the other end ring over the same peg as the first. Pull at the remaining ring until both sides of the cord are equally tensioned. The corner where you want the marked line to be then will be square (Fig. 6-5D). Push a peg into that further corner ring and you will have your square line (Fig. 6-5E).

You probably will not want to leave this cord in position when you start work on the garden. Mark the square line location with another cord between pegs, scratch a line in the soil, draw a line on the deck, or otherwise mark in a way that will ensure that the square-line position is indicated later if you have to measure other lines from it.

## TOOL BOX

A box to carry small tools, seed packets, gloves, and other odds and ends that a gardener needs is a worthwhile piece of equipment that is easy to make. Figure 6-6 shows a box with a handle made from a dibber that you can withdraw for use. You can hang the box from any long-handled tool that you will need for the work in hand. If you do not need this facility, the handle could be a piece of 1-inch dowel rod placed permanently in place.

Although sizes are suggested (Fig. 6-7), this is the sort of project that you could arrange to suit available materials or adapt to carry particular things. Almost any wood is suitable. This fact is especially true if it is finished with preservative or paint.

1. The key parts are the uprights with holes (Fig. 6-7A). Leave drilling the holes until you make the dibber.

2. Make the two ends (Fig. 6-7B) to lengths to match the first two pieces and the sides to match them (Fig. 6-7C).

3. Before assembly, drill holes to fit easily on the tool handle that will carry the box or to suit the dowel, if either is the chosen means of transport.

4. If a dibber is to double as a handle, make it (Fig. 6-7D). It could be a piece of 1-inch dowel rod nearly as long as the box, with a rounded point and a handle tenoned on.

5. Drill the uprights for an easy fit on the dibber. You should be able to remove it easily, but do not make it too loose.

6. Assemble the box parts and add a bottom (Fig. 6-7E). Nails or screws in the joints should be adequate, although if you are a woodworking enthusiast, you can

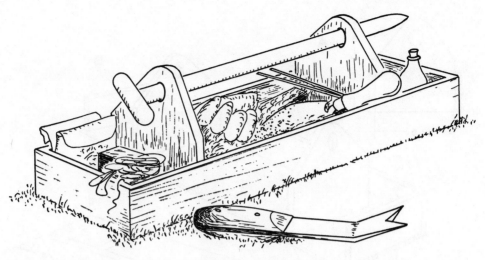

Fig. 6-6. A tool box will carry all the small things a gardener needs. This one uses a removable dibber as a handle.

**Table 6-3. Materials List for Tool Box.**

| | | |
|---|---|---|
| 2 uprights | 7 × 6 | × ⅝ |
| 2 ends | 6 × 3 | × ⅝ |
| 2 sides | 20 × 3 | × ⅝ |
| 1 bottom | 20 × 7¼ | × ⅜ |
| 2 cleats | 8 × 1 | × ⅝ |
| 1 dibber from | 26 × 1 diameter | |

dovetail the corners. If the bottom is plywood, that should be exterior or marine grade for damp resistance.

7. You can add cleats under the ends (Fig. 6-7F), if you wish.

## STACKING SEED BOXES

Many people prefer seed boxes in larger numbers than can be spread on the available shelf or bench space. It is then helpful if you can arrange the boxes with enough space between them for the contents to get air, to be watered, and to sprout. If the bottom box rests firmly, a stack of 6 or more would be quite feasible and make good use of available space.

By the nature of their use, people tend to neglect seed boxes and they do not last long. If they are made well—even from the least-expensive woods—you should get many years of use out of your boxes. It would be unwise to use paint or preservative on the wood because they might affect soil or seeds.

The boxes shown in Fig. 6-8 should suit average needs, but you can alter the sizes given (Fig. 6-9A).

1. For the sake of standardization, it is advisable to decide how many boxes

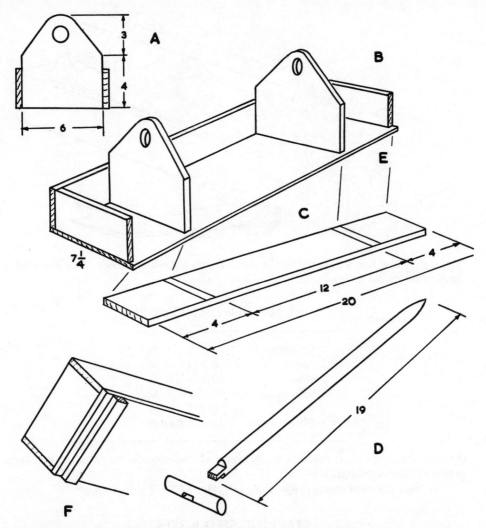

Fig. 6-7. *Nail parts of the tool box together and make holes large enough for the dibber to slide through easily.*

you need and make all the parts at the same time. You can make the bottoms of any number of narrow strips or single pieces of exterior plywood. If the wooden parts are sawn accurately, you need not plane them.

2. Have all the sides and ends ready and nail them together (Fig. 6-9B).

3. Nail on the bottoms. Check squareness as you do this. If you are assembling a large quantity, it will help to have a jig made from two strips square to each other attached to the bench (Fig. 6-9C).

4. Nail in the square corner posts (Fig. 6-9D). Be careful that these all finish at the same height.

5. Put strips across (Fig. 6-9E) to act as handles.

6. Make locating blocks (Fig. 6-9F) to go under the corners. When a box

*Fig. 6-8. Stacking seed boxes conserve space. You can separate them when needed.*

**Table 6-4. Materials List for
One Stacking Seed Box.**

| | |
|---|---|
| 2 sides | 18 × 3 × ½ |
| 2 ends | 11 × 3 × ½ |
| 1 bottom | 18 × 12 × ½ |
| 4 posts | 6 × 1 × 1 |
| 2 handles | 12 × 1 × ½ |
| 4 locating blocks | 2 × 2 × ½ |

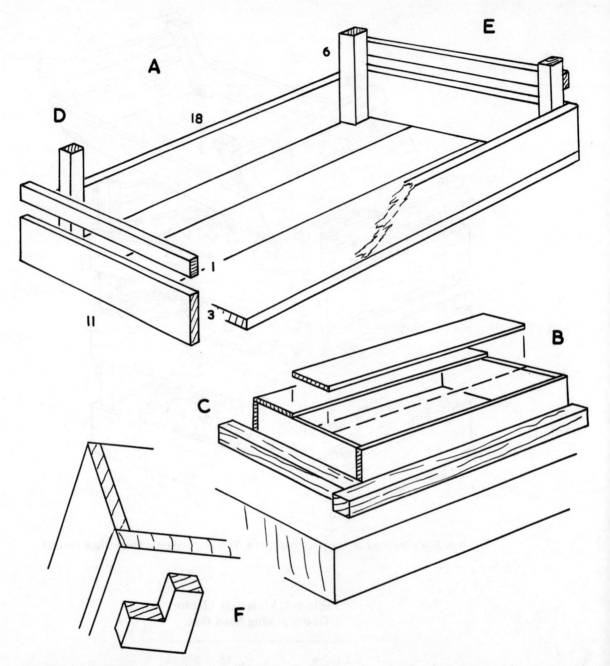

Fig. 6-9. Nail the boxes (A) together; a simple jig (B, C) keeps them square during assembly. Posts with handles (D-F) fit the boxes together.

stands alone, they act as feet; when stacked, they keep the boxes in place. They need not fit very closely to the posts. If the fit is loose, that will allow for slight variations in the construction of the boxes.

## KNEELER

It is usually unwise to kneel on damp ground, and it is always better to spread your weight if you are dealing with a prepared surface. It might be sufficient to use any available odd board, but many gardeners, even if fairly agile in other ways, have difficulty in getting up and down from a kneeling position. Gardeners usually welcome a board with handles.

Handles permanently in place could make a kneeler bulky for storage. The example shown in Fig. 6-10 has a handle stout enough to lean on at each end, but

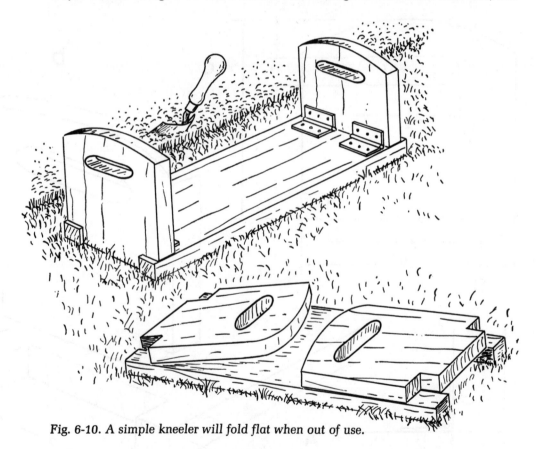

Fig. 6-10. A simple kneeler will fold flat when out of use.

**Table 6-5. Materials List for Kneeler.**

| | |
|---|---|
| 1 base | 18 × 9 × 1 |
| 2 handles | 9 × 9 × 1 |

when out of use, the two handles fold flat. Although the kneeler might be acceptable in almost any wood, it would be strong if made of close-grained hardwood. If
lightness is an important consideration, you can use softwood. For rigidity at the
joints, keep any wood to at least the specified thickness.

1. Prepare all wood to the same width and thickness.

2. Cut the piece for the base with notches that will let the handles set about
¼ inch (Fig. 6-11A).

3. Cut the bottoms of the handles to fit into the notches (Fig. 6-11B). They
must not project below the bottom surface and should be an easy, but a loose, fit.

4. Cut the finger holes (Fig. 6-11C) by drilling the ends and sawing between.
Round the tops (Fig. 6-11D), and then round the edges of the holes and outsides
where the hands will grip.

5. Use two 3-inch stout hinges at each end (Fig. 6-11E). There is no need to

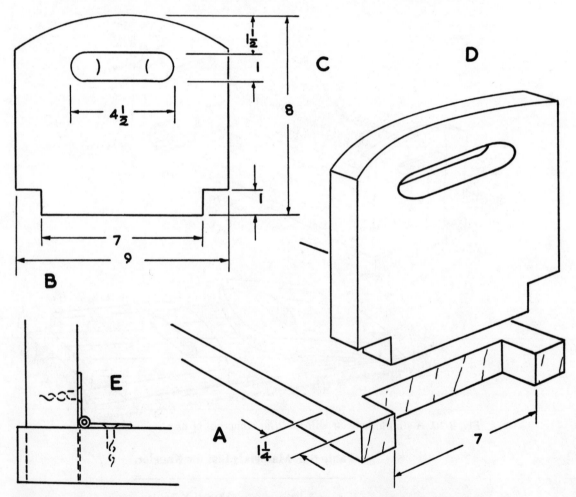

Fig. 6-11. The kneeler handles fit into sockets to give stiffness when they are leaned on.

let them into the wood. Fit them while the handles are held in position square to the base. Test the folding action. You can let the wood untreated or treated with preservative.

## KNEELER/TOOL CARRIER

No one needs to be uncomfortable while gardening. For anyone with difficulty in kneeling, close work on such things as flower borders becomes impossible without some aid. The combined tool carrier and kneeler shown in Fig. 6-12 is intended to give padded comfort under the knees, handles high enough to lean on when getting up and down, and boxes at the ends to carry hand tools, seed packets, string, and other small items.

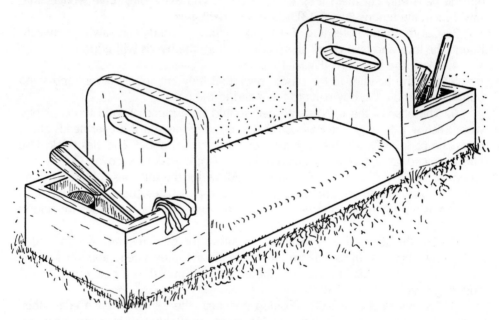

Fig. 6-12. This kneeler has an upholstered center and boxes at the ends to carry small tools and other equipment.

**Table 6-6. Materials List for Kneeler/Tool Carrier.**

| | |
|---|---|
| 1 base | 24 × 8 × ½ |
| 2 handles | 11 × 8 × 1 |
| 2 box ends | 8 × 4 × ½ |
| 4 box sides | 4 × 4 × ½ |
| 1 pad | 15 × 8 × ½ |
| 1 piece foam | 15 × 8 × 2 |

1 piece covering material 21 × 13

The base and boxes could be light softwood, but the handles are better made of hardwood. The base and the upholstered board could be plywood. Exact sizes are not crucial, but for comfort, do not reduce the gap for the knees between the handles.

You can alter the boxes and you can give them compartments for specific tools. Also, you can nail or screw the whole assembly together, but you can use dovetails or other appropriate joints at the corners. Even if you nail other parts, it would be stronger to tenon the handles into the base (as suggested below).

1. Set out the base (Fig. 6-13A) first because that controls many other sizes.

2. Cut the wood for the handles (Fig. 6-13B). If you are to nail or screw this through the base, cut the bottom square across. For mortise and tenon joints, mark out the parts and cut them (Fig. 6-13C). When you assemble, drive wedges into saw cuts in the tenons (Fig. 6-13D) to supplement glue.

3. Cut the hand holes (Fig. 6-13E) by drilling the ends and sawing between. Round the tops and take off all sharp edges where the hands will grip.

4. Make the box parts (Fig. 6-13F).

5. Join the handles to the base; check that they are square across and stand upright. Assemble the box parts to them and to the base.

6. The base of the upholstered pad should be a piece of solid wood or plywood. Screw it through the base, so that you can remove it if it ever needs attention. The padding is a piece of plastic or rubber foam about 2 inches thick. Use plastic-coated fabric that will be unaffected by dampness for the cover. Cut the pad wood for an easy fit between the handles. Allow for the thickness of the covering material. Drill two ½-inch holes in the base and pad. These holes are to let air in and out as the foam compresses and expands. Also drill for two holes for screws (Fig. 6-13G).

7. Cut the foam slightly oversize to allow for compressing. A thin-bladed knife, kept wet, will cut most foam. Bevel around the underside to about half thickness (Fig. 6-13H). This bevel allows the edge to be pulled to a neat curve by the covering material (Fig. 6-13J).

8. Use tacks (Fig. 6-13K). Position one near the center of each edge, then work out to the corners. A spacing of 1½ inches probably will be about right. Experiment with tensions of the material to get a good appearance on top, then cut off surplus material underneath and screw the pad in place.

9. If you are to paint the equipment, remove the pad until you are finished.

## ROW MARKERS

When you plant a row of seeds, you need to mark the ends to show where the row is and to indicate what seeds are in that row. Too often any odd stick is trust in and any marking soon becomes indecipherable. Better row markers are made easily in quantity if you have a table saw that will cut to at least 1 inch thickness.

Cut the profile you want on an offcut of wood. A thickness between ¾ inch and 1 inch and a length of 7 inches or so will do (Fig. 6-14A). Set the fence on the saw to about ¼ inch and cut off as many markers as you require (Fig. 6-14B). If the saw is fine and you feed the wood slowly, the surface left should be good enough

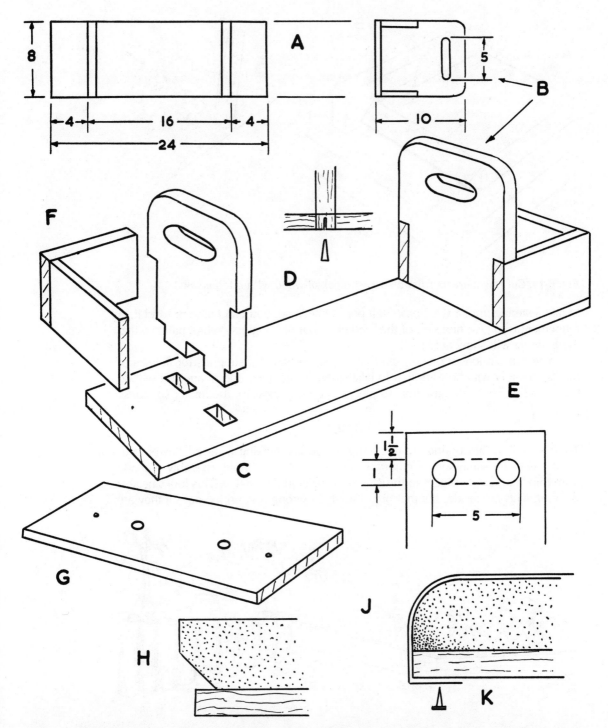

Fig. 6-13. Strength is given to the kneeler by tenons between the handles and the base (A-G). Use foam for the upholstery (H-K).

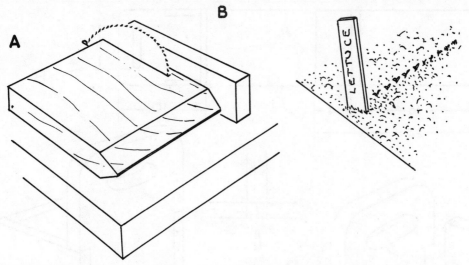

Fig. 6-14. Cut row markers from a shaped block of wood with a table saw.

to take lettering from a waterproof felt pen. Otherwise, you can plane or sand it. A refinement is to give one side of the marker a coat of nonglossy white paint so that the lettering will show better.

You can cut longer pieces, made in the same way, for supports for flowers or plants, possibly with holes drilled to take string. Although wood of any sort will do for markers, choose straight-grained pieces free from knots for the longer supports.

## EDGES

To keep soil within bounds, particularly if you are making a raised flower bed, there has to be some sort of edging to define limits. A simple assembly is made from thin boards with pieces to thrust into the ground (Fig. 6-15). This looks neatest if the uprights are inside, but that puts a load the wrong way on the nails if they are

Fig. 6-15. Make edges with boards or logs.

straight. It is advisable to take them through and clench the ends (Fig. 6-16A). It is better to use sections rather than try to make a long border piece. Allow for the lower edge to come sightly below the surface and give the uprights enough length to withstand the soil pressure, which could be considerable when you are digging or cultivating.

You can shape the top edge (Fig. 6-16B), but do not make the curves excessive or soil will escape over the top. Thickening a straightedge (Fig. 6-16C) will help to resist warping and can improve appearance. A painted finish should look attractive. If you have plenty of natural wood, you can drive a series of short stakes (Fig. 6-16D), about 2 inches or 3 inches in diameter, with level tops or arrange them in a pattern. For a corner, the tops can sweep down to the center (Fig. 6-16E). If your natural wood is thicker, you can split it and use it in the same way with the flat sides inward.

The edge of a lawn often is matched by a flower garden that might be a few inches lower. Trimming this edge can be a chore that you would rather not have. Grass grows out of the side and spreads into the garden. Periodically, you have to straighten the edge and generally tidy up. If you fit a wood or metal edge below the grass surface level, the lawn should keep a neat appearance for a long time.

If you use wood, pieces about 3 inches × ⅜ of an inch would be suitable, but they should be resinous or other durable types. Locate small supporting stakes about 9 inches apart (Fig. 6-16F). You need not attach all stakes to the lengthwise wood, but you can nail the end ones and some at about 24-inch intervals.

You can make a more durable lawn edge with a metal such as aluminum. Steel would rust but that is unlikely to matter. In both cases, a thickness of about ⅛ inch is advisable. Thinner metal would tend to buckle unless the supports were very close. Stakes can be 6-inch nails; hook the heads over the sheet metal to keep it in place (Fig. 6-16G). An occasional nail could be on the lawn side of the strip to help in retaining it. For neatness you can file the extending side of a nail head (Fig. 6-16H).

If you want to make a high support for soil, possibly behind a sloping bank of flowers, any wood structure is liable to bow outward after some time. Struts on the outside would prevent this. If you want to avoid struts, there will have to be some internal bracing. One way of arranging this is to fit diagonal, internal struts below what will be the soil level and have quite wide pieces across their bottoms (Fig. 6-16J) so that soil packed around them will resist the pull when the back tries to bow.

## BIRD PROTECTORS

Birds will devour many small seedlings. The usual way to scare them away is to arrange cotton thread stands which are almost invisible, above the rows of sprouting plants. This protector is often done with a few sticks pushed into the ground at the ends of the rows.

Something more substantial is worth making, and you can use the same parts year after year. Arrange the supports show in Fig. 6-17 at the ends of rows. On very long rows, you can use more intermediately. Position the supports soon after

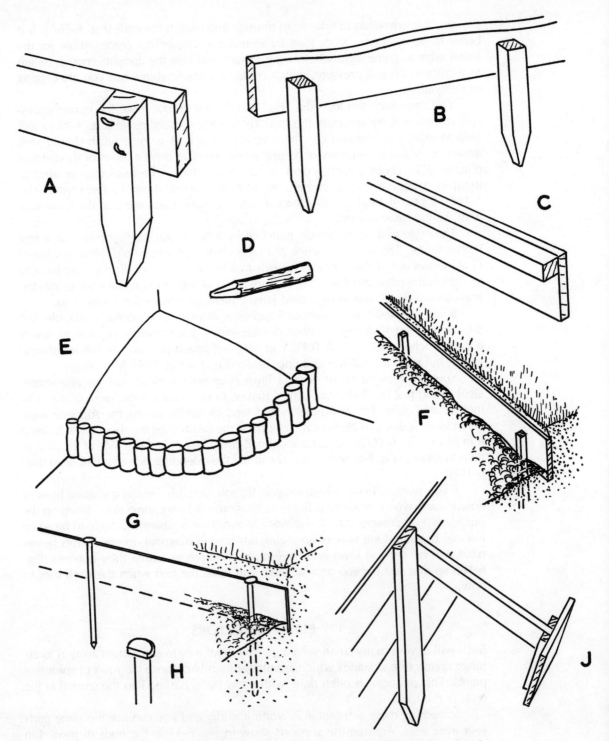

Fig. 6-16. Keep garden edges in place with stakes into the ground.

Fig. 6-17. Protect seedlings from birds with cotton strands on wooden ends.

### Table 6-7. Materials List for
### Bird Protectors.

First end: 1 piece 24 × 4 × 1 and 2 pieces 12 × 2 × 1
Second end: 1 piece 12 × 7 × 1 and 1 piece 18 × 2 × 1

sowing and string strands between them before the first shoots appear. The supports should be high enough for birds to tangle their legs before they are very close to the ground. Strands raised up to 6 inches should be satisfactory.

1. If there are two rows of seeds fairly close together, the simplest supports are straight pieces with legs to thrust into the ground (Fig. 6-18A). Round the ends, and then drive nails partly into the edges for attaching the strands (Fig. 6-18B).

2. Arrange the legs to come to the top edge (Fig. 6-18C). If you have to hit the supports to get them into the ground, your blows can come directly on these pieces.

3. Pivot the legs on bolts so that they will swing up to reduce bulk during storage (Fig. 6-18D).

4. For a single row, particularly if it is a crop that needs protection until the leaves are several inches high, it is better to make a semicircular end (Fig. 6-18E).

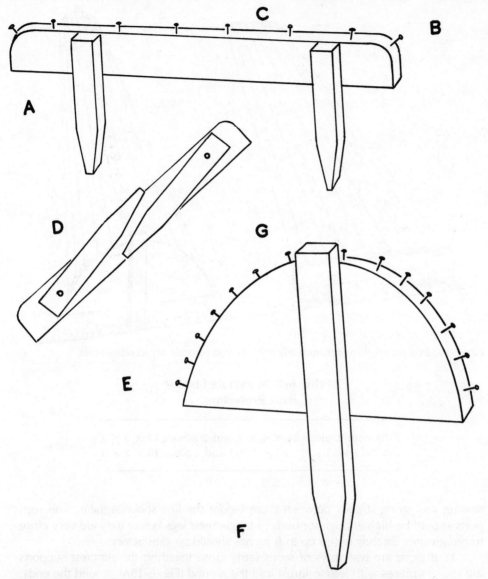

Fig. 6-18. Mount the wooden ends to support cotton strands on stakes that can be arranged to fold.

5. The end can have two legs, similar to those on the straight end, or there might be a central piece (Fig. 6-18F) extending a short distance above the shaped part (Fig. 6-18G), for thrusting or hitting into the ground.

6. You can carry the center leg higher if you want to mount a scarecrow, flag, or other additional bird scarer.

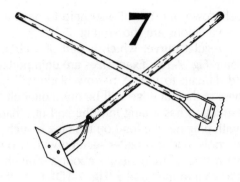

# 7

# Special Hand Tools

Y OU CAN DO MOST GARDEN WORK, PARTICULARLY ON THE LAND AROUND YOUR HOME, with a few standard hand tools. Such tools have stood the test of time and have evolved into patterns that generally are acceptable. They form the mainstay of gardener's tool kits. One advantage of making your own tools is that, besides these standard tools, you can make others that will do jobs better or are more suitable for your needs. You can have tools for which there is no manufactured alternative. Some of the tools might be similar to those found in a tool store, while others might be special designs.

The tools described in this chapter are not all new designs. They are mostly the types of hand tools that can be regarded as extra to the basic gardening tools that every gardener should have. You might not find a need for all of them, but others will be preferable to some basic tools. A special tool does not have to be difficult to make while allowing you to perform a task better than the tool it replaces.

## TURF EDGER

You can trim the edges of the grass alongside a flower border with a spade, but because of its curved cross section, it will not produce a uniform line when you look along the edge of the turf. A spade is not a sharp-cutting tool; its edge does not go easily through matted turf. It is better for straightness of cut and ease of working to have a turf edger (a cutting tool made straight in section). This tool has a blade made from a piece of steel taken from discarded farm machinery. You can make the edger from new tool steel, but mild steel is not stiff enough and would not keep its edge for long.

You use the edger with a double action. Thrust it down to make the first cut, and then rock it both ways to lengthen the cut. Its top should have a handle suitable for your hand to push down and it will also help to have a foot position to give a greater thrust. Some variations are shown (Fig. 7-1).

1. Cut the blade to a regular curve, which is part of a circle (Fig. 7-1A), or take the end to a slight point (Fig. 7-1B). Exact sizes are unimportant, but too wide a blade will be weak and difficult to use. A narrow blade will have to be thrust more often, and straightness of the cut edge will be more difficult to maintain.

2. The simplest construction has a tang into the end of a handle with a tube ferrule (Fig. 7-1C). Even with brazing, the load on the tang is such that it should be wider than on many other tools, and it is better secured with two rivets.

3. For the tang, have a strip of mild steel—about a $5/8$-inch $\times$ $3/8$-inch section—and forge one end to go into the handle (Fig. 7-1D). Cut off with enough left to make the palm, and hammer this down to a piece wide enough for two $1/4$-inch rivets (Fig. 7-1E).

4. Clean the meeting surfaces, and then rivet the parts together and braze or weld them. See that the tang is square to the blade in both directions.

5. Another method of attaching the blade puts handle and blade between steel-cheek strips (Fig. 7-1F). With a $1\frac{1}{4}$-inch diameter handle the strips can be about $7/8$-inch $\times$ $3/16$-inch-section mild steel.

6. Taper both sides of the end of the handle for about 6 inches to the thickness of the blade (Fig. 7-1G). Cut the strips to fit against the wood and the blade. One might have its top straight and the other turned out for a step (Fig. 7-1H). Round the ends of both pieces and bend them slightly to fit closely in position.

7. Drill for $1/4$-inch rivets through the handle and blade in the steel strips and the blade. Rivet and braze the strips to the blade.

### Table 7-1. Materials List for Turf Edger.

| | |
|---|---|
| 1 blade | 9 $\times$ $4\frac{1}{2}$ $\times$ $5/32$ or thicker tool steel |
| **If tang is used:** | |
| 1 tang | from 6 $\times$ $5/8$ $\times$ $3/8$ mild steel |
| 1 ferrule | 2 $\times$ $1\frac{1}{4}$ $\times$ $1/16$ mild steel tube |
| **If cheeks are used:** | |
| 1 strip | 7 $\times$ $7/8$ $\times$ $3/16$ mild steel |
| 1 strip | 9 $\times$ $7/8$ $\times$ $3/16$ mild steel |
| 1 rod | for rivets 10 $\times$ $1/4$ diameter mild steel |
| **In both cases:** | |
| 1 wood handle | 30 $\times$ $1\frac{1}{4}$ diameter |
| 1 step, if required | 8 $\times$ $3/8$ diameter mild steel |

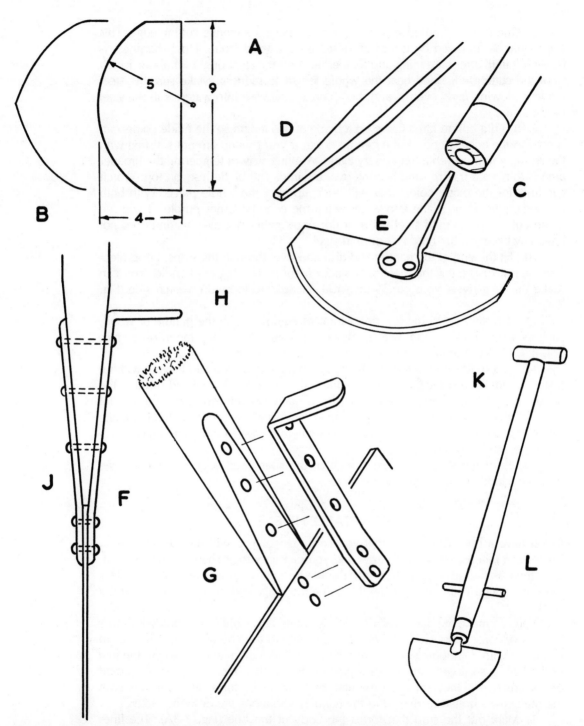

Fig. 7-1. Rivet the blade of the turf edger to its tang (A-E) or you can use a double arrangement of cheeks (F-J). The handle (K) can be given a step (L) for foot pressure.

8. Grind the curved edge on both sides to make a knifelike cutting edge. This step could be followed by use of an oilstone or a water stone. Final sharpness is better left until after hardening and tempering. Rub the steel bright for about 1 inch from the cutting edge and heat the whole length to redness. Make sure the steel blade is glowing fairly evenly, and then plunge edgewise into water. Rub the steel bright again.

9. It is difficult to fan a flame on a blade of this length so the oxide colors can spread to the edge evenly, but it can be done. If you try and are not satisfied with the result, you must reharden and try again. Another way of tempering the broader area is to have a tray of sand heating over a flame. The blade rests on top. Watch carefully for the oxide colors that will build up over the whole piece. With both methods, plunge the blade into water when the edge becomes purple. If you see oxide colors on the mild steel strips, it does not matter because heating does not have any effect on the hardness of mild steel.

10. Fit the end of the handle and drill and rivet through the strips. For protection against rust, paint the meeting surfaces before attaching the handle. You can make the long rivets from cut ¼-inch rod. Heads are formed on each side (Fig. 7-1J).

11. To stand up to the levering action of cutting, make the handle of wood, such as ash or hickory, that withstands flexing loads. At the top tenon on a cross grip (Fig. 7-1K), thoroughly round all the wood for comfort.

12. If you attach the blade to the handle with a tang, you can leave it without a step for foot pressure. One way of adding this is to put a steel rod through the handle (Fig. 7-1L). It should be satisfactory to put a ⅜-inch rod through a parallel 1¼-inch diameter handle. To compensate for any weakening due to drilling, make the shaft of the handle about ¼ inch thicker where the hole comes and taper off toward top and bottom.

13. Paint the steel to within 1 inch of the sharpened edge and varnish the wooden handle to complete the turf edger.


## ADAPTABLE HOE

If you have a hoe with blades that you can change, you will increase its scope. Blades can then be of different sizes and you can vary their shapes. Constructionally, there is the advantage that only the blade need be made of tool steel. This type construction simplifies hardening and tempering. The other part can be mild steel.

You can make the hoe shown in Fig. 7-2 in two possible forms, and with some alternative constructions. The blade can be square to the line of the handle, so you can use it with a chopping action, or it can be set at a more acute angle to the line of the handle so it will function as a push-pull or Dutch hoe. The general method of construction is the same, but the first instructions are for a push-pull hoe with the metal parts bolted or riveted to the handle. Variations are described later.

1. Mark out the strip that forms the body of the hoe (Fig. 7-3A). The lines across for the bends diagonal to the edges can be at 60 degrees, but these affect the

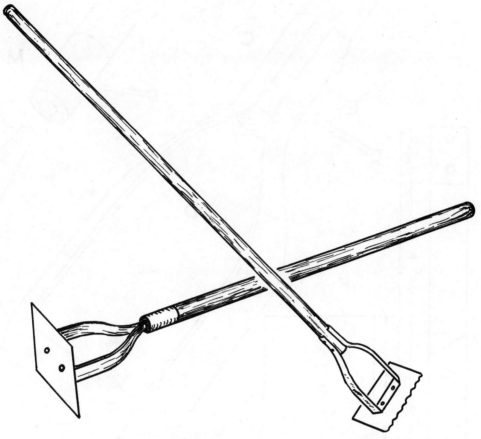

Fig. 7-2. You can make a hoe adaptable if you can bolt different blades on.

**Table 7-2. Materials List for Adaptable Hoe.**

| | |
|---|---|
| 1 frame | 15 × 1 × 3/16 mild steel |
| 1 or more blades | 6 × 3 × 16 or 18 gauge tool steel |
| 2 bolts with nuts and washers | 3/4 × 1/4 diameter |
| 23/16 rivets to suit handle | |
| 1 wood handle | 48 × 1 1/8 diameter |

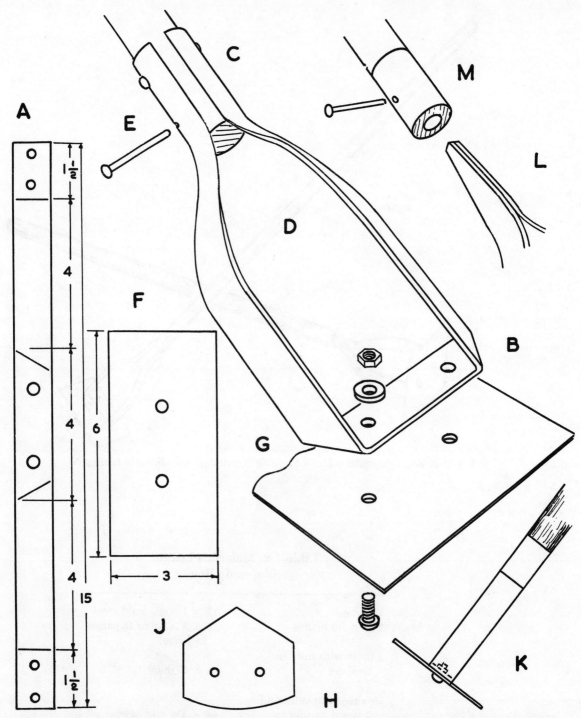

A

$1\frac{1}{2}$

4

6

4

4

15

$1\frac{1}{2}$

E

C

M

D

L

F

B

3

G

J

H

K

Fig. 7-3. *Rivet the strip part of the hoe (A-E) to the handle and drill the blades (F-K) so they bolt on. Alternatively, the strip can fit into the handle (L,M).*

98

angle at which the blade will be to the handle. You might want to try bending a strip of paper or card to find what angle would suit your needs best.

2. Mark the positions of holes and drill those for the bolts through the blade. It is better to leave the holes for rivets through the handle until after shaping, or only drill one side, so that you can drill through the handle and the other side at the same time during fitting.

3. Bend the strip on the diagonal lines (Fig. 7-3B) by hammering over in a vise.

4. Curve the ends that will fit against the handle (Fig. 7-3C). You can create this curve by hammering a rod over the hot metal resting on a partly open vise.

5. Bend the two sides in toward the handle equally (Fig. 7-3D). They also will have to be given a slight twist to bring the ends into line at the handle.

6. Fit the end of the handle between the frame sides and drill through for rivets or bolts (Fig. 7-3E). Paint or varnish where the metal and wood meet, and then join these parts together.

7. The basic blade is a piece of tool steel cut to a rectangular shape (Fig. 7-3F). If you make it slightly thicker than if you intend to heat treat it, you can use it without hardening and tempering. Drill for the bolts and make a trial assembly. Sharpen the cutting edges. If you harden and temper, bring the edges to purple oxide colors.

8. It helps in cutting some small surface weeds if you serrate the cutting edge like a saw or cut with small curves (Fig. 7-3G). The edges do not have to be straight across. You might prefer to have an edge cut diagonally so that there is one long corner for digging into stubborn weeds. You can curve (Fig. 7-3H) or point (Fig. 7-3J) the edge.

9. If you want to make a chopping type of hoe, instead of making bends at an angle across the body strip, bend them squarely. The part across the end will finish square to the handle and you can bolt on a blade that can chop from either side (Fig. 7-3K).

10. Riveting and bolting the sides through the handle will provide sufficient strength for the push-pull action of hoeing. This structure will be satisfactory for a chopping action if the handle is hardwood and is taken far enough through the metal sides to resist splitting.

11. You can have a tubular ferrule on the end of the handle and the sides of the tool frame brazed to it. The ferrule compresses the wood and resists any tendency to split.

12. You can bring the two ends of the frame together and point them (Fig. 7-3L), then strengthen the handle end with a long ferrule. After driving the metal into the hole, a rivet through the ferrule and all parts will secure it (Fig. 7-3M).

## SIMPLE TOOLS

Several very simple tools might not be available through a manufacturer, yet the craftsman/gardener can make them to aid his hobby. Some of these tools are appropriate to use with window boxes, hanging plant holders, and other small gardening situations where tools of standard size would be too bulky. Sometimes toylike tools are offered for the purpose, but it would be better to have substantial tools within their limitations. You might alter and develop the tools to suit your needs.

**Reversible Hand Hoe.** You can make a reversible hand hoe from a strip of mild steel that is ¾ inch × ⅛ inch and about 10 inches long. Bend one end to make the hoe and file its edge thin (Fig. 7-4A). You can leave the other end square as a little Dutch hoe or file it to a rounded point (Fig. 7-4B). You can make a handle by binding with electrician's tape, but it would be better if you fit two wooden slabs (Fig. 7-4C) about 4 inches long. Drill the top slab and the steel to clear two screws, and then drill undersized holes for the screw threads in the lower slab. Partly shape the slabs before assembly.

**Hook Tool.** In its smallest size, a hook tool acts as a hoe or cultivator. It has about a 2-inch cut when flat or a 1-inch cut when on edge for use in confined spaces. You can make it larger for more general use. For the small version, use steel 1-inch × ¹⁄₁₆-inch section. Bend to shape (Fig. 7-4D) and file the cutting edges thin. The example is shown with a tang to fit into a file handle (Fig. 7-4E), but you could make it with a wooden slab handle (Fig. 7-4F).

**Paving Stone Hook.** When you form a path with stone slabs, whether squared blocks or natural shapes as crazy paving, weeds will grow in the gaps. You can remove these weeds with the paving stone hook. It should reach into even the narrowest crevices. The hooks are on a strip of ¼-inch-diameter steel about 15 inches long. Tool steel is advisable if the double hook is to have a long life. The handle is

### Table 7-3. Materials List for Simple Tools.

| | |
|---|---|
| Reversible hand hoe | |
| 1 blade | 10 × ¾ × ⅛ mild or tool steel |
| 2 slabs | 5 × ¾ × ⅜ wood |
| | |
| Hook tool | |
| 1 blade | 10 × 1 × ¹⁄₁₆ mild or tool steel |
| 1 handle: | either 2 wood slabs 5 × 1 × ⅜ or a file handle |
| | |
| Paving stone hook | |
| 1 rod | 15 × ¼ diameter tool steel |
| 1 handle | 5 × ¾ diameter wood |
| | |
| Paving stone knife | |
| 1 blade | 10 × 3 × ⅛ tool steel |
| 2 slabs | 5 × 1 × ⅜ wood |

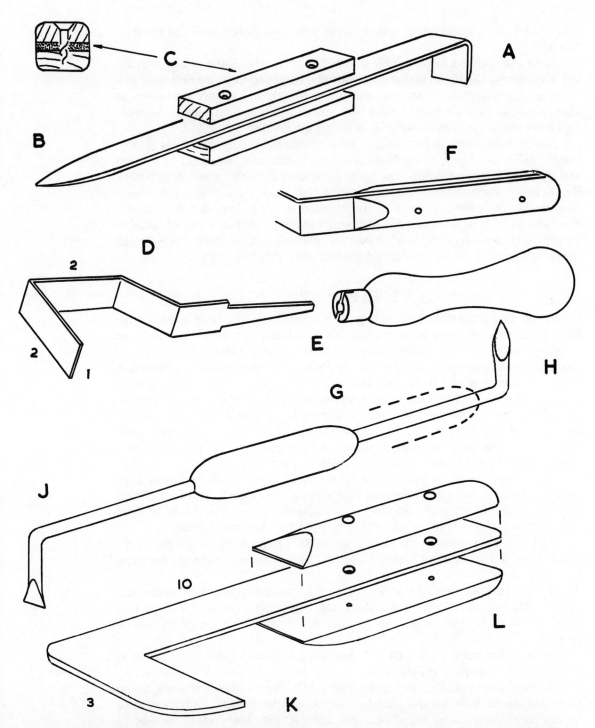

Fig. 7-4. *The reversible hand hoe has flat, slab handles (A-C). A hook tool can fit into a round handle or have slabs (D-F). The paving stone hook has a wooden handle (G-J). A paving stone knife can have a slab handle (K,L).*

a piece of ¾-inch wood dowel rod, 5 inches long, and drilled to fit the rod (Fig. 7-4G).

Bend one end and forge and file it to a thin blade (Fig. 7-4H) in line with the rod. Slide on the handle up to that end while you bend and forge the other end to a chisel section (Fig. 7-4J). If you use tool steel, harden and temper the cutters to blue or purple. Slide the handle out of the way as you heat treat each end. Smear the center of the rod with epoxy glue to secure the handle.

**Paving Stone Knife.** A hook might not be substantial enough for weeds in large cracks. The knife shown in Fig. 7-4K is more capable of standing up to hacking and chopping to greater depths. The blade is cut from sheet tool steel (⅛ inch thick should be satisfactory) and it is shown with a slab handle (Fig. 7-4L). There is no need to thin the edge because it is not intended to cut in line, but its tip works more like a chisel or tiny hoe. It is the temper at the point that is crucial. Harden the end, and then temper by heating near the angle so that the oxide colors spread slowly to the point, which you should quench when purple.

## BULB PLANTER

When you must plant something as large as a flower bulb, you need a rather large hole. If you make the hole by pushing a stick or a dibber into the ground and then levering it round to make the hole bigger, the effect is to compress the soil around the hole. Compressed soil makes it hard for the delicate roots to enter, and there is a risk that the roots will be broken as you insert the bulb. It is better to remove enough soil so that what is left is at its normal consistency. If you use a trowel to dig a hole, you remove more soil than is necessary. You can thrust a piece of parallel tube in, but there would be difficulty in removing soil from inside it each time. It would be better to make a tapered, tubular planter. The hole it makes is better for planting, and any soil inside is easily pushed through.

The planter shown in Fig. 7-5 should suit most flower bulbs and other large seeds or plants. It will make a tapered hole up to 6 inches deep. The conical tube part has a dowel-rod handle attached with strip-steel pieces (Fig. 7-6A). Riveted construction is shown, but you can braze or weld the sheet-metal cone.

1. Draw a side view of the cone (Fig. 7-6B). Based on this, draw the developed shape as described in Chapter 3 (Fig. 3-5). Allow enough metal for the edges to overlap about ½ inch.

2. Mark a centerline on the development for the position of the handle strip opposite the joint. Drill rivet holes along one edge before rolling the metal to a cone. Allow for two 3/16-inch rivets for each handle strip, but the others can be ⅛ inch.

3. Bend the conical tube. Drill through for the ⅛-inch rivets and fit them to hold the tube in shape (Fig. 7-6C).

4. Bend the strips for the handle (Fig. 7-6D). They follow the slope of the cone, but should have parallel ends to take the wooden handle. Drill those ends for central wooden screws (Fig. 7-6E). Drill and rivet the other ends to the tube.

5. Cut and fit a piece of dowel rod between the strips and screw it in place. If you have a wood lathe you might prefer to turn a shaped handle.

Fig. 7-5. A bulb planter removes sufficient soil without disturbing the surrounding area.

**Table 7-4. Materials List for Bulb Planter.**

| | |
|---|---|
| 1 tube | from 12 × 9 × 18 gauge mild steel |
| 2 handle sides | 7 × ¾ × ⅛ mild steel |
| 1 handle | 5 × 1 diameter wood dowel rod |
| | |
| Rivets and screws to suit | |

6. Not everything you plant will need to go the full depth of the tool. It is helpful to know how much of the tube is in the ground, by making deep scratches at 3 inches, 4 inches, and 5 inches from the bottom (Fig. 7-6F).

7. You can let the handle parts plain or you can paint them, but the tube should be left untreated.

## RIDGER

For planting seeds, you have to make a groove or furrow in the ground. When plants are growing in rows, you will have to scoop soil from between the rows to build up around the plants. A *ridger* or furrower is a tool primarily used for the second purpose, but it also will make planting furrows or drills.

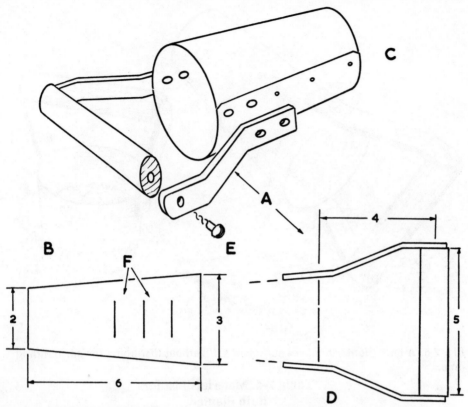

Fig. 7-6. The bulb planter has a conical body with strips to join to a handle.

The tool can be small and short-handled for some work, but for most jobs it should be long enough to use when standing and wide enough to form grooves and ridges where rows of plants are 12 inches or more apart. Some tools have a blade like some snow plows and large farm double ploughs. You use them with a pulling action so that you do not walk on the part you have worked.

1. The blade shown in Fig. 7-7A is cut from a square piece of sheet metal. This square shape gives a corner folded at 45 degrees. Other angles are possible. You can experiment with paper and use the shape you prefer as a template. You do

**Table 7-5. Materials List for Ridger.**

| | |
|---|---|
| 1 blade | from 10 × 10 × 18 gauge mild or tool steel |
| 1 stem | from 15 × ⅜ diameter mild steel |
| 1 ferrule, as needed | |
| 1 handle | 48 × 1⅛ wood |

104

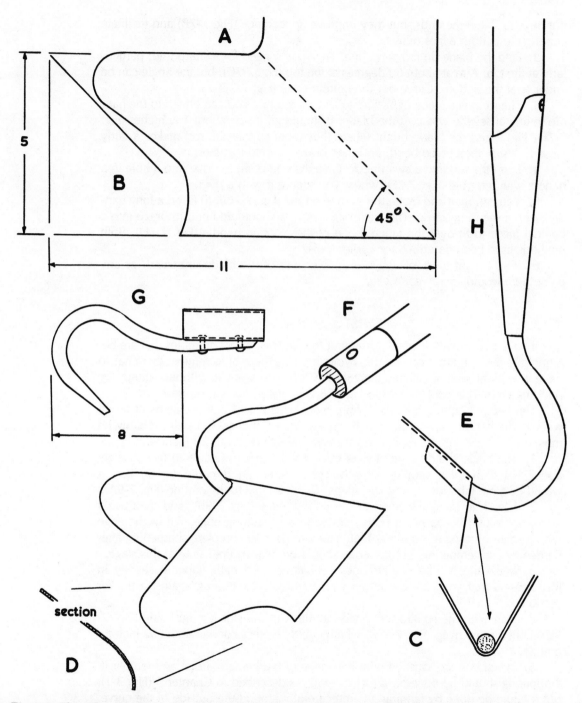

Fig. 7-7. The ridger blade is cut square and bent to shape (A-E). The stem curves to fit and can go into the handle, be riveted to a ferrule, or be continued into a conical socket (F-H).

not have to shape the ends, but they improve appearance (Fig. 7-7B) and facilitate curving the bottom edges outward.

2. Fold the blade on the bend line. There is no need for a sharp fold, particularly at the top. Aim at about 60 degrees at the top (Fig. 7-7C), but the angle can be wider near the bottom. Curve out the bottom edge (Fig. 7-7D).

3. The stem is a piece of ⅜-inch-diameter rod that you can attach to the handle in any of several ways. At the blade, it should go inside about 1½ inches (Fig. 7-7E). File it and the blade bright where they meet so that the rod makes a fairly close fit inside the curved bend, and then braze or weld together.

4. Form the rod into a swan neck. Give the end point to drive into a hole in a handle with a ferrule (Fig. 7-7F), where you secure it with a rivet.

5. You can rivet and braze the stem to a tube (Fig. 7-7G), to fit on a long handle, with a securing screw. The stem might have a shoulderd end to braze into a conical piece to fit over the tapered end of the wooden handle (Fig. 7-7H). Both methods have been described for earlier tools.

6. If you paint the tool, leave the lower half of the blade untreated, as any paint there would soon wear away.

## THISTLE HOOK

If you have to deal with a small amount of thistles, nettles, or brambles that are beginning to overrun the crop you are trying to grow, the tool to remove them has to have a working end small enough to go where you want it without cutting the standing crop. This hook shown in Fig. 7-8 is intended for that purpose.

The hooked cutting edge has sharp teeth to grip and cut the stems of tough weeds. The handle can be any length greater than 6 inches, but will probably be most useful if it is 15 inches (giving an overall length of about 20 inches).

1. The blade should be tool steel thick enough not to buckle in use. A sheet about 1/16 inch thick should be satisfactory. Although it could be thicker, it would be more laborious to cut and shape. Cut the metal to the outline (Fig. 7-9A).

2. File large triangular teeth in the hollow edge (Fig. 7-9B), and then use a large, half-round file to bevel both sides to make a cutting edge. Finish the edge with a small oilstone (used like a file). You will have to complete sharpening after hardening and tempering, but the edge should be near its final state at this stage.

3. Make the handle of hardwood. Whatever its length, taper it slightly in thickness so that you can strengthen your hand grip by pulling against a thicker section.

4. Start with the square-sectioned handle. Cut the slot for the blade (Fig. 7-9C). Drill for two rivets (Fig. 7-9D), which could be pieces of nail about ⅛ inch diameter.

5. When you are satisfied with the shape of the blade, harden and temper it. Tempering should be done on a tray of sand, as described in Chapter 3 (Fig. 3-1), but it could be done by fanning a flame carefully around the outside of the curve. Stop when dark brown or purple oxides reach the cutting edge.

6. Complete the shaping of the handle before assembly or leave final shaping

Fig. 7-8. A thistle hook will pull and cut off tougher weeds.

**Table 7-6. Materials List for
Thistle Hook.**

| 1 blade | from $7 \times 3 \times \frac{1}{16}$ or thicker tool steel |
| 1 handle | from $16 \times 1\frac{1}{2} \times 1\frac{1}{2}$ hardwood |

until after riveting. You can round the section fully, or you could leave it with a square section with rounded corners.

7. The loads on the rivets mainly are across them and the heads have to do little more than prevent them from falling out. Countersink the holes only lightly and cut the rivet ends with just enough projecting to hammer into them (Fig. 7-9E).

8. Paint or varnish the handle. Leave the steel untreated.

## WOOD AND NAILS RAKE

To be successful, a tool does not have to be complicated or difficult to make. You can make a satisfactory rake from wood and nails for ordinary garden use or for gathering large grass cuttings and weeds.

The rake shown in Fig. 7-10 has eight tines made from nails spaced about 1½ inches apart (it could be made to other sizes). The head is in two parts so that the nails will not be forced back if they strike stones or if you drop it on hard surfaces.

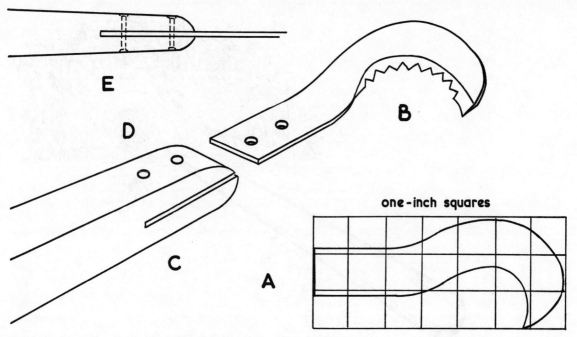

one-inch squares

Fig. 7-9. Rivet the thistle-hook blade (A,B) into its handle (C-E).

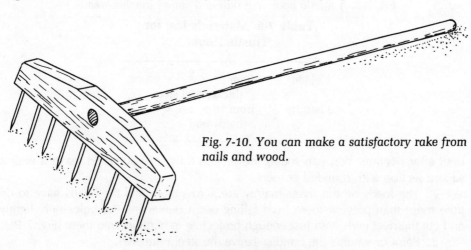

Fig. 7-10. You can make a satisfactory rake from nails and wood.

### Table 7-7. Materials List for Wood and Nails Rake.

| | |
|---|---|
| 1 head | 14 × 1 × 1 |
| 1 head | 14 × 2 × 1 |
| 1 handle | 48 × 1⅛ diameter |
| | |
| nine 4-inch nails | |

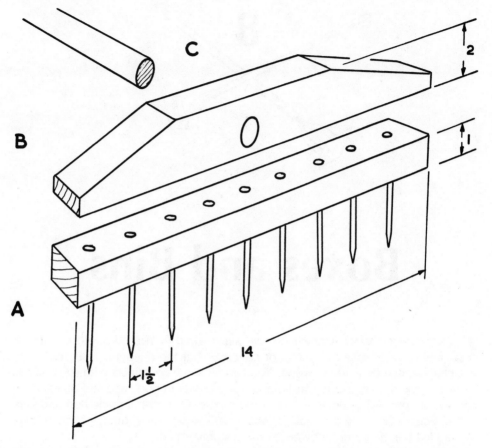

Fig. 7-11. *The nails in the rake go through one piece of wood, and their heads are covered by the other piece that you have drilled for the handle.*

You might want some weight in the head, but a light hardwood is recommended. The nails suggested are 4 inches long.

1. Start with the strip to take the nails (Fig. 7-11A). Mark the positions of the nails and drill for them before cutting the ends to length. This drilling will reduce the risk of end-grain splitting. The ends need not be cut off until after assembly. Drill the nail holes slightly undersize (how much smaller depends on the wood). It will be worthwhile to experiment on a scrap piece of the same wood to see what size gives a tight grip on the nail without splitting. Drill squarely, with the aid of a drill press, if possible. Lightly countersink for the nail heads.

2. Make the cover piece (Fig. 7-11B) and drill it for the handle (Fig. 7-11C).

3. Drive the nails so the heads finish level with the surface.

4. Join the two parts of the head with glue and screws (which you can drive from below between nails). Four screws should be enough.

5. Glue in the handle. For further security, you could drive a screw down through the head or you could saw a cut across the end and drive in a wedge.

6. Paint the rake if you prefer.

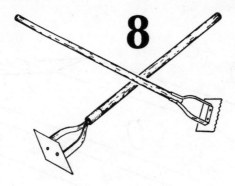

# 8

# Boxes and Bins

CONTAINERS OF MANY SIZES AND SHAPES ARE NEEDED IN THE YARD AND GARDEN. A few of these might be metal or concrete, but the majority, as described in this chapter, can be made of wood. You can fill some containers with soil and use them to grow things, others can hold or carry plants in pots, and still others hang and either hold soil or enclose one or more pots. Compost is made best and kept within bounds by using a container. Many tools and other equipment can be kept in a lidded box if you do not want to use a storage shed.

When you use containers for growing plants, you can extend your garden and provide attractive edges for decks or patios. They allow flowers to be grown on the tops of walls that would otherwise be bare. For anyone with limited garden space, window boxes, hanging containers, and other arrangements of flowers in boxes can extend the apparent size of a garden and make an attractive display where there would otherwise be a barren outlook.

Open boxes or trays have their uses for starting seedlings indoors or in a greenhouse. Too often these are crude and simple things that might not even survive one use. It is preferable to use better wood and a little more skill and care to produce longer-lasting trays. The stacking seed boxes shown in Fig. 6-8 are one way of dealing with seed growing, but you also need boxes and trays of other sorts in the well-equipped garden.

You need some boxes to contain plants in pots for permanent display or to transport plants from greenhouse to garden. The containers do not have to be soiltight and are better with some gaps for cleaning and ventilation. Some containers even might appear to have more gaps than wood.

Tool storage boxes need to be substantial, and it might be necessary to provide a lockable lid if the garden is remote from the house. The box could be a horizontal chest with a lid that serves as a seat or one that slopes to shed rain. The tool storage container might be upright and more like a shed, but not so large that you could get into it.

The wood used might be a resinous type that has a good resistance to moisture, but you can use other woods that you can protect with paint or preservative. If seeds are to be grown in soil close to the wood, check that there is no risk of the particular preservative affecting the crop. It is possible to use plywood, but that should be exterior or marine grade plywood that has a glue unaffected by moisture. Where solid wood is difficult to obtain in suitable sections, plywood will make satisfactory boxes. It needs care in cutting to avoid ragged edges and it is more difficult to form corner joints.

Much can be done with natural wood or boards that are not prepared to the stage where they would be suitable for better carpentry or cabinetwork. You can build pieces cut from poles or branches into attractive containers. When a lumberyard cuts planks and boards from round logs, it removes slabs from the outside. The slabs are flat inside and curved outside. Much of that outside wood is discarded and burned. You can use it for parts of plant pot stands.

When boards are cut through the log, one or both edges will have an outline following the profile of the log. This *waney edge* would be cut off and the edge of the board made straight, but in some boxes or wall troughs, a board with the natural edge would look attractive and more in keeping with its surroundings than a straight board.

## BASIC BOX VARIATIONS

Boxes are not necessarily all "hammer and nail" projects. You can build boxes that way in some cases, but for others it is better to cut joints. You need variations from the simple box for special purposes. Most boxes are rectangular, but sloping sides improve appearance and help if you have to tip the contents out. The basic method of construction allows for a great many variations (Fig. 8-1).

1. If the box is longer than it is wide, it is usual to nail the longer sides to the ends (Fig. 8-2A) and to nail the bottom underneath (Fig. 8-2B). This procedure is satisfactory for most purposes.

2. At the corners, the nails have to go into end grain, which does not provide the best grip. Penetration into end grain should be at least twice the thickness of the wood. Instead of straight nailing, it is stronger to alter the angles of the nails or use dovetail nailing, with the top two nails closer than the others (Fig. 8-2C).

3. Attach the pieces making up the bottom to the sides and ends, with dovetail nailing, using closer spacing across the ends than you need at the sides.

4. If you use plywood for the sides and ends, it does not provide a very good grip for nails and it tends to split. It is better to cut the corners with tongues to fit into each other (Fig. 8-2D). You can use thinner nails to reduce the risk of splitting, and you will lock the joints by having nails both ways.

5. The greatest load comes on the bottom of a box and that has to be taken in the usual construction by nails end-on, in the direction most likely to slip.

6. It is better to enclose the bottom within the sides (Fig. 8-2E). This enclosure should be done for any heavily-loaded box, but it involves more careful workman-

Fig. 8-1. Garden boxes have several sizes and patterns.

ship and a bottom thick enough to take nails in its edge. The nails take the load across their thickness (Fig. 8-2F), instead of end-on, and the bottom is more secure.

7. Cleats under the ends of a box (Fig. 8-2G) are not essential, but they serve at least two purposes. If the box is to stand on damp earth, they keep the bottom clear and they help to strengthen the attachment of the bottom to the ends.

8. If you want to provide a box with handles for lifting, the easiest way is to put strips across the top edges at the ends (Fig. 8-3A). If you nail the ends of the strip into the ends of the sides, it will help to prevent the sides from being forced out.

9. Form more comfortable handles on a box or tray used for carrying pots or equipment by building up the ends so you can cut slots (Fig. 8-3B). If the ends are fairly thick and the slots are about 5 inches long and at least 1¼ inch deep and well-rounded you can carry heavy loads comfortably.

10. If you want to make a box of thin wood, particularly if it is plywood that you cannot expect to take nails safely in its edges, frame the box ends (Fig. 8-3C) so that the nails from the sides have thicker wood to grip.

11. This box is shown with the framing outside. That gives a clean, smooth surface inside and the top part of the framing also acts as a handle. If it is more important for the outside to be smooth, the end framing would be just as strong inside.

12. There might be a problem of nailing a bottom to a thin side. If so, you can add framing strips on the sides—either outside (Fig. 8-3D) or inside—after you have assembled the other parts of the box.

13. Sloping sides can improve the appearance of a box or trough containing

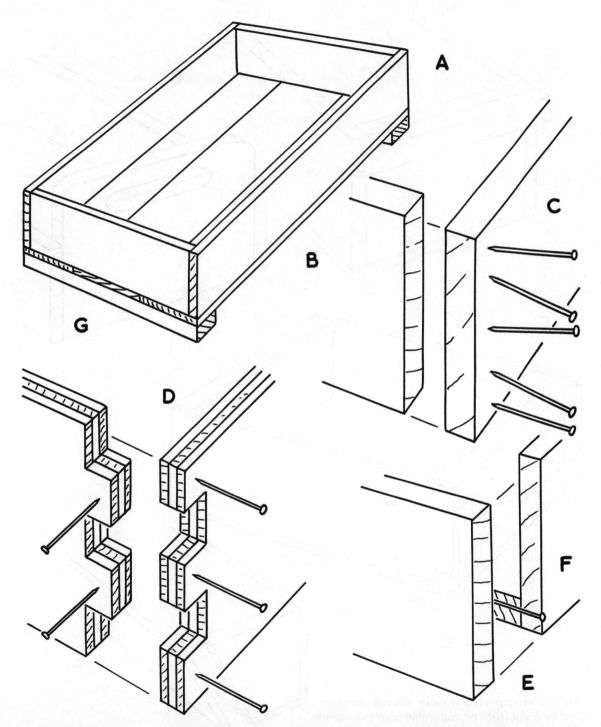

Fig. 8-2. Strengthen a nailed box (A-C) with interlocking ends (D). The bottom is better held if it is inside (E,F).

113

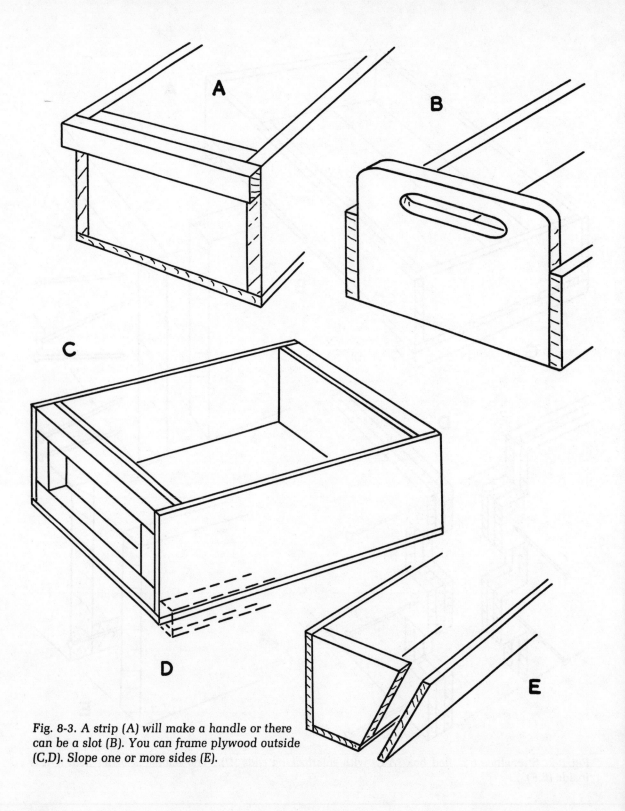

Fig. 8-3. A strip (A) will make a handle or there can be a slot (B). You can frame plywood outside (C,D). Slope one or more sides (E).

plants. You can slope the front of a window box (Fig. 8-3E). You also can slope the back of a box without having any structural problems, but it is inadvisable to slope all four sides—at least, not very much. If a box is to be made flaring out, so the top is much larger than the bottom, you will have compound angles at the corners. If you merely cut ends square across, the joints will be poor. You can accept this or alter the angles by trial-and-error, but getting the angles correct by geometry is not really worthwhile for garden woodwork.

## WINDOW BOX

Flowers growing in a box under a window enhances the appearance of the house, and it adds an extra area for the enthusiastic gardener to use. How you arrange the box in relation to the window depends on the house construction. In some town houses, there is a fairly wide sill under the window. Even if this slopes, it is possible to wedge a box level on it. A 6-inch width is about the minimum if a box is to have enough room in it for spreading roots. If the window is not set back much, you can support the box on the wall below it. In that case, you do not restrict its length and a longer box full of colorful flowers can make a very effective display.

A long box full of earth is quite heavy. This weight puts a strain on the box and on its supports (which might not be immediately apparent). After some time, boards in the box might warp or sag while brackets or other supports might collapse or buckle. In any case, the box should be deeper than the amount of soil you intend to put in it, in order to provide stiffness and to retain its contents as plants grow. With a width of at least 6 inches, soil could be 3 inches deep for small plants. If you want to make a good, large display, there should be a soil depth of 6 inches.

Mount the box securely, but do not have it against the wall. If you attach a box tightly to a wall, it would encourage rot and might harm the wall (whatever its construction). An air gap would prevent harm to the wall. It would be advisable to make the box removable, which would make it easier to turn out soil, paint the wood, or service the wall behind or below. A typical box and various supports are described as follows, with some suggested sizes as guides to proportions. Adapt sizes to suit circumstances.

1. The section of a box can be parallel. That will be appropriate for a shallow one standing on a window sill, but in most cases, the box looks better if the front slopes. The back can be slightly higher (Fig. 8-4). Do not make a considerable slope (Fig. 8-5A). The available wood will govern sizes. Allow for the bottom coming inside the back and front (Fig. 8-5B). Nailing from below might put more load on the nails than they could stand over a long period. Cut the two ends.

2. Nail the parts together. It is preferable to use nails with zinc or other coating to resist rust. Drive in a dovetail-nailing pattern at the ends. Screws instead of nails would provide extra strength into the ends near the tops of front and back (Fig. 8-5C).

3. Drill some holes in the bottom for drainage. To prevent soil from falling through, tack fine, metal mesh, perforated zinc, or something similar over each

Fig. 8-4. A window box is decorative and provides additional space to grow plants.

hole. An alternative is to merely put suitably-shaped pieces of stone or tile in place when you fill the container with soil.

4. Most window sills slope in order to shed rainwater. Bring the box level with wedges (Fig. 8-5D). Secure to the window framing with screwed blocks or metal brackets.

5. Make unobtrusive supports for a box below a window of mild steel, almost wholly behind the box (Fig. 8-5E). The supports have to be fairly stout; bending them might require more heat than a propane torch can produce. If the supports were too light, they would gradually sag under the load. One way of reducing the tendency to sag would be to screw the backboard to each bracket. So you can re-

### Table 8-1. Typical Materials List for
### Window Box.

| | | |
|---|---|---|
| 2 ends | 10 × | 8 × 1 |
| 1 back | 48 × | 10 × 1 |
| 1 front | 48 × | 8 × 1 |
| 1 bottom | 48 × | 6 × 1 |
| | | |
| For each bracket: | | |
| 1 bracket back | 24 × | 2 × 1 |
| 1 bracket rail | 10 × | 2 × 1 |
| 1 bracket strut | 15 × | 2 × 1 |

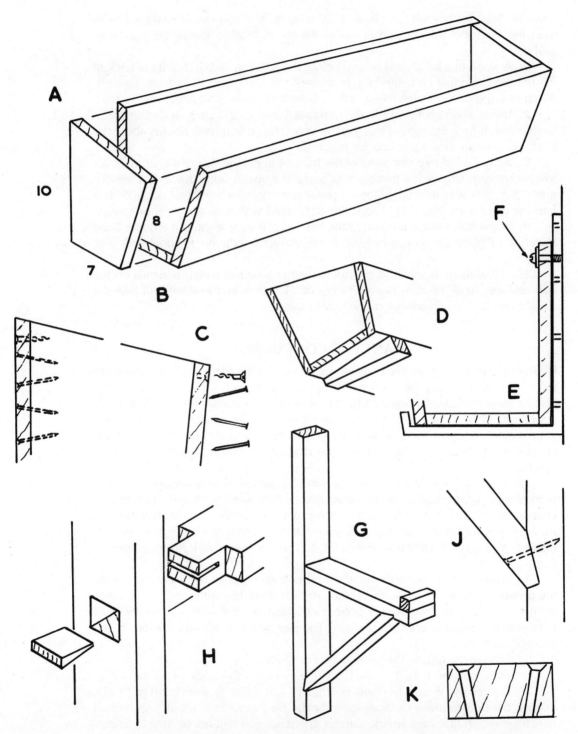

Fig. 8-5. Nail the window box and support it on brackets.

117

move the box, the bracket must have a threaded hole so you can drive the screw in from the front. Put a large washer under the screw head to spread the load (Fig. 8-5F).

6. A wood bracket should extend below the box (Fig. 8-5G), but if the back of the bracket extending up behind the box keeps the rear board away from the wall, it requires one or more high fixing screws (where they are most effective).

7. Use a tenon joint between the horizontal and upright parts, with glue and a wedge (Fig. 8-5H). Strength at this joint is important. If you have doubts about the joint, put a small steel angle bracket inside it.

8. Set out a full-size side view of the bracket to get the size of the strut. To allow for settling, arrange the piece across under the box to slope upwards a few degrees. The best way to arrange the diagonal piece to take the thrust is to notch it into the other parts (Fig. 8-5J), where it can be held with glue and nails or screws.

9. Screw holes in the top part of the bracket can be straight, but arrange those lower at a slight angle so you can use a screwdriver beside the diagonal strut (Fig. 8-5K).

10. How many brackets to provide, whether wood or metal, depends on the size and weight of the box, but a spacing of 24 inches to 30 inches will take the weight and limit any tendency of the box to sag.

## PLANT POT CONTAINER

Flowers and plants in pots need something more than the plain pot to complement the foliage. If they have been grown in the pots, however, it might be unwise to disturb them by transplanting into boxes. A wooden container for the plant in its pot can stand on a deck or patio, and a number of similar containers will enhance your outlook over the yard. When one plant has passed its prime, you can exchange it for another in the box without digging up one and replacing it with another.

The container shown in Fig. 8-6 is intended for the more enthusiastic woodworker who favors traditional construction. A container described later in this chapter provides a similar effect with simpler methods. If the container is to be well made, it is worthwhile starting with a good hardwood that can be finished by varnishing. You can use softwood and paint it to match other work in the garden or yard.

1. The choice of plywood will affect other parts. Groove the legs centrally for the plywood (Fig. 8-7A). A depth of ⅜ of an inch should be sufficient. The grooves do not need to extend below the bottom rail position, but with most methods of grooving, it is easier to cut right through. The part below is not very obvious in the finished container.

2. Groove the rails in the same way (Fig. 8-7B).

3. Mark out the legs (Fig. 8-7C). Cut tenons on the ends of all rails (Fig. 8-7D). The tenons should be long enough to just meet in the legs (Fig. 8-7E); deepen the slots to make mortises accordingly. Be careful to mark all legs and all rails together, so that sizes are the same. Otherwise, you will not be able to assemble the container squarely.

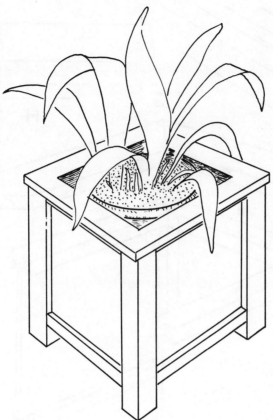

Fig. 8-6. You can make a plant-pot container with plywood panels in solid wood.

4. The bottom is a piece of plywood resting inside the side plywood panels on the bottom rails (Fig. 8-7F). Cut this to size before completing assembly. You will not be able to fit it in after you join all four sides.

5. Assemble two opposite sides. Waterproof glue alone should be sufficient, particularly if you clamp the assemblies until the glue sets. Drive thin nails from inside into the tenons if you prefer. Check that they are square, without twisting, and that they match each other.

6. Assemble the parts the other way and include the bottom. That will keep the assembly square (as viewed from the top). Check squareness the other way,

### Table 8-2. Materials List for Plant Pot Container.

| | | | |
|---|---|---|---|
| 4 legs | 16 | × 2 | × 2 |
| 8 rails | 12 | × 2 | × 1 |
| 4 tops | 14 | × 3 | × 1 |
| 4 panels | 12½ × 11½ × ½ plywood | | |
| 1 bottom | 11 | × 11 | × ½ plywood |

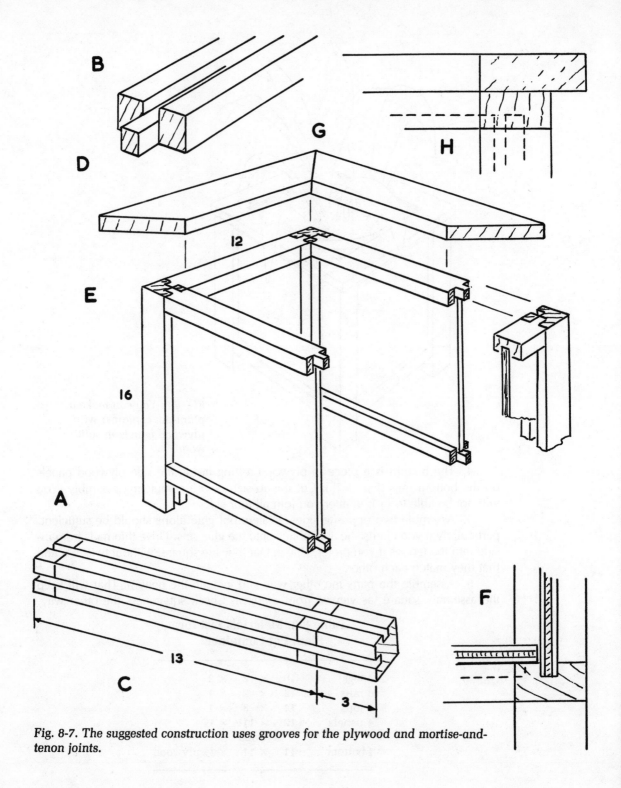

Fig. 8-7. The suggested construction uses grooves for the plywood and mortise-and-tenon joints.

and stand the container on a flat surface, with a weight on top if necessary, so that the legs stand without wobbling.

7. The top (Fig. 8-7G) has its inner edges level with the insides of the legs and rails (Fig. 8-7H). Miter the corners and fit the parts with glue and nails or screws.

## NAILED PLANT POT CONTAINER

If you prefer a simpler construction than mortise and tenon joints with plywood grooved in, it is possible to make satisfactory containers using a mainly nailed construction. This container looks very similar to the one shown in Fig. 8-6, but uses simpler methods. You fit the framing wood to the surfaces of the plywood and join two pairs of assemblies together to make the box.

The suggested construction uses ½-inch plywood and strips of 1-inch × 2-inch wood. You could use softwood finished with paint. The completed container is comparable with the previous example, but you can alter sizes easily. The container does not have to be square, but if it is square, the assemblies one way have to be narrower by the thicknesses of the two assemblies the other way. It would help to make the container stronger and more durable if you use waterproof glue, as well as nails, for all joints.

1. Cut the plywood panels for the two larger sides (Fig. 8-8A).

2. Join the legs and rails to them by nailing from inside.

3. Deduct twice the total thickness of one assembly to get the width to cut the plywood for the other panels (Fig. 8-8B). Make up these sides in the same way. Check that all legs are the same length. Put the bottom support strips on the narrow panels only at this stage (Fig. 8-8C). If necessary, plane leg and panel edges true.

4. Join the parts by nailing the wider assemblies to the narrower ones (Fig. 8-8D). Below the overlapping panels, fill in the gaps between the legs with pieces of plywood.

5. Put bottom support strips on the wider sides between the strips already on the narrow panels. Fit the bottom plywood to these supports (Fig. 8-8E).

6. You make the top from four mitered strips similar to those in the previous example, but they should come about ½ inch inside the top of the box (Fig. 8-8F).

### Table 8-3. Materials List for Nailed Plant Pot Container.

| | |
|---|---|
| 8 legs | 16 × 2 × 1 |
| 4 rails | 9 × 2 × 1 |
| 4 rails | 6 × 2 × 1 |
| 4 tops | 14 × 3 × 1 |
| 4 bottom supports | 9 × ¾ × ½ |
| 2 panels | 13 × 12 × ½ plywood |
| 2 panels | 13 × 9 × ½ plywood |
| 1 bottom | 9 × 9 × ½ plywood |

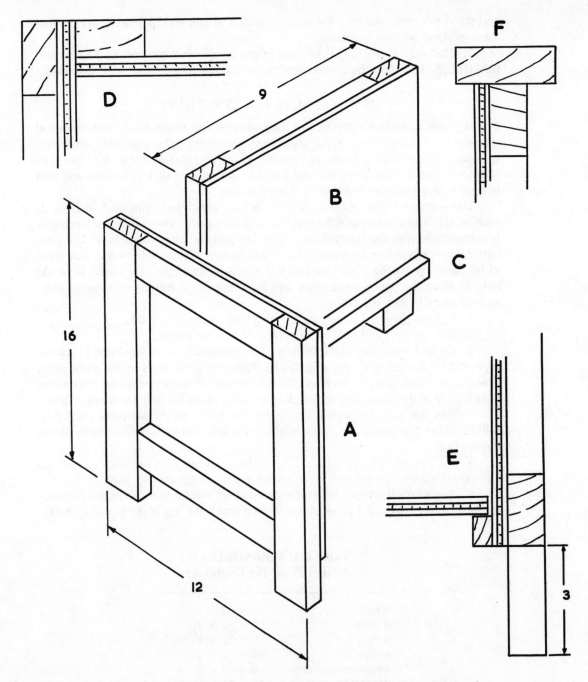

Fig. 8-8. For a simpler plant-pot container, nail the plywood inside the solid wood.

# WALL BOX

A box on top of a wall holds a display of flowers where there would otherwise be a rather blank expanse of brick or stone. You can make the box of planed boards, but this is a place where wavy-edged boards would look attractive. Perhaps you could have the front board showing waney edges at the top and where it overhangs the wall (Fig. 8-9).

A box could be any length, but practical difficulties limit it to not more than about 60 inches because of weight and the availability of suitable boards. Unless it is quite a small box, the wood should be at least 1 inch thick. If only the front of the box normally will be visible, the bottom of the back can be straight above the wall (Fig. 8-10A). If you will see both sides, it will be better to have the back extending below (Fig. 8-10B) in the same way as the front. In any case, there will be sufficient weight to keep the box in place without any special attachments.

1. Make the bottom first. It is a parallel board and governs the sizes of other parts (Fig. 8-10C).

2. Drill some drainage holes in the bottom and add two or more cleats (Fig. 8-10D) to raise the bottom off the top of the wall and allow water to run away.

3. The ends could be straight across the top or have wavy edges (Fig. 8-10E).

4. Front and back could have straight ends that are either level with the box ends or projecting slightly. If two or more boxes are to fit against each other, you must finish their ends level.

5. Alternative ends carry on the wavy edge theme by cutting to irregular curves (Fig. 8-10F).

*Fig. 8-9. A box to mount on a wall can have the natural, waney edges of the boards.*

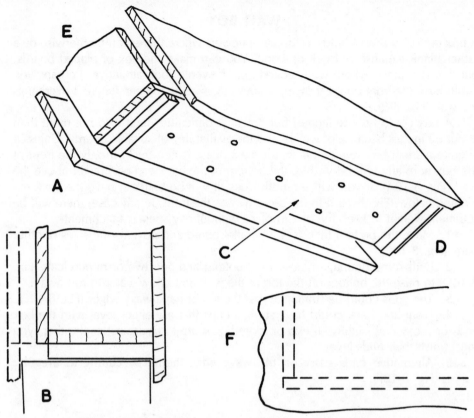

*Fig. 8-10. Nail the wall box together, but raise the bottom and provide drainage holes.*

6. Protect nails with zinc or other coatings. The box will be stronger if you drive the nails in a dovetail manner, possibly with screws at the tops, as suggested for the window boxes.

## ROD HANGING POT HOLDER

Hanging plant or flower holders are broadly divided into those that actually have soil contained in them and those that are containers for potted plants. Both can be in various sizes, but in this example we are referring to one which is intended to hold a pot of moderate size such as might hang in a porch, either alone or as a series of similar ones, to give a colorful display of potted flowers. An advantage is that you can use the same holders for other flowers, with minimum trouble, when the first ones are finished. Such a hanging holder also can be taken indoors for further use when the outside weather becomes unsuitable.

The base of the holder is a piece of plywood. The sides are made of wood rod, which is conveniently cut from dowel rod, although you can use old broom handles or similar things. Thread the parts on rope.

1. The guiding shape is the truncated cone that passes through the base and the rods (Fig. 8-11A). Measure the diameters of the rods and set out the shape to al-

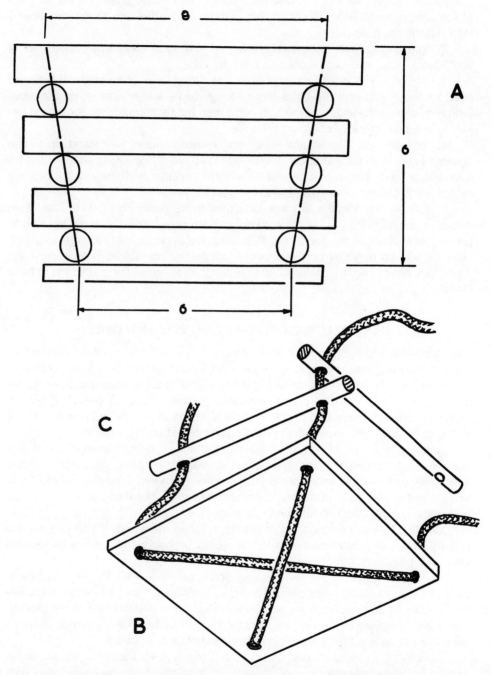

Fig. 8-11. Drill the rods of the hanging pot holder so that the assembly tapers to suit the pot.

low for the chosen number of these thicknesses. This shape gives you the location of the centers of the holes in each layer of rods. Allow the rods to extend about 1 inch outside the holes.

2. You can cut the ends squarely across and sand away any raggedness. If you have a lathe, you can bevel or round the ends.

3. Although you would have to drill close-fitting holes at an angle, there is no need for this if you drill the holes large enough to be a very easy fit on the rope. Drill the holes in the rods and the base, and then lightly countersink above and below to reduce the risk of chafe on the rope.

4. You can use almost any rope, but synthetic fibers will stand up to the weather better than natural fibers. Quite light cord would be strong enough, but for appearance, it is better to use rope ³/₁₆-inch or ¹/₄-inch diameter. It does not matter if it is plaited or three-strand construction.

5. Cut double lengths to cross underneath the base (Fig. 8-11B), and then thread on the parts (Fig. 8-11C). Tie a knot in each rope close above the top rods to prevent movement of the parts, and then continue up to tie all four parts together. How far you go depends on the situation where the pot holder is to hang. Long ropes look better and are easier to arrange among foliage (if there is space to have them).

## NATURAL WOOD HANGING POT HOLDER

You can make a hanging holder for a plant pot that looks very similar to the one made from dowel rods with natural wood. That is more suitable for larger construction, and possibly for a situation where the holder is to hang among trees or from a rustic arch rather than in a porch or similar position. Because pieces of natural wood vary, design the holder to suit the available pieces of pole or branch. The pot that is to be held will govern the approximate internal measurements.

Although you can obtain an interesting pattern by using pieces of wood that are not straight, too many varying shapes will make it difficult to get a holder that is reasonably symmetrical and looks right. Fir poles will yield a good supply of fairly straight and almost parallel pieces. There will be tapers, but if you reverse alternate layers, the overall effect should be fairly true.

Whether to leave the bark on or not depends on the wood. If you can remove it fairly easily, that is advisable. If left, it would probably come away in sections later and it tends to harbor insects.

The holder shown in Fig. 8-12 is intended to be made with 1½-inch to 2-inch-diameter wood to hold a pot about 12 inches in diameter and 14 inches high. Because it would be difficult to set out the shape in the way described in the preceding project, because of the varying wood sizes, it is better to work upside down—using the pot as a guide to the progressing shape that is built up.

1. Select the piece of wood and cut the first pieces for the top to length. So far as possible, have opposite pieces in each layer of matching thickness. Start with the top four pieces and arrange them to easily fit around the top of the pot.

2. Drill for nails (Fig. 8-13A). The hole should be clearance size in one piece

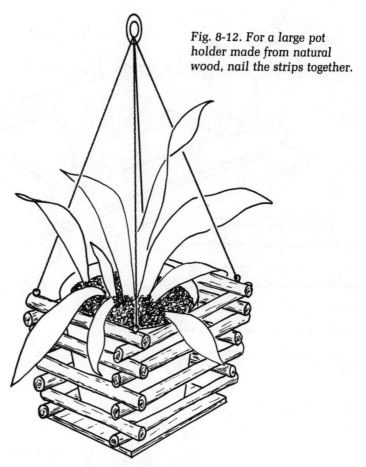

*Fig. 8-12. For a large pot holder made from natural wood, nail the strips together.*

**Table 8-4. Materials List for Rod-Hanging Pot Holder.**

| | |
|---|---|
| 1 base | 8 × 8 × ½ plywood |
| Rods from | 240 inches of 1 inch dowel rod |

and slightly undersize in the other piece. How much undersize depends on the wood, but the nail must grip without splitting the wood. Use zinc-coated nails.

3. Check squareness by measuring diagonals, although do not expect perfection. Drive the nails (Fig. 8-13B) so you bury the heads.

4. As you build up the pile, use the inverted pot as a guide to the amount of taper (Fig. 8-13C). The number of pieces of wood will depend on their diameters.

5. The bottom is a piece of exterior plywood (Fig. 8-13D). Give it a good bearing surface on the bottom two strips by planing flats on them. It might be better along these joints to use screws instead of nails.

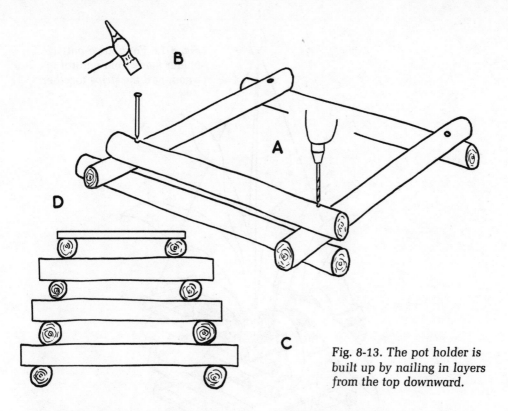

Fig. 8-13. The pot holder is built up by nailing in layers from the top downward.

6. Put large screw eyes in the corners at the top and attach hanging ropes to them, taken up to be knotted together or to a metal ring.

## PLYWOOD HANGING POT HOLDER

Anyone interested in the use of a scroll or jigsaw might welcome an opportunity to decorate a hanging plant holder. Plywood is the most convenient material for this type of decoration. This project is a box with plywood sides to hold the usual plant in a pot (Fig. 8-14). You can use exterior plywood, and then paint it so that the cutouts show a contrast. Fir plywood will not allow for much detail in the shaping so a bold treatment is advised. Mahogany or similar plywood will take all the fine detail you want, but a pot holder is something normally viewed at a distance so fine work would not be appreciated.

Suggested sizes are given in Fig. 8-15. If you join the parts with waterproof glue, only fine nails or panel pins need be used in assembly.

1. Two plywood panels overlap the edges of the other two (Fig. 8-15A), so the two inner ones (Fig. 8-15B) should be narrower if the box is to finish square.

2. For the outlines of the top edges (Fig. 8-15C), make a card template of half the shape and use it each side of centerline on the plywood.

3. The cutouts can be leaf shapes or anything else you prefer (Fig. 8-15D). Clean off any raggedness of the edges.

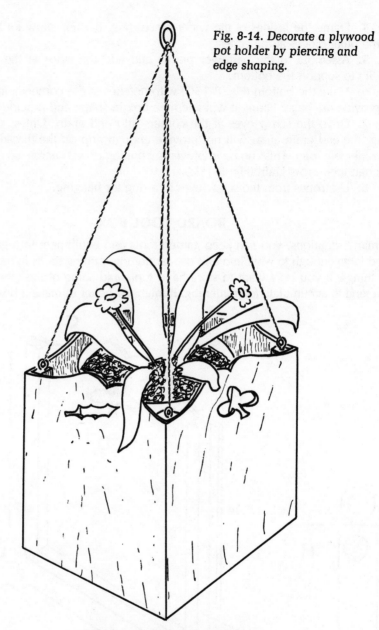

Fig. 8-14. Decorate a plywood pot holder by piercing and edge shaping.

**Table 8-5. Materials List for Plywood-Hanging Pot Holder.**

| | |
|---|---|
| 4 panels | 16 × 12 × ½ plywood |
| 1 bottom | 12 × 12 × ½ plywood |
| 4 corners | 14 × 1 × 1 |
| 4 bottoms | 12 × 1 × 1 |

4. Frame the insides of the wider pieces (Fig. 8-15E); allow for the thickness of the other pieces at the edges.

5. Assemble to the narrower pieces and add the strips at the bottom (Fig. 8-15F) to support the bottom.

6. Make the bottom (Fig. 8-15G) with notches at the corners and a few holes to provide drainage. Fitting it will keep the box in shape and provide rigidity.

7. Drive the screw eyes at the corners into end grain. Unless they are very long, the end grain areas will not provide enough grip on the threads to take the considerable load. This can be improved by putting dowels across so the screws go through their cross grain (Fig. 8-15H).

8. Use ropes from the screw eyes to a ring for hanging.

## BOARD TOOL BOX

In many situations, you can keep garden tools and equipment in a garage or in a shed large enough to walk into and use for potting, putting seeds in trays, and similar things. If you only want to store hand tools and some of the other equipment you tend to accumulate for gardening, it might be better to make a box or locker. If

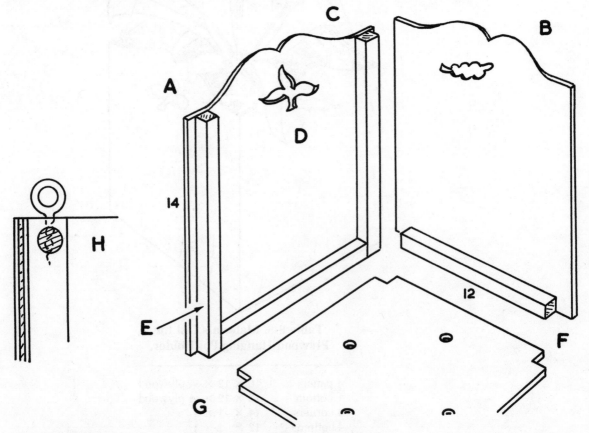

Fig. 8-15. Nail the plywood panels of the pot holder to strips inside.

the garden or yard is extensive, you will be glad to have such a box at some point distant from the main storage area.

You can make the box with solid wood or plywood. Plywood construction is described in the next project. The boards you use could have square edges, but if you are able to get tongue-and-groove boards, they will make a weatherproof box. Check what stock sizes of boards are available and scheme the overall sizes to make the best use of them without wasting much. If you have tongue-and-groove boards, you must allow for cutting tongue or groove off some boards that come at edges. Measure the longest tools you will want to store. Some long handles might fit in diagonally if you want to keep the length to the minimum.

As shown in Fig. 8-16, the lid slopes slightly to shed rain, but it also comes at a height that makes it suitable for a seat. When open, it is held just past upright by ropes.

1. The pair of ends are the key pieces that settle several other sizes. Frame the

Fig. 8-16. A large tool box will store tools near where you use them and you can use it as a seat.

ends with strips, but leave gaps at the corners for the lengthwise pieces (Fig. 8-17A). If you are using square-edged boards, bring the edges tightly together as you assemble. If they are made of normally-seasoned wood, they will expand a little outdoors and become even tighter. With tongue-and-groove wood, it is better to not force the edges very tight.

2. Join the ends with the four lengthwise strips (Fig. 8-17B). Make sure outer surfaces come level. Nails into end grain at the corners will be sufficient at this stage because the boards fitted next will secure the corner joints.

3. Check squareness by measuring diagonals.

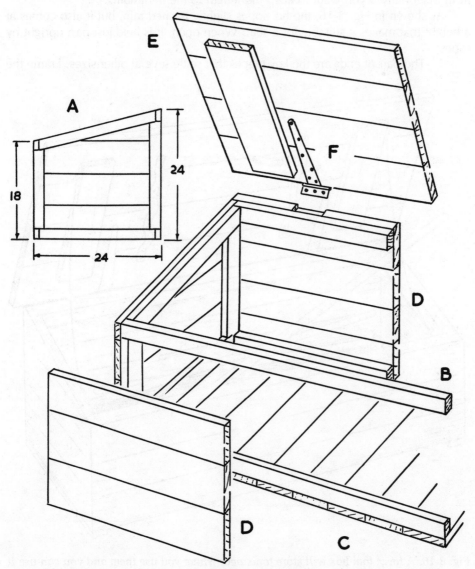

*Fig. 8-17. The large tool box is made with boards on framing.*

## Table 8-6. Materials List for
## Board Tool Box.

| | |
|---|---|
| 8 end frames | 24 × 2 × 1 |
| 8 end boards | 24 × 6 × 1 |
| 4 lengthwise strips | 60 × 2 × 1 |
| 7 lengthwise boards | 60 × 6 × 1 |
| 10 bottom boards | 24 × 6 × 1 |
| 4 or 5 lid boards | 63 × 6 × 1 |
| 2 lid cleats | 24 × 6 × 1 |
| 2 bottom cleats | 26 × 2 × 2 |
| 2 T hinges to suit | |

4. Nail on the bottom. This pattern is shown with boards across the narrow way. You could use long boards, but by using short pieces, there is less risk of the bottom warping and the assembly will be slightly stronger (Fig. 8-17C). With the bottom boards on, the assembly should keep its shape. Further check squareness as you fit the other boards.

5. Nail on the front and back boards (Fig. 8-17D). If the box is very long and there might be a risk of the boards warping later, fit one or more uprights intermediately. These boards should overlap the bottom.

6. The lid comes level at the back, but it should overlap the ends and the front by about 1 inch. Cut the boards to suit and join them with pieces across (Fig. 8-17E). It might be sufficient to put a piece near each end, but for extra strength, particularly with square-edged boards, you could have another piece at the middle.

7. Large T hinges are recommended (Fig. 8-17F.) Preferably, the hinges should reach halfway across the lid. They can go on the surface of the lid, but let the other part in enough for the lid to shut with only a small gap along the back.

8. Put screw eyes in the lid and ends for supporting ropes (Fig. 8-16).

9. You can screw strips of leather or plastic with loops under the lid to take small tools.

10. If the box will stand on concrete or be supported on stones, you can leave the bottom unaltered. To keep it away from earth, and the risk or rot, fit cleats across at the ends and perhaps intermediately.

11. Finish the wood with paint or preservative. There could be a handle and a hasp and staple for a lock, as described for the next project, if you like.

## PLYWOOD TOOL BOX

Plywood is convenient to use. Exterior or marine grades will withstand exposure to the weather. The box shown in Fig. 8-18 is similar in form to that described in the previous project, but the main parts are ½-inch plywood. Framing is shown on the outside of the plywood. This framing gives a smooth interior and offers protection to many plywood edges, where moisture might otherwise seep into the veneers if inadequately protected by paint or other finish.

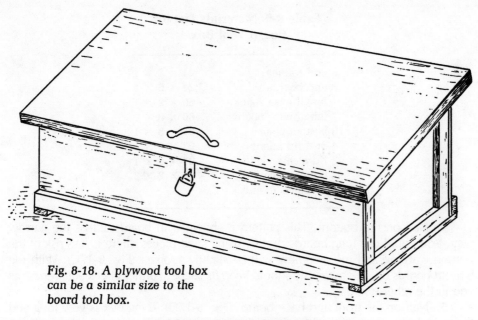

Fig. 8-18. A plywood tool box can be a similar size to the board tool box.

**Table 8-7. Materials List for Plywood Tool Box.**

| | |
|---|---|
| 2 ends | 24 × 24 × ½ plywood |
| 8 end frames | 24 × 2 × 1 |
| 1 back | 48 × 24 × ½ plywood |
| 1 front | 48 × 24 × ½ plywood |
| 4 lengthwise strips | 48 × 2 × 1 |
| 1 bottom | 48 × 28 × ½ plywood |
| 2 cleats | 28 × 2 × 1 |
| 1 top | 51 × 1 × 1 |
| 2 top frames | 29 × 1 × 1 |
| 2 top frames | 8 × 1¼ × 1¼ |
| 3 hinge blocks | |
| 3 four-inch hinges | |
| 1 handle to suit | |
| 1 hasp and staple | |

Suggested sizes are intended to allow you to cut many parts economically from the usual 48-inch × 96-inch plywood sheet. If your long tools will not go into a box this size, you will have to cut the plywood to suit and find other uses for some of the offcuts.

1. Start by making the pair of ends (Fig. 8-19A, B). You could use waterproof glue as well as nails, for this and other framing. Plane the framing pieces level on the edges where other parts must fit.

2. Cut the front and back plywood to size and stiffen top and bottom edges (Fig. 8-19C).

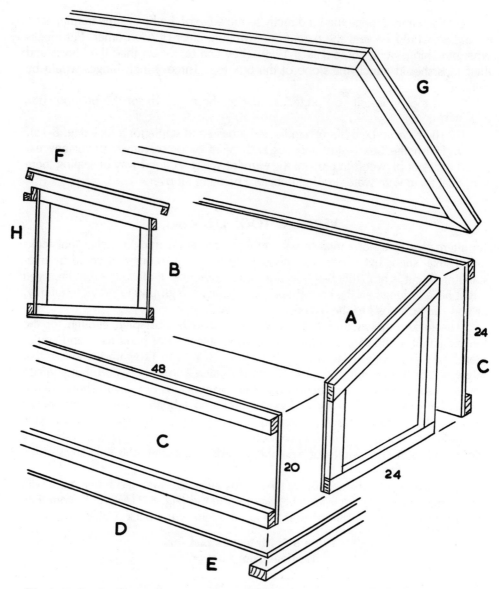

*Fig. 8-19. Frame the plywood on the outside and raise it on battens from the ground.*

3. Join these parts to the ends and check squareness.

4. The bottom could be a piece of plywood (Fig. 8-19D) overlapping the other parts. This bottom could be vulnerable in a very damp situation, and it might be preferable to fit a solid wood bottom, as suggested for the previous project. In any case, put cleats across underneath (Fig. 8-19E) to raise the bottom slightly.

5. Frame around the plywood lid so it fits loosely over the top of the box (Fig. 8-19F). For neatness, miter the strips at the corners (Fig. 8-19G), and round the edges of strips and plywood.

6. You cannot hinge the lid directly to the edge of the box as the framing strip on the lid would prevent the parts from swinging clear of each other. Put blocks where the hinges will come (Fig. 8-19H). They can be longer than the hinges and their tops should match the slope of the box top. Three 4-inch hinges would be suitable.

7. Fit tool loops, if you prefer, similar to those shown for the previous box (Fig. 8-16).

8. There could be a lifting handle and a hasp and staple for a lock (Fig. 8-18).

9. Finish the box inside and out with paint or preservative. Cover any exposed edges of plywood to prevent the entry of water. A good way of sealing them is to coat them with waterproof glue before painting all over.

## VERTICAL TOOL LOCKER

An alternative to a horizontal box for tool storage is an upright locker that looks like a small shed, but is not large enough for a person to enter. It could be freestanding, but it is probably better against a wall or fence. If made freestanding, you might have to lengthen the corner uprights to enter the ground to provide stability, or you can bolt posts to the outside.

The locker shown in Fig. 8-20 is intended to be just high enough for the longest handles and roomy enough for a good selection of hand tools and equipment. You can make it larger for power tools. If it is to fit against a fence, that might decide the height. The locker is shown made from solid wood, but you can cover it with plywood. A comparison of the two previous boxes will show the differences in construction. If you use tongue-and-groove boards, the covering should be more weatherproof than if you use square-edge boards. The roof is shown made up of boards, but that could be plywood and you can cover it with a waterproof roofing material. The widths of available boards might settle the final sizes of the sides of the locker.

1. Make a pair of sides. Bring the boards close together and frame them with strips on all edges. At the front, cut back for the top (Fig. 8-21A) and bottom (Fig. 8-21B) strips. Allow for the strips at top and bottom of the back (Fig. 8-21C).

**Table 8-8. Materials List for
Vertical Tool Locker.**

| | |
|---|---|
| 6 side boards | 60 × 6 × 1 |
| 4 side frames | 60 × 2 × 1 |
| 6 side frames | 18 × 2 × 1 |
| 3 back boards | 60 × 6 × 1 |
| 3 back frames | 18 × 2 × 1 |
| 4 roof boards | 22 × 6 × 1 |
| 3 door boards | 50 × 6 × 1 |
| 2 door boards | 15 × 6 × 1 |
| 2 four-inch hinges | |
| 1 latch or lock to suit | |

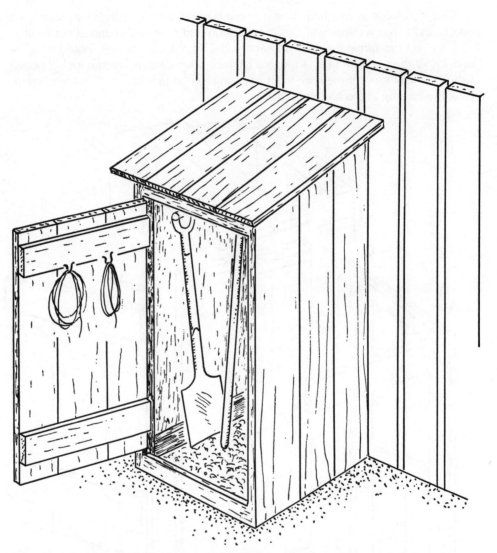

*Fig. 8-20. A vertical tool locker provides storage, but is not large enough to enter.*

2. Make the back assembly (Fig. 8-21D). You can cut the central-cross member to fit between the side framing. You do not need to notch it into the uprights.

3. Cut the top and bottom front pieces to fit into the notches and hold the assembly to the same width at the front as at the back.

4. Join all these parts. The locker can stand directly on the ground without a bottom of its own, but if you want a closed bottom, nail boards across. Check squareness (particularly in the door opening).

5. Make the roof with boards level at the back and overhanging at the sides and front (Fig. 8-21E).

6. Assemble a door (Fig. 8-21F) to fit easily into the opening. Except for not

making it so loose as to admit vermin, there is nothing to be gained by making it a precision fit. The weather will cause expansion and contraction and affect its fit.

7. You can hinge the door on either side. Two 4-inch hinges should be satisfactory. At the opposite side, arrange a latch or other fastener (with a lock if necessary). You can prevent the door from swinging too far in with strips inside overlapping the framing at top and bottom.

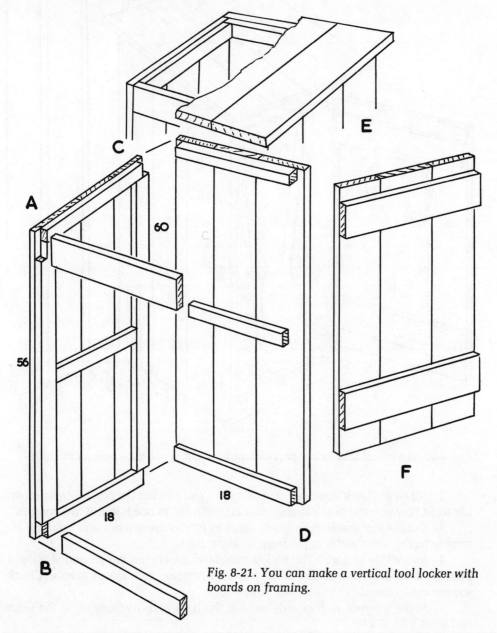

Fig. 8-21. You can make a vertical tool locker with boards on framing.

8. Fit racks and hooks for tools inside and to the back of the door. If there are many tools to stow, more can be put in if they are kept loose.

9. Finish the wood with paint or preservative.

## SECTIONAL COMPOST CAGE

Making compost is not always a year-round activity. It is convenient to have a compost container that you can take down and pack flat when you do not need it. The compost cage shown in Fig. 8-22 consists of four identical frames that you can hook together for use or reduce to a pile about 10 inches thick for storage. The suggested sizes are for a cube about 36 inches each way, but you can vary sizes to suit your needs and the amount of composting you expect to do.

In each section, the wood frame has its corner joints made with plywood gussets. If you want to show your carpentry skills, you can mortise and tenon the corner joints. You need good access for air. You can provide this access by making

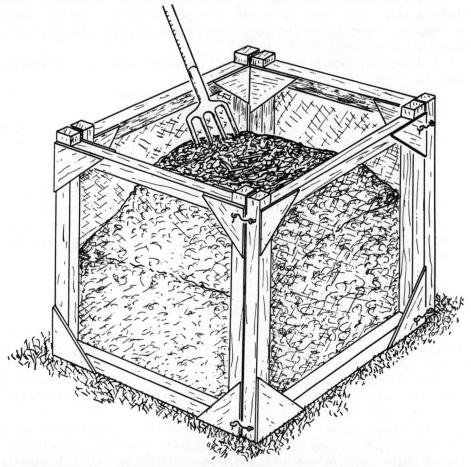

Fig. 8-22. This cage for making compost has four sides hooked together so that they can be taken apart and stored flat.

## Table 8-9. Materials List for Sectional Compost Cage.

| | |
|---|---|
| 4 posts | 36 × 2 × 2 |
| 4 posts | 42 × 2 × 2 |
| 8 rails | 32 × 2 × 2 |
| gussets from 8 pieces | 8 × 8 × ½ plywood |
| 8 hooks and eyes, about 2 inch. | |

the main area of a side of a mesh about ½-inch size. You could use chicken wire or any of the other metal mesh obtainable from a hardware store. The sections are shown with one leg pointed for driving into the ground and the tops of the legs extended slightly so you can hit them. If your compost cage will be on a hard surface, cut off the points.

1. Cut the wood for the posts and rails (Fig. 8-23A, B). Allow for the posts standing about 1 inch above the top rails. The amount you allow for the pointed end into the ground depends on the softness of your soil, but a projection of 6 inches should be enough (Fig. 8-23C).

2. Make the gussets by cutting squares of plywood and dividing them diagonally (Fig. 8-23D).

3. Join the posts and rails with the gussets on the outside only, checking squareness and that the four sections match (Fig. 8-23E).

4. Trim the wire mesh so it comes within about ½ inch of the outsides of a section. Attach it with staples or by partially driving nails and turning over their heads. You can obtain further security by nailing the inside gussets over the mesh (Fig. 8-23F).

5. Make the temporary corner joints with hooks and eyes screwed to the posts. Bring a corner together and get the positions for the screwed eyes by experiment (Fig. 8-23G), so the parts are held reasonbly close. There is no need to have to force the hooks and eyes tight, particularly if the posts go into the ground to provide rigidity.

6. Finish all parts with several coats of paint.

## STACKING COMPOST BIN

Compost is something that is often plentiful at one time and sparse at another time. A large bin to hold the maximum quantity is a nuisance when you have very little compost with which to deal. Therefore, it is helpful to have some means of enlarging or reducing a bin to suit your needs. The bin shown in Fig. 8-24 is made in sections that you can be assemble to make a structure of any height, depending on how many sections you make.

If the sections are to stack in any position, there has to be some uniformity of size. Assembly can be fairly loose, but even then there is not much tolerance to allow for discrepancies of size. One way of reducing the problem is to avoid a square shape. With four sides supposed to be equal, there are four ways each sec-

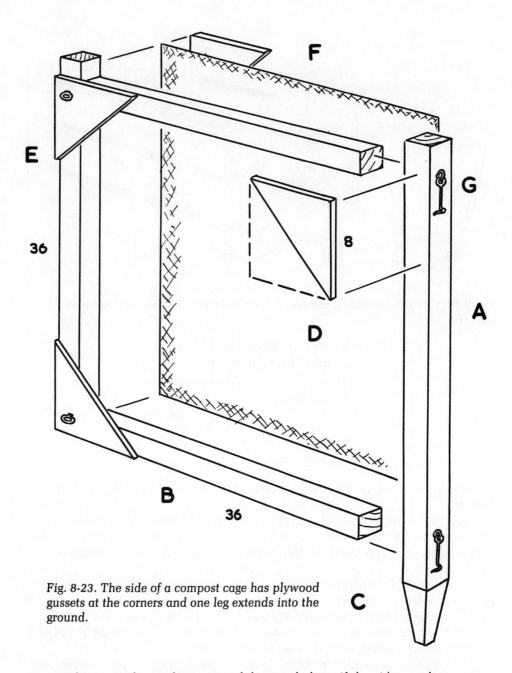

Fig. 8-23. The side of a compost cage has plywood gussets at the corners and one leg extends into the ground.

tion needs to match any four ways of the one below. If the sides are longer one way than the other, there are only two ways you can expect each section to match. The sections have short posts in the corners, and these fit on to each other so there is a gap of 1 inch between the boards. This gap should be enough to allow air to the contents. If you need more air, drill holes in the boards. That would be

Fig. 8-24. You can assemble a compost bin made like open boxes to any height required.

**Table 8-10. Materials List for Stacking Compost Bin.**

| | |
|---|---|
| (for one section) | |
| 2 sides | 30 × 6 × 1 |
| 2 ends | 24 × 6 × 1 |
| 4 posts | 7 × 2 × 2 |

better than widening the gaps (which might then let too much of the contents slip through).

Rest the bin on the ground, and press the post extensions of the bottom section into the ground. If the bin is to rest on a hard surface, cut the posts off flush on the bottom section. If you want the bin to be self-contained, nail a bottom on the lowest section.

1. Decide on the number of sections you want and make all parts at the same time so that sizes match. Suitable sizes are suggested (Fig. 8-25A). You do not need to plane the wide boards, but the posts will make a better fit if you plane them.

2. Make the posts so they will come 2 inches below the top edges and extend 3 inches below the bottom edges (Fig. 8-25B).

3. Taper the outer surfaces of the bottom extensions of the posts so they will fit easily inside the section below (Fig. 8-25C).

4. Screw or nail the parts securely together and use the first assembly to check subsequent ones. Check that they will fit together either way. If you do not succeed in making all parts interchangeable, mark those which fit together best.

5. Finish the wood with preservative.

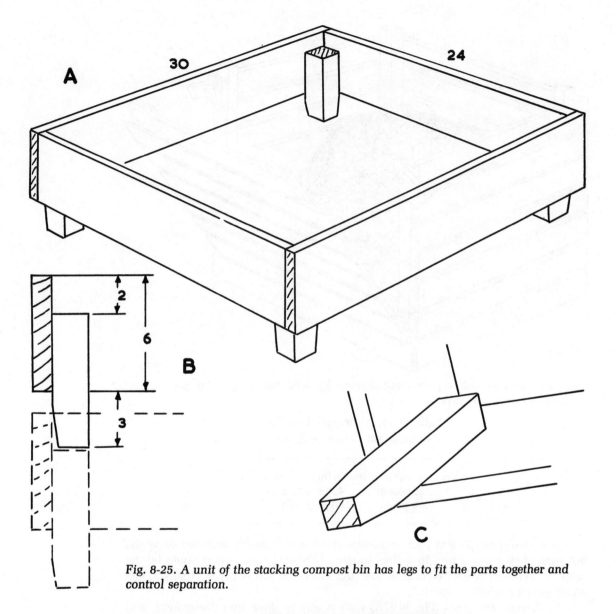

Fig. 8-25. A unit of the stacking compost bin has legs to fit the parts together and control separation.

## PERMANENT COMPOST BIN

If there is a corner of the garden where you will always make compost, it might be better to assemble a permanent means of keeping it all together than to rely on take-down or other semi-temporary structures. The obvious way to do this is to drive posts into the ground and fit covering around them, but there has to be some means of access. This fact is particularly true when the contents are low. The permanent bin shown in Fig. 8-26 is all wood, and it has a front that will swing down or lift away completely.

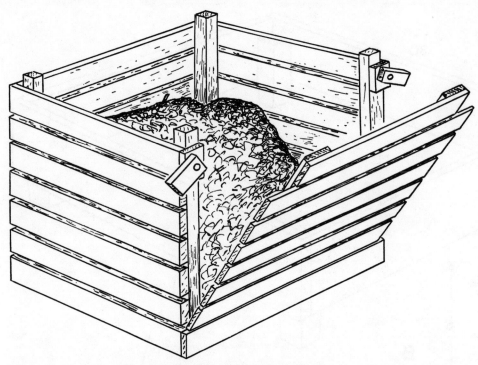

Fig. 8-26. You can make a permanent compost bin with boards nailed to posts. A removable side allows access.

**Table 8-11. Materials List for
Permanent Compost Bin.**

| | |
|---|---|
| (sizes are for approximate 36 inch cube capacity) | |
| 32 boards | 42 × 4 × 2 |
| 4 posts | 60 × 3 × 3 |

Sizes will have to suit your available space and probable required capacity, but sizes shown suit a bin 36 inches square. The sections of wood could be the same up to nearly twice that overall size, but this is the sort of project that you can adapt to suit available materials.

1. Prepare the posts (Fig. 8-27A) with points to drive into the ground, and probably too long, so you can trim the tops level later if all posts do not penetrate to the same depth.

2. If the ground is not level already, bring it to a reasonably level surface for the area the bin is to cover. Otherwise, it will be difficult to assemble the parts. Boarding around the sides that are not near horizontal will look unsatisfactory, even if it does the job just as well.

3. Measure the size you want on the ground and start holes for the posts with a spike or other tool so that the posts enter in the correct places. Check that the posts are upright as you drive them.

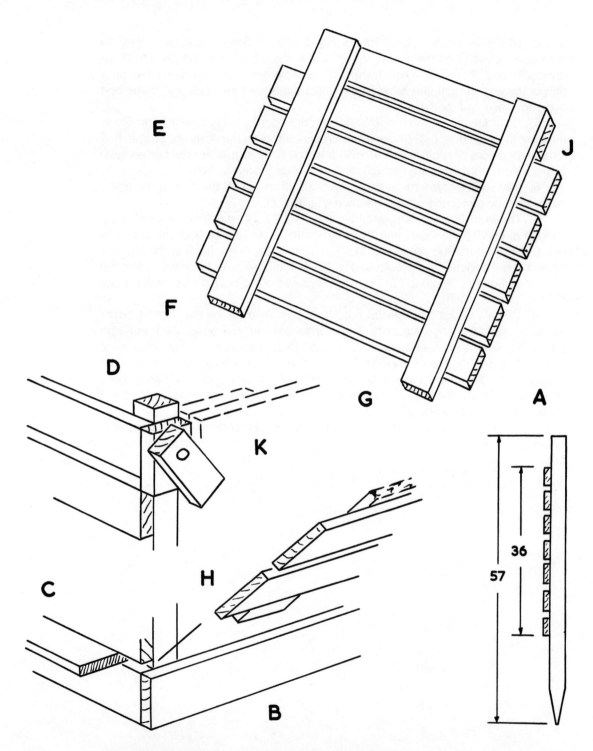

Fig. 8-27. Arrange one side of the compost bin to lift out.

145

4. Fit the lowest boards all round (Fig. 8-27B). It does not matter if they do not make a close fit on the soil all round. It is more important to get them level individually and with each other. It probably will be advisable to drive a few nails part of the way in until you have checked that the boards are level and in the best positions; then nail them flush.

5. Continue up the three sides, adding more boards, using a board on edge to measure the gaps (Fig. 8-27C). As hammering could push the posts out of true, nail temporary pieces of scrap wood across their tops to keep them in the correct relative positions until there are enough outside boards to steady them.

6. Nail sufficient boards to three sides, and then cut off the tops of the posts, either level or projecting a short distance (Fig. 8-27D).

7. The front is a separate assembly (Fig. 8-27E). Have sufficient boards long enough to overlap the sides. Join them with strips at a distance from the ends that will fit easily inside the posts (Fig. 8-27F). These strips come level at the top, but project about 2 inches at the bottom (Fig. 8-27G) to hook over the piece across the bottom of the front (Fig. 8-27H). Have the ends of the top boards level with the upright strips (Fig. 8-27J).

8. When you put the front in, hold its bottom in place by the hooked extensions. At the top there have to be large turnbuttons on the posts. Pack out with pieces the same thickness as the boards, and then use strips turning on bolts or screws (Fig. 8-27K). The outward pressure on the front of a large, full bin could be considerable. Therefore, the pivots should be long, stout wooden screws or bolts taken right through the posts. Use washers under the heads to spread the load and others between the turnbuttons and the posts to ease turning.

9. It would be advisable for most woods to treat the bottoms of the posts with preservative before driving into the ground. Treat all woodwork before using the bin.

# 9

# Display Equipment

ALTHOUGH MUCH OF THE BEAUTY OF A GARDEN OR YARD COMES FROM WHAT IS actually growing in the ground, additional attraction can come from flowers, plants, and ferns growing in boxes, troughs and pots such as those described in Chapter 8. If the amount of ground is limited or nonexistent, you will have to arrange the entire display. Some of the boxes might not need special support or have legs built-in. If you intend to hang the plants, suitable supporting places might exist or you might have to provide brackets. You will have to provide other containers with supports if you want to raise the plants above ground level.

Thought given to arranging displays can increase the growing potential of your existing available area considerably, and the total effect of what you provide in additional display facilities can give you a more effective and satisfying garden.

There can be a certain amount of improvisation. Supporting a box or pot on bricks might be just as satisfactory as building a special support. You might be uncertain about what display arrangements will be best and have to assemble temporary shelves or other supports. In any case, whatever you build as display equipment only has a secondary role to play to the display of flowers or foliage. Build permanent display equipment strongly. In many cases, it should not be treated as a decorative feature in its own right. There are exceptions—such as designs like miniature paling fences around pots—but in general, what you are making is just functional.

You can expect that what you make probably will be ignored and neglected once it is in position. This fact means that it should be made strong and able to fulfill its purpose without much maintenance.

Untreated softwood is unlikely to last long if left outside throughout the year. Treating it with preservative will lengthen its life, but it is better to start with a more durable hardwood or a softwood containing resin.

Consider loads. A long trough that extends over supports might not have much effect on a shelf, but if you stand individual pots along a shelf, each applies a more localized load. Large pots full of soil are heavy. A new shelf might appear to be supporting them adequately, but in six months time you could see a definite sag and pronounced downward curve. Make sure your shelves are thick enough to be stiff and arrange supports fairly close together. The two requirements are related. If the only support locations have to be wide apart, you need a stiffer board for the shelf than if supports are more frequent.

## WALL SHELVES

The simplest shelf is a board supported on two brackets, screwed to the wall (Fig. 9-1A). If screws through the bracket can get a good grip into something capable of supporting the weight, this is satisfactory. Make sure you are not just screwing to cladding (that will pull away) or plugging a brick or stone wall that is so soft that it will crumble around the screws.

Check that the shelf is level. You can measure up from the floor, but it is not always level. It is better to use a level on the shelf, as you fit it, or on a line drawn on the wall as a guide. Put one screw through a bracket and move the shelf up and down, pivoting on it to a level position before marking the first screw hole at the other end.

1. In many situations, strong points in the wall or fence and the positions you want to drive screws will not coincide. It is better then to attach battens to the wall and screw the brackets to them (Fig. 9-1B). You can arrange the battens long enough to allow for driving screws in the best positions. Leveling the shelf on its bracket becomes easier. Make the battens thick enough to take screws long enough through the brackets to support the intended weight.

2. You could notch the shelf around the battens, and then fit a strip under it between the battens (Fig. 9-1C). This type construction does two things: it helps the shelf resist sagging, and it is a place to put more screws into the wall. Alternatively, the shelf could come against the battens so that its rear edge is away from the wall. This position would be better for cleaning. You can stiffen the front of a shelf with a strip underneath (Fig. 9-1D) that is either level with the front or set back a short distance. Round or bevel the ends of the shelf and this stiffener (Fig. 9-1E).

There could be a single stiffener near the center of the shelf width. This stiffener makes a good place to put hooks for hanging plant holders (Fig. 9-1F).

3. You can arrange several shelves on the same battens. It is a good idea to let the battens reach the floor (Fig. 9-1G) because this gives additional vertical support.

4. Although steel brackets are convenient shelf supports in many situations, it is possible to make satisfactory wooden brackets. If solid wood is used, the grain should run diagonally for maximum strength. You can decorate the front by shaping (Fig. 9-2A). Fix this type of bracket by screwing through the shelf and batten (Fig. 9-2B).

That means you must attach the bracket to the battens before you screw them

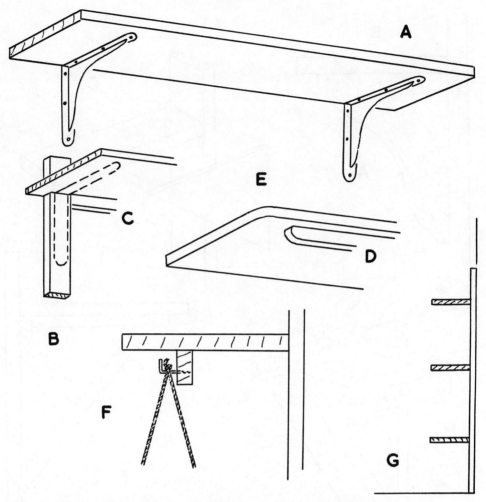

*Fig. 9-1. Bracket the shelves to the wall. They will require stiffening.*

to the wall. Screwing down through the shelf can be done in position. If you are certain you will not want to take the assembly apart later, it is worthwhile using waterproof glue as well as screws.

5. You can make a cruder bracket with plywood. Arrange a batten under the shelf, the same width as the upright batten, and nail plywood to one or both sides (Fig. 9-2C). If you like, fill the space between with solid wood. When making this or any other bracket, it is advisable to assume that the front edge of the shelf will sag slightly under load. If the bracket is made to lift the front edge a little in the first assembly, it should settle level eventually. If the wall batten is truly upright, that means making a bracket that is about 92 degrees instead of square. If the wall is not plumb, use a level to check the actual angle needed.

6. A wide, heavily-loaded shelf is better supported with brackets having diag-

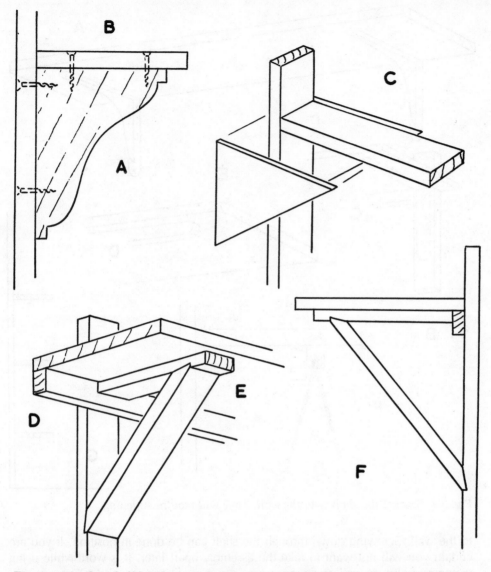

Fig. 9-2. Wooden shelf brackets might be solid (A,B), made with plywood gussets (C), or built up (D-F).

onal struts. Attach the shelf to the upright batten with a lengthwise strip (Fig. 9-2D) and arrange another batten under the shelf (Fig. 9-2E). Set out the full size of the shape of the bracket. Allow for the slight rise of the front of the shelf. The angle of the strut can be about 45 degrees, but is better when slightly more upright.

7. You should notch in the ends of the strut (Fig. 9-2F). Keep the notches shallow and cut their outer ends square. Secure these joints with nails or screws, but the notches will take the thrust.

# SHELF END SUPPORTS

It might be better to support some shelves with uprights at one or both ends. There could also be brackets along the shelves, but an upright support would be better near an external wall corner. The upright then can carry hooks or brackets for hanging displays.

End supports usually take the load to the floor and so relieve the wall fasteners of some of the load. An end can be solid or open and might be plain or shaped. It does not have to be the full width of the shelves, but that would provide the best support.

1. The simplest end support is a board the same width as the shelves (Fig. 9-3A). You could support the shelves with dado joints (Fig. 9-3B), but for most outdoor assemblies it will be sufficient to nail pieces across (Fig. 9-3C). Probably the best arrangement is a combination of the two with a shallow dado locating the shelf end (Fig. 9-3D).

2. If the end is not as wide as the shelves, carry supporting pieces forward to prevent the shelves from sagging (Fig. 9-3E). Pieces inside the ends, either from shelf to shelf or only as required, can take screws into the wall.

3. For an open end, use two narrow uprights (Fig. 9-3F) with dadoes or supporting strips across. You can take them above the shelf and cap them in order to prevent anything slipping off the end (Fig. 9-3G).

4. It might be that brackets provide ample support, but an exposed corner of a block of shelves needs to be supported and strengthened. If you do not require a full end, there could be a fairly light upright (Fig. 9-3H). This upright is best let in, with each shelf and the upright notched (Fig. 9-3J), so that the parts cannot move under load. The upright could be at the end of a short distance along the shelves. You can use the same method if you need intermediate support for the front edges elsewhere along the shelves.

5. A plain, full-width end might be considered ugly, and it might restrict the view of plants displayed or limit the amount of sunlight getting to them. You can scoop out the front edge between shelves (Fig. 9-3K) or give it a decorative outline and holes to let light through (Fig. 9-3L).

# FREESTANDING WALL SHELVES

If you screw shelves to a wall or fence, there is no reason to fear them falling over and wrecking the pot plants or other display, but you might not always want to have shelves permanently in position or you might not want to make holes in the wall. If you can have a stack of freestanding shelves, you can move the whole assembly to another position if you want to alter the layout of a deck or garden. You could move the assembly under cover for the winter.

For stability, it is important to give freestanding shelves a broad base. You cannot have a stack of narrow shelves, similar to those attached to a wall, without providing feet that extend some way. Such feet could be a nuisance; it is better to make the lower shelves wider. This way, you can avoid the need for extending feet. The arrangement shown in Fig. 9-4 will go flat against a wall, but the spread

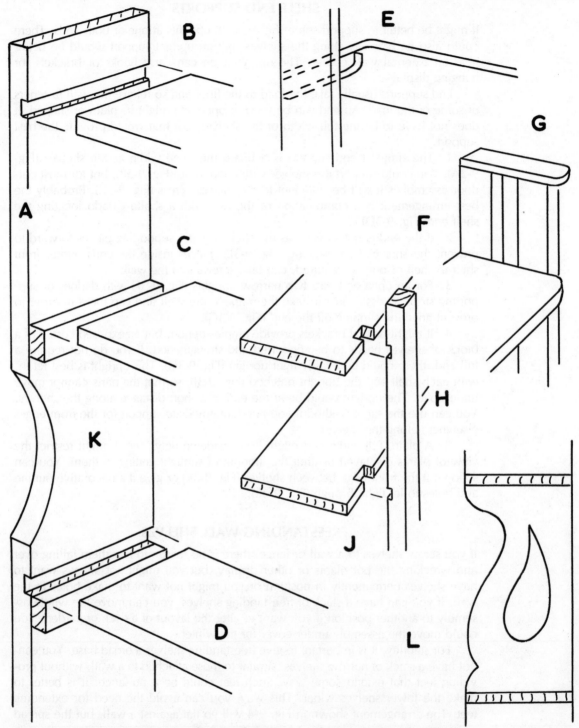

Fig. 9-3. End supports are better than brackets for providing strength and stiffness.

Fig. 9-4. Support freestanding
wall shelves on end frames,
with diagonal bracing at the
back for stiffness.

**Table 9-1. Materials List for
Freestanding Wall Shelves.**

| | |
|---|---|
| 4 legs | 50 × 3 × 1 |
| 2 tops | 8 × 3 × 1 |
| 8 shelf supports | 14 × 3 × 1 |
| 1 shelf | 48 × 9 × 1 |
| 1 shelf | 48 × 10 × 1 |
| 1 shelf | 48 × 12 × 1 |
| 1 shelf | 48 × 15 × 1 |
| 2 braces | 56 × 2 × 1 |

front legs prevent tipping forward (except with the most abnormal usage).

1. Decide on the end view that will suit your purpose. Suggested sizes are given as a guide to wood sizes (Fig. 9-5A). Set out one leg assembly.

2. Make up a pair of leg assemblies. It probably will be sufficient to arrange battens across to support shelves (Fig. 9-5B). There could be another at the top, but that part will look better if you halve the two parts together (Fig. 9-5C). Use dadoes at the shelf positions if you prefer.

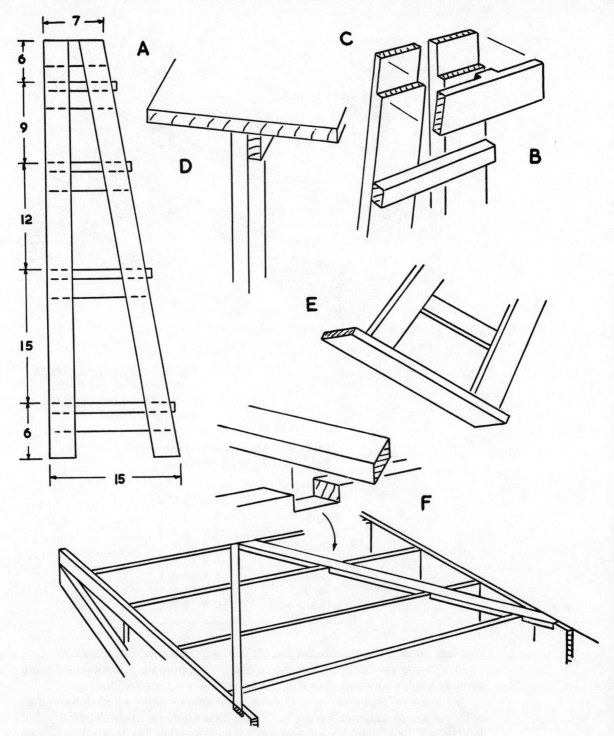

Fig. 9-5. Nail the shelf assembly; notching parts together provides mutual support.

3. Make the shelves by building up widths as necessary. There could be battens across intermediately to prevent the boards warping in relation to each other. If the shelves are fairly long, stiffen them with lengthwise pieces and put struts between shelves (Fig. 9-5D).

4. If the legs are to rest on a hard surface, there is no need to do anything to them. If they are going on soil or other soft surface, put feet under them to spread the load (Fig. 9-5E).

5. Nail or screw the shelves to the end assemblies. Besides nails into the supporting battens, you can put screws through the legs into the end grain of the shelves. Keep the rear edges of the shelves level with the edges of the uprights.

6. The block of shelves might seem steady after the first assembly, but they would tend to loosen if not given extra stiffness lengthwise. Brackets between the ends and the shelves would help, but it would be better to provide diagonal bracing at the back (Fig. 9-5F). This bracing is best done after you assemble the other parts and check for squareness.

7. Lay the pieces that will make the braces across the other parts and pencil where they come. Notch for them, screw them in place, and then cut off their ends level.

## STEP SUPPORT

If you are going to display pot plants, many of them need to go higher than the usual gap between shelves. It is necessary to arrange the shelves so that a lower one is clear of the next one above and the foliage or flowers can stand in front of the upper shelf. It might be satisfactory, as in the previous example, to have the shelves only partially overlapping. If you want the whole shelf width to be clear of the one above, a series of shelves will have to project a long way from the wall. Unless there is a considerable amount of space available, it would be wise to limit this arrangement to two shelves.

A simple way of supporting shelves against a wall is with sloping ends (Fig. 9-6). You can screw them to the wall at each side. There should be no need to secure the lower ends to the ground, but there could be similar blocks for screws into wood or concrete, or you can use small stakes into soft ground. Besides the two shelves, pots or boxes can stand between the legs and the whole assembly of three layers of plants can make a very decorative display. You can modify the suggested sizes, but it is unwise to use this method for a very big or a multishelf stand.

1. Set out an end view full size (Fig. 9-7A). Draw the end views of the shelves first (Fig. 9-7B) with their supports and let the sloping ends follow through to match their positions.

2. Make the pair of ends and mark on them where the other parts come (Fig. 9-7C). Attach blocks at the top that will screw to the wall (Fig. 9-7D). Fit the supporting blocks for the shelves.

3. Make the lower shelf to fit between the sides and the top long enough to overlap the screw blocks (Fig. 9-7E). Attach them to their supports.

4. When attaching to the wall, use your full-size drawing height to check the

Fig. 9-6. For plants that reach higher than one shelf to the next, slope supports and screw them to the wall.

### Table 9-2. Materials List for Step Support.

| | |
|---|---|
| 2 legs | 36 × 6 × 1 |
| 1 shelf | 30 × 6 × 1 |
| 1 shelf | 26 × 6 × 1 |
| 4 shelf supports | 7 × 2 × 1 |
| **If free-standing** | |
| 2 legs | 24 × 2 × 1 |
| 2 rails | 12 × 2 × 1 |

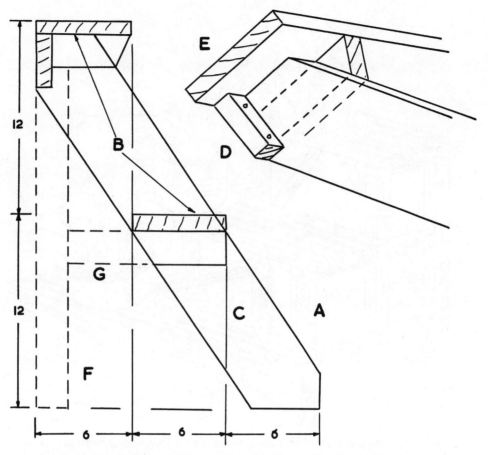

*Fig. 9-7. Blocks hold the step support parts together and to the wall.*

position of the top shelf on the wall and use a level on the top shelf to see that it does not slope forward.

5. You can make the assembly freestanding. Fit rear legs vertically (Fig. 9-7F) and extend the lower shelf supports to join them (Fig. 9-7G).

## SLATTED PLANT STAND

Pot plants require frequent watering, and considerable water will land on the shelves. Therefore, it is a good idea to have gaps in the shelves for water to run through. These gaps are done by arranging a series of strips—that have to be thicker than the board you would otherwise use—to resist warping unevenly. The use of strips or slats makes the building up of shelves of any width easier. If the stand is to take larger plants in tubs or other big containers, you can make stepped supports to any required size.

The plant stand shown in Fig. 9-8 has three wide-slatted shelves that are clear

*Fig. 9-8. A slatted plant stand will drain water away. This arrangement allows for high growth.*

**Table 9-3. Materials List for
Slatted Plant Stand.**

| | |
|---|---|
| 4 legs | $36 \times 2 \times 2$ |
| 2 legs | $24 \times 2 \times 2$ |
| rails from four pieces | $36 \times 2 \times 2$ |
| 2 struts | $15 \times 2 \times 2$ |
| 15 slats | $36 \times 2 \times 2$ |
| 2 struts | $48 \times 2 \times 2$ |

of each other, when viewed from above, so foliage on any level can extend upwards without hindrance. The construction suggested has the lower front shelf supported by diagonal struts. The weight of the assembly, plus any pots on the other shelves, should prevent any risk of tipping, but if you place very heavy loads on the lowest shelf, it could be given vertical legs at the front.

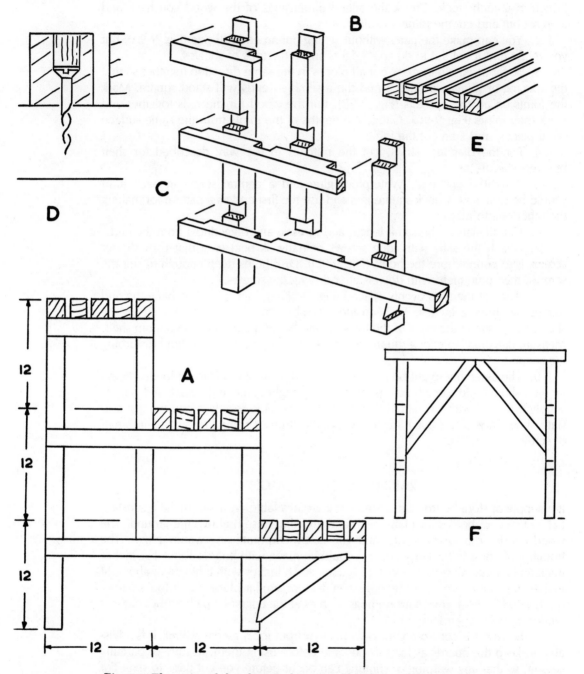

Fig. 9-9. The parts of the slatted plant stand are halved together.

1. Get all the wood first. The whole assembly is intended to be made of 2-inch × 2-inch stock. Check the actual dimensions of the wood you have and then set out and cut the joints to suit.

2. You can make the parts without setting out an end full size (Fig. 9-9A), but you might find it helpful to do so. Heights are to the tops of shelves.

3. So far as possible, mark out all pieces in the same direction together so that the spacing of joints will match and the assembled ends will stand square. Mark the joints on all the uprights (Fig. 9-9B). Put the wood for the rails together and mark their joints (Fig. 9-9C). Gauge the depths of the joints from the same surface of all pieces, and then cut the joints.

4. For the diagonal struts, cut the notches in the way described for shelf brackets (Fig. 9-2).

5. Assemble one end. Waterproof glue and a central screw in each joint should be sufficient. Check squareness and use the first end as a pattern for making the other one to match.

6. Cut all slats to the same length and remove any raggedness from the ends.

7. Attach the slats with long screws or nails. A neat way that uses shorter screws is to counterbore the holes (Fig. 9-9D). Drill holes deep enough to suit the screws, then plug them with dowels after driving the screws.

8. Arrange the slats evenly spaced (Fig. 9-9E) and let them overhang the end frames by about 2 inches. To keep the assembly in shape while making up the shelves, fit a slat at the back of the top and another at the front of the bottom shelf. Measure diagonals to check squareness, then add the other slats without disturbing the shape.

9. The assembly might be rigid enough, but if the stand is to be loaded heavily, you should add some bracing. This bracing might come at the back and is most simply arranged with two struts (Fig. 9-9F) between the rear legs and the top rear slat. Although you can notch in the ends of the struts, it should be sufficient to nail or screw them in place.

## RAISED RUSTIC TROUGH

If a supply of stout boards cut across a log are available, you can make a substantial rustic-effect holder for plants with end legs that raise it above the ground. The wood can have a sawn surface and you can incorporate any waney edges. The trough looks best if it is fairly large. It could be made with boards about 1½ inches thick and an overall size of about 72 inches × 18 inches with a height of about 24 inches. It can then stand on the edge of a deck or similar place, but it looks particularly good in less formal surroundings such as at the edge of a path further out in a wilder part of the garden.

If the wood is cut from your own trees or from local recent felling, it is advisable to keep the boards as long as possible before using them, to fully or partially season, so that any warping or splitting can occur before you cut parts to size. For this type of assembly, regard natural flaws as decorative if changes of shape or size and any opening of shakes are not too pronounced. Usually it is the ends of boards that open in cracks. Keep pieces over length until you have seen what is likely to happen before final cutting to size.

1. The trough is shown with legs splayed outward slightly and the lower edges of the side pieces with waney edges (Fig. 9-10). Proportions and sizes will have to suit the available wood and the location of the finished trough.

2. The key parts are the two ends (Fig. 9-11A). Make them symmetrical about centerlines. Recess the sides to take the long pieces, and then spread below to widen the legs and give increased stability.

3. You can make the center V cut by just two saw cuts meeting, but it helps to drill first and saw into the hole (Fig. 9-11B). This drilling and sawing makes cleaner cuts, looks decorative, and reduces the risk of a split starting from the opening as the wood dries out further.

Fig. 9-10. You can make a trough with natural boards and can raise it on its own legs.

**Table 9-4. Materials List for Raised-Rustic Trough.**

| | |
|---|---|
| 2 ends | 25 × 25 × 1½ |
| 1 bottom | 72 × 18 × 1½ |
| 2 sides | 72 × 12 × 1½ waney edge |
| 2 strips | 22 × 4 × 1½ |

4. The lengthwise spread of the legs need only be slight (possibly 2 inches further at the bottom than the top). This measurement is not really enough to affect the angle at the bottom of the recesses (which could be cut square across).

5. Make the bottom to fit between the sides (Fig. 9-11C), using the ends as a guide to its width.

6. Cut the two sides (Fig. 9-11D). Keep their tops level with the ends. You might have to notch the waney edges to fit into the ends. Mark on the sides the intended splay of the ends. It probably will be best to leave cutting off any extensions until after nailing the parts together.

7. Put a few drain holes in the bottom.

8. Assemble with nails, but screws at the top corners will provide extra strength where the greatest loads come.

9. You could leave the trough at this stage, but you can minimize warping of the ends and you can strengthen the corner joints if strips are put across (Fig. 9-11E), with screws into the sides as well as the ends.

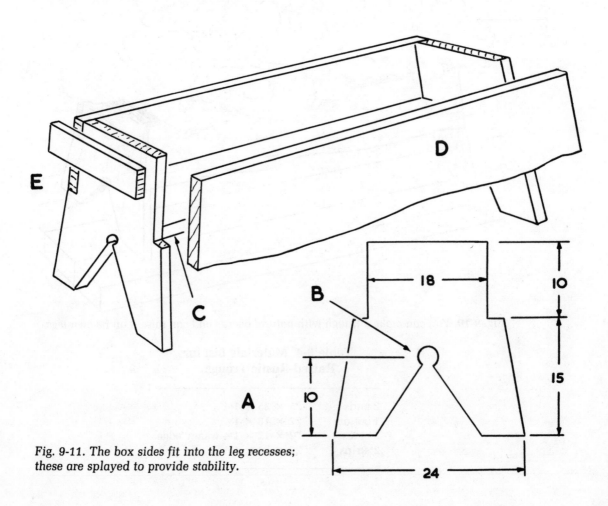

Fig. 9-11. The box sides fit into the leg recesses; these are splayed to provide stability.

## FORMAL RAISED TROUGH

A trough on legs, which has been made of planed, seasoned boards and finished with white or other paint, is more appropriate to the patio or deck than the rougher trough just described. It could be used to contain plants in pots or there could be soil put directly into it (Fig. 9-12).

Many sizes are possible; much depends on where you want to locate the trough. If it is going near a wall, it might be made higher than if it is free and could be knocked over. The height and width should not be very different. The trough should have enough dead weight to be quite stable. Length does not affect stability and can be anything reasonable. Remember the weight if the trough has to be moved. Great length will result in bulging sides after long use. Stiffeners inside will reduce this risk. The sizes suggested in the materials list are intended as a guide to proportions.

1. The sides and ends are shown as made up of two boards (Fig. 9-13A).

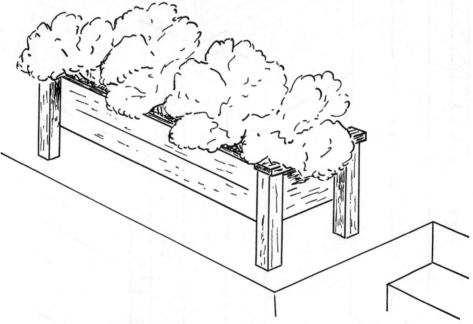

Fig. 9-12. You can make a raised trough with boards on square legs.

### Table 9-5. Materials List for Formal-Raised Trough.

| | |
|---|---|
| 4 sides | 48 × 6 × 1¼ |
| 4 ends | 14 × 6 × 1¼ |
| 3 bottoms | 48 × 6 × 1¼ |
| 4 legs | 16 × 3 × 3 |
| 2 caps | 16 × 5 × 1 |

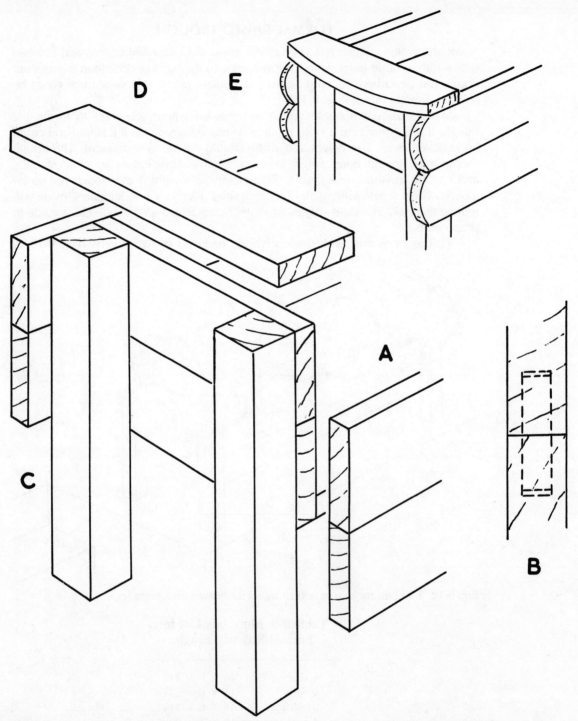

Fig. 9-13. You can glue or dowel the boards (A,B), and then nail them to the legs (C) with top cover pieces (D) and shaped ends (E) if you prefer.

There should be no need to glue the boards together, but it will help to keep them in line along the sides if there are dowels at about 12-inch intervals (Fig. 9-13B). The bottom can be two or three boards with dowels arranged in the same way. Prepare the boards before marking out and cutting to size.

2. Nail the end boards to the legs, checking squareness and seeing that opposite ends match.

3. Prepare the bottom width to fit between the sides. Drill drain holes.

4. Nail in the bottom between the ends and the sides to ends and bottom (Fig. 9-13C). Assemble on a flat surface and check that the trough stands firmly and without twist.

5. Fit capping pieces at the ends (Fig. 9-13D), level with the inside surfaces, but extending about ½ inch outside.

6. The main drawing shows the ends cut square, but you can provide some decoration by curving the ends of the side boards and the edges of the capping pieces (Fig. 9-13E).

7. If the trough is to stand on a soft surface, the load can be spread by putting strips across below each pair of end legs.

8. Finish the trough with paint inside and out.

## PALING POT CONTAINER

Although most supports, boxes, and troughs for pot plants are made to be inconspicuous, there are many places where the container will draw more attention to itself and be attractive even when you have removed pots temporarily. The container shown in Fig. 9-14 is intended to be more of a decoration than some others. The front and back are arranged like the upright palings of a fence. This container is intended to hold several fairly large pots. Their contents should grow to at least twice the depth of the holder.

It would be advisable to decide on the pots that usually will be put in the container. Make sizes to suit so that the pots almost reach the tops of the surrounding rails and a convenient number can be put in the length. The suggested sizes comfortably would take three pots of about 16-inch diameter and depth. The wood sizes are light, but the parts depend on mutual support when built into the complete assembly. The splayed legs are decorative. You could fit upright legs if the container is to stand near a wall or fit into a limited space and you do not want the rear legs to extend behind. As shown, the container is intended to stand where it might be viewed from any direction.

1. Choose the wood sizes. In particular, get the wood for the palings. This container is shown 3 inches wide with 3 inches between pieces (Fig. 9-15A). Both could be wider or narrower. Space out the chosen wood in relation to the length you estimate you will need and settle on the overall length in that way. The width between the sides should give ample space for the pots to be put in and out.

2. The design is based on two identical frames (Fig. 9-15B) that you should join securely at the corners. Nails only there would not be strong enough.

3. Join the corners with small, metal, angle brackets (Fig. 9-15C).

4. Alternatively, cut joints. Glued dovetails will resist pulling apart if the tails

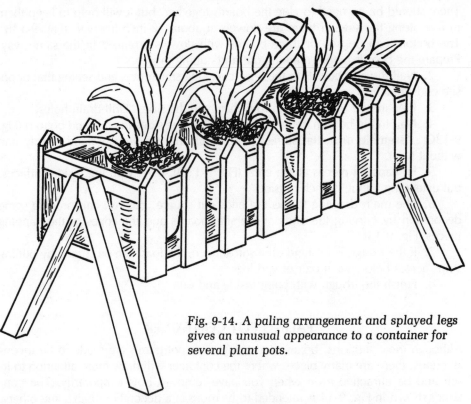

Fig. 9-14. A paling arrangement and splayed legs gives an unusual appearance to a container for several plant pots.

**Table 9-6. Materials List for Paling Pot Container.**

| | |
|---|---|
| 2 sides | 46 × 2 × 1 |
| 2 ends | 18 × 2 × 1 |
| 1 bottom | 46 × 18 × ½ plywood |
| 16 palings | 20 × 3 × 1 |
| 4 legs | 40 × 2 × 2 |

are on the crosswise pieces (Fig. 9-15D). Another suitable joint is a comb or tongue (Fig. 9-15E) that gives a good area for waterproof glue. There could also be a nail or screw down through most of the tongues.

5. The bottom (Fig. 9-15F) can be solid boards in either direction, but it is most simply made from exterior plywood. Put a few drain holes in it and attach it to the bottom frame. Do not make up the whole assembly and try to put the bottom in last; that cannot be done.

6. The upright palings should be identical (Fig. 9-15G). You can cut them by the use of square and miter fences on a table saw, or you can mark out and carefully cut by hand. Take the sharpness off exposed edges.

7. Space the palings evenly on the sides of the frames. Fit the end ones on both sides and check squareness before adding the other pieces.

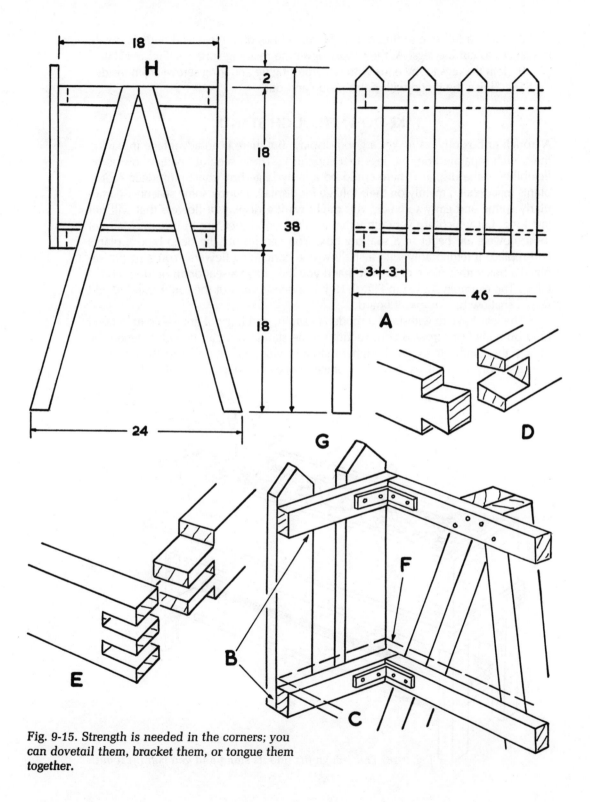

Fig. 9-15. Strength is needed in the corners; you can dovetail them, bracket them, or tongue them together.

167

8. Make a full-size setting out of the main lines of the legs and ends to obtain the angles to cut the legs. At their tops, bevel the meeting surfaces (Fig. 9-15H).

9. Join the legs to the ends with waterproof glue and long screws from inside.

10. Finish the wood with paint inside and out.

## TAKE-DOWN TROUGH STAND

A trough or box on legs makes a good display, but there is an advantage in having the trough separate from the legs that support it. These separate parts allow some flexibility in the display. There could be a fairly large box containing deep-rooted plants that depend mainly on their foliage for display. During some seasons, particularly spring and early summer, you might want a display of flowers that will not last long, but which are very attractive for the period they are in bloom. Many of these flowers are better in a shallow box. You can lift out the deep box of plants and replace it temporarily with a shallow one containing flowers. You also can replace a box with a piece of plywood and you then have a seat or an outdoor coffee table. The example shown in Fig. 9-16 has a deep box, but the same stand would take a shallow box or a seat board.

The legs have to withstand a moderate strain, and it is not advisable to depend only on nailed or screwed construction in the stand. You can dowel or tenon the rails. If the stand is to be much higher than it is wide, a shelf underneath will stiffen the assembly as well as provide storage space. Although a durable hardwood

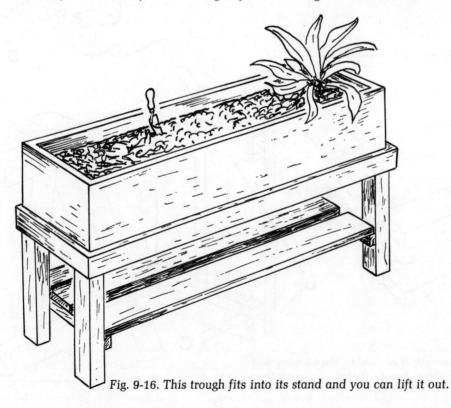

Fig. 9-16. This trough fits into its stand and you can lift it out.

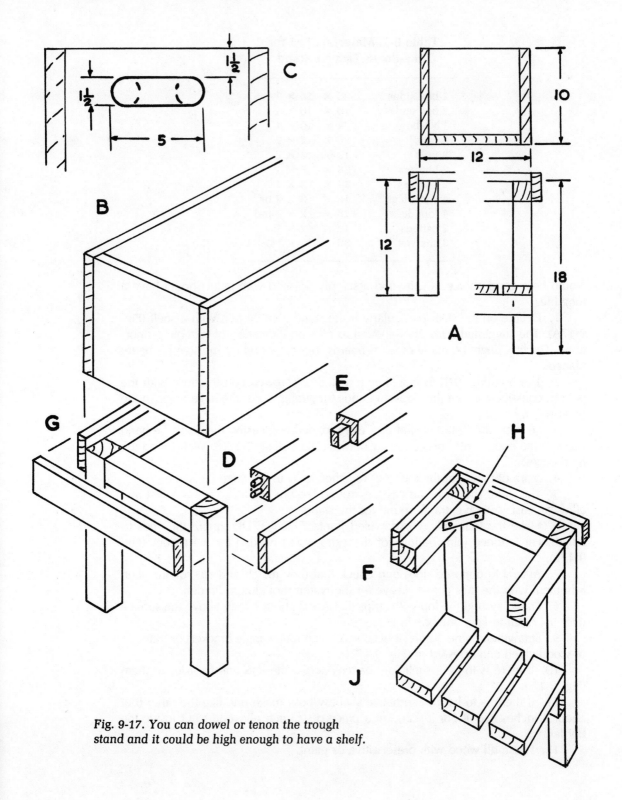

Fig. 9-17. You can dowel or tenon the trough
stand and it could be high enough to have a shelf.

169

## Table 9-7. Materials List for Take-down Trough Stand.

| | | | |
|---|---|---|---|
| 2 box sides | 36 × | 10 × 1 | |
| 2 box ends | 10 × | 10 × 1 | |
| 1 box bottom | 34 × | 10 × 1 | |
| 2 rails | 36 × | 2 × 2 | |
| 2 rails | 12 × | 2 × 2 | |
| 2 borders | 38 × | 3 × 1 | |
| 2 borders | 14 × | 3 × 1 | |
| 4 short legs | 12 × | 2 × 2 or | |
| 4 long legs | 18 × | 2 × 2 and | |
| 2 battens | 12 × | 2 × 1 | |
| 3 shelves | 36 × | 3½ × 1 | |

would be a good choice, a softwood assembly finished with paint should have a long life.

1. Decide on the size, particularly if the stand is to be tall, with a shelf (Fig. 9-17A). The suggested sizes are intended to give an indication of suitable proportions. The box might be made of sawn boards, but the wood for the stand is better planed.

2. The box (Fig. 9-17B) is a simple nailed or screwed construction, with the bottom contained within the sides and ends for strength. Put drainage holes in the bottom.

3. So you can lift the weight of a deep-loaded box easily, there can be hand holes in the ends. Drill holes and saw between them (Fig. 9-17C). Well round the hold edges.

4. Mark out and cut the four legs together so as to get them the same.

5. The stand should be an easy fit around the box, so make the box first and allow at least ¼ inch extra all round for the stand.

6. Make the four rails. For doweled joints (Fig. 9-17D), square the ends to length. For tenoned joints, allow for the extra wood needed for the tenons (Fig. 9-17E).

7. Assemble opposite sides and check that they match and are square, then join them with the rails across. Leave for the waterproof glue to harden.

8. Frame around the top with strips that stand about 1 inch above the surface (Fig. 9-17F,G) to keep the box in place.

9. Strengthen corner joints, if necessary, with metal angle brackets or triangles of wood glued and screwed in (Fig. 9-17H).

10. If there is to be a shelf, put battens across the legs and fit strips to them (Fig. 9-17J).

11. If there is to be an alternative shallow box, make one like the other (but about 4 inches deep). For a seat, cut a piece of ½-inch plywood to fit inside the border.

12. Finish all wood with preservative or paint.

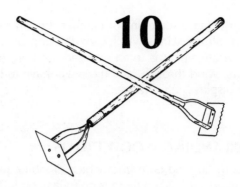

# 10

# Climbing Supports

**M**ANY THINGS THAT GROW CLING TO SUPPORTS AS THEY CLIMB UPWARD. THIS concept applies to flowers, vegetables, vines, and other growths. For vegetables, the supports can be temporary and as simple as possible, without much thought for appearance. If the support is for climbing flowers, it should be designed better and made permanent so that it looks attractive when nothing is climbing on it. If the support is for a vine or climbing tree, it might have to be fairly massive and built more like the structure of a building.

You can make the supports for the flower garden and vegetable garden entirely of wood, but there is a use for fiber rope and wire in single strands or as nets or meshes. You can use planed wood or natural poles for the wood structure.

Supports for climbers also can provide backgrounds or dividers between parts of a garden, and perhaps even to the extent of being more like fences with archways and gates. Arranged in this way, climbers look better than unadorned fences and gates between such things as a formal garden and a natural one, or between the vegetable patch and a flower garden. A divider covered in foliage or blossoms makes a good background to the garden as viewed from the house windows. This fact is true even when it is almost bare in winter.

Plan the larger arbor or support for vines or trees as an extension of a building, as a shelter for seats, or as a roofed avenue from one part of the garden to another.

You can make temporary supports for such things as a vegetable crop of almost any wood. Place the parts in a dry store when not needed. Make more permanent supports that have to withstand winter weather of more durable wood. This concept is particularly important for the uprights that enter the ground; treat them with preservative.

It might be better to use short, concrete posts in the ground and bolt the wood to them above the surface. A common fault is to not take the posts deep enough. A height of 6 feet or so of fairly dense screening or climber support can offer considerable obstruction to wind. Strong winds will loosen the grip of shallow posts in the ground. If the display arrangement is in an exposed position, there should be plenty of gaps in it to let the wind through, and there will have to be some diagonal struts. For most floral displays, an arrangement that is not too tightly packed looks better in any case.

## EXPANDING WOOD TRELLIS

Crisscrossing trelliswork forms a good base from which climbing plants can cling. Its diamond pattern looks good even when there is no foliage on it. It will not stand unaided, but it is attached easily to a few uprights or more extensive framing for a large area. You also can attach to a fence or wall permanently or just for the growing season. If you must take it down, this trellis will fold to a compact bundle for storage. If you make it as described, it also gives you scope for adjusting overall sizes. You can pull or push it to the width you want. This flexibility is accompanied by variations in the height, but it is possible usually to change sizes of a particular piece of trellis within a fairly wide range to get a shape to match a particular area you want to cover.

In most circumstances, this type of trellis looks best when you open it to a diamond shape (Fig. 10-1). You might prefer top angles about 60 degrees (Fig. 10-2A), but it is still attractive with squares (Fig. 10-2B). It is less satisfactory when you pull it too wide and the diamonds are the other way (Fig. 10-2C). If you know the area you want to cover, it probably is best to scheme the laths to form the trellis so you allow for opening to square shapes. You can add one or two pieces, depending on the overall size, so that you do not have to pull the assembly to the full width and the openings will finish taller than they are wide.

The wood chosen should have fairly straight grain and be free of large knots. Convenient sections are between ¾ inch × ⅛ inch and 1¼ inch × ⅜ inch. You might have to cut your sections down from larger stock. If you cannot get wood in single lengths to suit a large area, you can make the trellis in several sections. Two sections that open to matching shapes might not be much different in appearance from one large trellis. They will be easier to make and fit. For convenience in making, use strips no more than 60 inches wide.

1. Decide on the size mesh you want and draw the centerlines of the strips on a layout. Meshes at 5-inch centers are suggested and the lines are at 45-degrees to the borders (Fig. 10-2D).

2. At the outside, allow for the ends extending about half a mesh size (Fig. 10-2E).

3. With the layout as a guide, mark sufficient strips of full length (which are the same both ways) and others to make up the shorter pieces at the ends (Fig. 10-2F). Be careful that the distances between hole centers are exactly the same or the trellis will not submit to expanding and contracting or complete folding. Cut the ends to 45 degrees, which will come level when the meshes are square. The slight unevenness will be attractive if you push the meshes to a diamond shape.

Fig. 10-1. An expanding trellis attached to a wall provides a base for climbing plants.

4. Make the joints with nails driven through and clenched. Drill all the hole positions slightly undersize. Then you can drive all, or most, of the nails and the fibers will grip them while you turn the trellis over and clench them. Choose nails that will project about ¼ inch.

5. At each nail position, support the driven nail on an iron block and curve the end over a spike (Fig. 10-2G) in a direction diagonal to the grain. Turning along the grain might split the wood. Remove the spike and bury the point in the wood (Fig. 10-2H). There is no need to knock the whole nail thickness into the wood.

6. Try moving the section of trellis from the mesh-square shape to the fully folded shape, with the intermediate diamond shape, to settle on which suits the situation. Arrange the supports accordingly.

7. Nail or tie the trellis panel in position, but it is best to fit it with brass screws in drilled holes. This way, even after long exposure, you can take it down without damage.

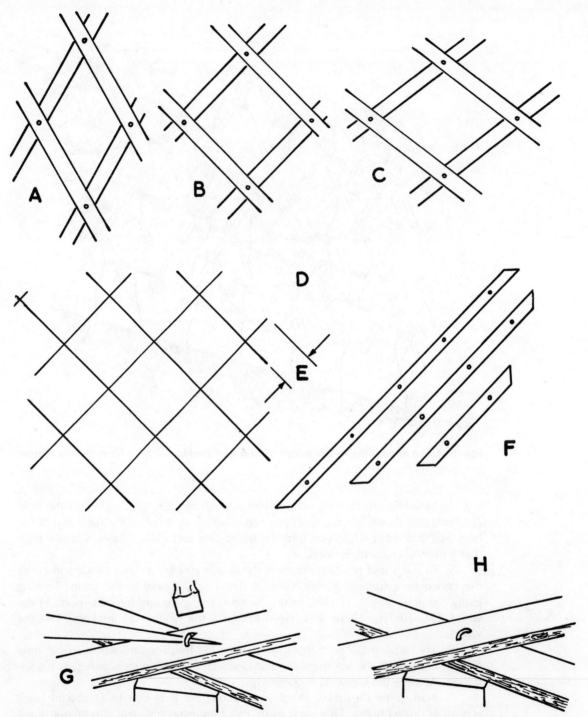

Fig. 10-2. Although a trellis can have different shapes (A-C), plan it square (D-F). Clench nail the crossings (G,H).

# TRELLIS SUPPORTS

If the trelliswork just described is to support climbing plants efficiently, you must support it so that the plants and their tendrils can work their way up without interference. They should be able to go all round and through, that means mounting the trellis away from a solid backing such as a house wall. Holding out about 2 inches should be enough. For the best appearance, any supports should be kept in from the edges (possibly at the first crossings of the laths).

The simplest supports on a surface are strips arranged horizontally (Fig. 10-3A), but the climbing plants will be coming on the trellis square to them and will not cross these obstructions unaided. Vertical pieces are better (Fig. 10-3B), but you will need more of them if the trellis is wide. Locating the strips behind trellis crossings makes them less obvious, but once foliage has started spreading, they will be hidden.

For free-standing, trellis supports should go into the ground and have horizontal rails attached. Get adequate penetration in the soil for stability and treat the wood with preservative before driving. As posts are unlikely to go in the same amount, start with them overlong and make any joints after driving. Although shallow notches might be cut (Fig. 10-3C), it should be sufficient to nail the parts together. If you want to avoid horizontal rails obstructing climbers, there could be light, vertical pieces between them and the rails (Fig. 10-3D). In a typical assembly with trellis up to 72 inches square, the posts could be up to 3 inches square, the rails 2 inches square, and the upright strips 1 inch × 2 inch section.

In some assemblies, it is advisable to brace the supports to keep them square. Diagonal braces that match the angles of the trellis will do the job and be inconspicuous (Fig. 10-3E). You can cut and nail them after you have erected the other parts. Unless the structure is very shaky, one at each end should be sufficient.

If the ground is sandy or soft and the posts are not given much support by it, you can dig holes and set the posts in concrete. If there is a risk of wind moving the trellis, add diagonal struts. The greatest rigidity comes from having them large and at 45 degrees or even a flatter angle (Fig. 10-3F), but that means they could extend so far as to be a nuisance. A more upright angle will still give enough support (Fig. 10-3G), but in many cases, struts at a reasonable angle lower down will stiffen enough and be out of the way (Fig. 10-3H).

For a strut to be most effective, it needs something to thrust against (Fig. 10-3J). That object could be a piece of board or sheet metal, but you have to dig a hole and bury it. Another way to get a similar effect is to drive in a stake and notch or bolt to it (Fig. 10-3K). At the post, you can notch in (Fig. 10-3L) or bolt through (Fig. 10-3M) the strut. It is unwise to depend only on nails or screws into the side of the post.

Struts are best able to take a load in compression. Arrange them so wind pressure is toward them. If there is a possibility of strong winds in both directions, there will have to be struts both ways. If you plan to arrange the trellis at an angle, possibly with two panels meeting at a corner, there is mutual support in the arrangement and the posts are unlikely to need struts to resist wind pressure.

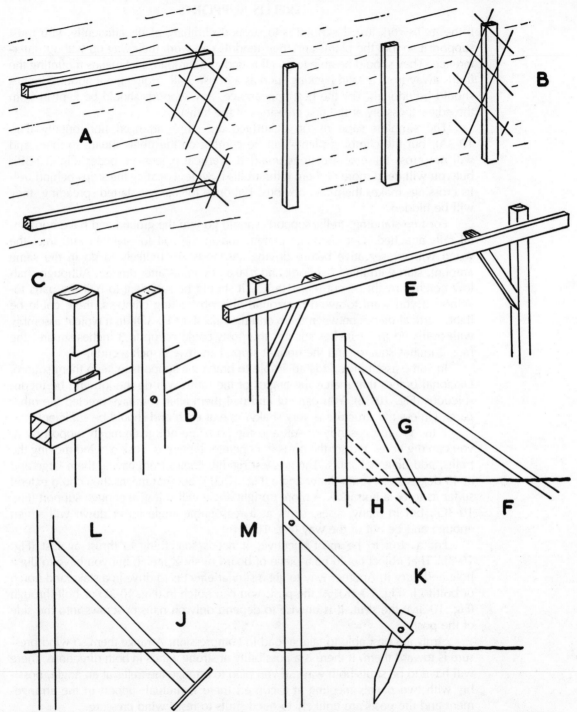

Fig. 10-3. Attach trellis supports to a wall or they can be freestanding, with posts into the ground.

# LARGE ARBOR

An arbor is a support for vines, climbing trees, or anything more substantial than a simple creeper or climbing flowering plant. It usually is intended to be a permanent feature because what climbs it is expected to grow there for many years. How you arrange it depends on the situation. You can attach it to a house or form an extension of a shed or other existing feature. You do not roof it and it is not intended to form a shelter, but in many cases, the foliage growing over it becomes almost a complete cover. An arbor often provides shelter from the sun so it might contain seats that are separate or built in to the structure of the arbor.

One attractive form of arbor has four or more legs, and it supports a framework that the vine will grow over. The space below could be a path, possibly leading to a gate, or it could be a summer shelter. Some vines that grow over supports can become quite large and heavy. Wisteria and other climbers will develop strong trunks and spread their branches in all directions. Therefore, the basic support has to be quite strong. This statement means that whatever you erect should be capable of standing there for many years with only the minimum of attention. A major repair after a few years probably would be impossible to make without damaging the vine that is being supported.

This design is the basic form of a large arbor that should be able to support any large climber (Fig. 10-4). Arrange sizes to suit the situation, but keep the parts to large sections so that there will be little fear of breakages or sagging after long use. You could use softwood in stock sections, but a durable hardwood, if available, would be a better choice. The uprights are shown as square-sectioned wood,

Fig. 10-4. A large arbor needs substantial framing to support heavy growth over a long period.

Table 10-1. Materials List for
Large Arbor.

| | |
|---|---|
| 4 posts | 108 × 4 × 4 |
| or | 108 × 5 or 6 round |
| 2 stringers | 144 × 8 × 2 |
| 8 cross members | 84 × 6 × 2 |

but they could be round poles with the bark removed. Treat poles in the same way with similar joints at the top.

1. Prepare the posts by allowing for at least 18 inches in the ground. In some soil, it will be possible to drive the posts in directly or into prepared holes. If soft soil will later let the posts sink deeper under load or there is a risk of them moving, it would be better to dig larger holes and set the posts in concrete (Fig. 10-5A). Treat the wood with preservative and slope the top of the concrete away from the wood so that you will drain rainwater away from the post.

2. Lay out the post positions while checking that they are parallel and square. Although you will have decided on a size, precision is not important, providing the posts will make a satisfactory pattern. Because of this fact, it is unwise to make the upper parts until you locate the posts. Then you can allow for variations. Make the posts overlong at first because the ground might not be level and they might not enter the same amount. Check that the posts are plumb and put temporary stays between them for mutual support while you fit the other parts.

3. Get the tops of the posts level. Use a temporary board across, with a level on it, using the lowest post as a guide for marking and cutting the others.

4. Mark down 6 inches for the notches (Fig. 10-5B). Use the board and level across where you have marked the notches before cutting them. It is these notches that settle the levels of the upper parts and it is less important if the tops of the posts are not level.

5. Cut the notches and bevel the tops of the posts to shed water (Fig. 10-5C).

6. Make the two stringers (Fig. 10-5D). With most assemblies, they can over-hang the posts by up to 24 inches. In the example, it is assumed that a length of 12 feet will do. If you space the cross members at 18 inch centers, the end ones can then be 9 inches from the ends of the stringers (Fig. 10-5E).

7. There is no need for deeply-cut joints between the stringers and the cross members, but shallow notches in the stringers serve to locate the other pieces and ensure accurate assembly. Without the notches, the parts tend to slide during nailing. Put the two stringers together and mark the notches across them. A depth of 1 inch should be enough (Fig. 10-5F). Bevel the undersides of the stringers at the ends (Fig. 10-5G), but a small amount left square is stronger than cutting to a sharp angle.

8. Mount the stringers on the posts, using two bolts at each place (Fig. 10-5H). Saturate the meeting surfaces with preservative before assembly. It is where water accumulates in joints that rot might start.

9. Make all the cross members to match each other and bevel their ends to match the ends of the stringers (Fig. 10-5J).

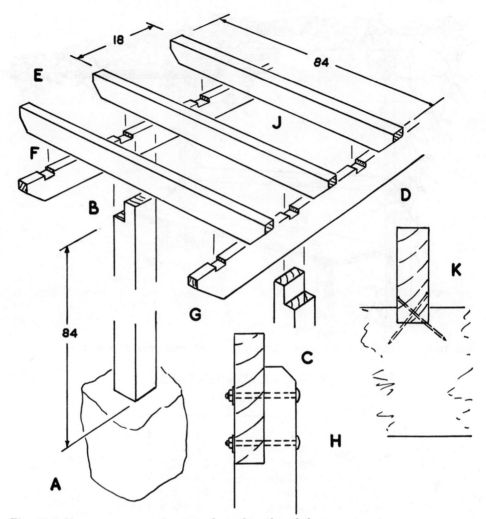

*Fig. 10-5. You can concrete posts and notch and nail the upper parts.*

10. Join the parts with nails driven diagonally both ways (Fig. 10-5K).

11. Treat all the wood with preservative or thoroughly paint it. Leave the assembly long enough for the finish to become absolutely dry before allowing growing plants to come into contact with it.

## ROSE ARBOR

An arbor might be needed with a vista one way only and it might not have to support heavy vines or similar things that develop large trunks and branches. Such an arbor would suit climbing roses or similar climbing plants that need many years to develop. It is convenient to locate such an arbor at the boundary of a lawn or flower garden and provide it with a seat so that it is possible to sit in the shade and enjoy the views. The arbor shown in Fig. 10-6 is intended to be about 6 feet in

Fig. 10-6. You can arrange a rose arbor on two posts and provide a seat.

**Table 10-2. Materials List for
Rose Arbor.**

| | |
|---|---|
| 2 posts | 90 × 4 × 2 |
| 2 cross members | 72 × 4 × 2 |
| 2 braces | 54 × 2 × 1 |
| 2 packings | 4 × 4 × 1 |
| 6 purlins | 72 × 2 × 2 |
| 1 seat back | 60 × 6 × 1 |
| 2 seat supports | 20 × 2 × 2 |
| 2 legs | 24 × 2 × 2 |

each direction and be strong enough to take most kinds of climbing plants (except the heavier vines and trees).

Most of the top cantilever is forward, but its weight is balanced by the extensions at the back, tied to the uprights with diagonal braces. Besides ensuring the top keeps its shape, this allows the roses or other climbers to spread behind as well as in front and make an attractive canopy.

1. The posts are shown as 2-inch × 4-inch pieces, but they could be more substantial. They are shown sunk into the ground 18 inches (Fig. 10-7A), but how you support them depends on the ground. You might have to concrete them as described for the previous project. It might be advisable to make a concrete platform to include the posts and extend along in front of the seat.

180

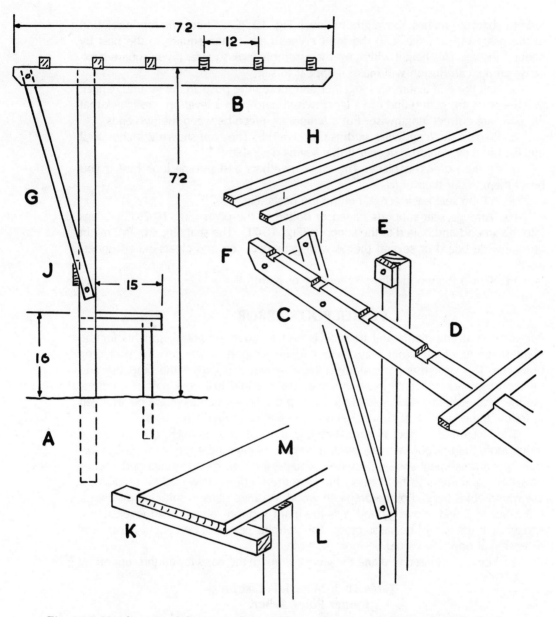

Fig. 10-7. Notch parts of the rose arbor and brace the top with diagonals at the back.

2. Make the cross members (Fig. 10-7B,C) the same and with ½-inch notches to locate the lengthwise pieces (Fig. 10-7D).

3. At the top of each post, attach a packing the same thickness as the brace (Fig. 10-7E). Drill through these and the cross members for ½-inch bolts.

4. Drill near the ends of the cross members for ½-inch bolts into the braces (Fig. 10-7F).

5. Temporarily bolt a post to its cross member and make a brace from the end

hole to about 20 inches above ground level (Fig. 10-7G). Check the top in relation to the post, and arrange it so the front comes higher than square to the post by about 3 inches. This height will make the assembly look square. If you square it exactly, an optical illusion will make it appear to sag.

6. Bolt the end assemblies together and mount the posts in the ground. Check that the posts are plumb and use a lengthwise board with a level on it to check that the parts are correct lengthwise. Put a temporary piece between the two ends.

7. Prepare the lengthwise purlins (Fig. 10-7H). They are shown 2 inches × 2 inches, but they could be deeper if that seems desirable.

8. Fit the purlins in place. The cross members and purlins look best if you bevel them under their ends.

9. Put the seat back across behind the posts (Fig. 10-7J).

10. Arrange seat supports nailed or bolted to the posts (Fig. 10-7K) and legs into the ground and bolted to the supports (Fig. 10-7L). The seat (Fig. 10-7M) might be one wide board or several pieces with gaps between and cleats across underneath.

11. Finish the wood with preservative or paint.

## CENTER POLES ARBOR

For some climbing plants and trees, it is best to arrange central uprights for the plant stems to climb. That way there will be support at the top for spreading branches. This design is particularly suitable where you expect the branches and foliage to spread and hang in abundance. There could just be a pair of uprights, but the arrangement also is suitable for a long display—such as might be arranged to follow the edge of a path—that is not necessarily straight (Fig. 10-8).

The suggested project is comparatively light. If you arrange supports at not much more than 5-foot intervals, with a climber planted near the base of each upright, the arrangement should provide adequate support. If you expect fairly heavy growth or spacing is to be greater, increase the sections. It would be possible to use round poles instead of the prepared wood. Arrange sizes to suit circumstances, but a height 7 feet above ground puts the main supports above head level, and a spread of 4 feet would be satisfactory. The uprights need not be central if a greater extension at one side would be more suitable.

1. You do not need to plane the wood. Prepare the parts for all the supporting

### Table 10-3. Materials List for Center Poles Arbor.

Parts for one support:

| | |
|---|---|
| 1 upright | 90 × 4 × 2 |
| 1 crossbar | 48 × 4 × 2 |
| 2 joint covers | 12 × 4 × 1 |
| 2 struts | 48 × 2 × 1 |
| Lengthwise pieces | 2 × 2 as needed |

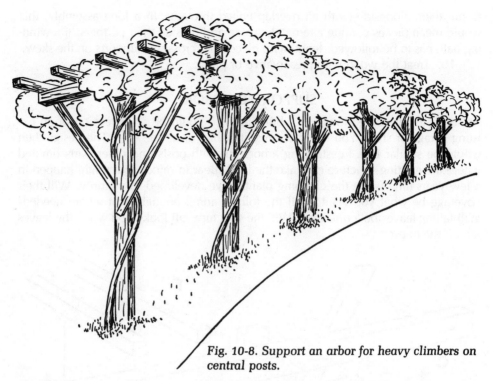

Fig. 10-8. Support an arbor for heavy climbers on central posts.

assemblies at the same time so that they are all the same. The crossbars (Fig. 10-9A) and the uprights (Fig. 10-9B) are the key pieces. Allow for the uprights entering the ground sufficiently (probably 18 inches). If necessary, dig a hole for bedding the foot of the post in concrete.

2. Drill for ½-inch bolts a few inches from the ends of the crossbars (Fig. 10-9C) and mark where the uprights will connect.

3. Make joint covers (Fig. 10-9D) to nail or screw both sides.

4. Assemble these parts by checking squareness between the top and upright.

5. Arrange two diagonal struts (Fig. 10-9E). They will provide most support if the angle is slightly more upright than 45 degrees. If that angle makes a hazard for the head of anyone walking nearby, they could be brought to a flatter angle.

6. Bolt on the struts. Preferably, you should use large washers under the nuts and bolt heads to spread the pressure. It is advisable to put plenty of preservative in these and other joints before tightening in order to resist the onset of rot.

7. This arbor is shown without locating notches for the lengthwise parts, but you can cut shallow notches, if you prefer, in the same way as previous projects allow for joints in long assemblies (see step 9).

8. Arrange the lengthwise parts at spacings to suit the expected growth, but having the outside pieces level with the ends of the crossbar and the others spaced at the 12-inch centers should suit most needs. At the ends, let the strips overhang their supports by about 12 inches (Fig. 10-9F).

9. In a series of supports, lengthwise pieces should overlap three supports. Further pieces need not have fitted joints to the others, but it should be satisfactory

to put them alongside (with an overlap nailed through). In a long assembly, that would mean pieces coming alternately inside and outside their partners. If a winding path has to be followed, lengthwise pieces can cross the supports on the skew.

10. Treat the wood with preservative or paint.

## SUPPORTED ARBOR

An arbor might come alongside a building or it could be an extension of an existing garage or shed. You might arrange it in line or at one side. The design then would be similar to a freestanding arbor, but with posts and other parts omitted where the existing structure can take the load. Bear in mind what might happen in a few years time when the climbing plants have developed to maturity. Will their coverage be what you want? Will the foliage admit enough light where needed? Will falling leaves be a nuisance? Will the structure still look good when the leaves are off the trees?

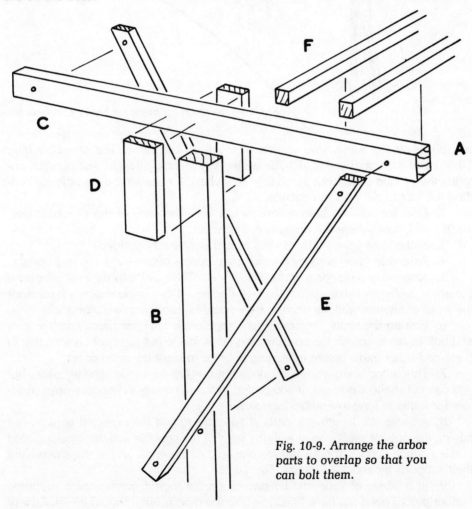

Fig. 10-9. Arrange the arbor parts to overlap so that you can bolt them.

Supports for climbing vines and trees can improve a patio or deck. If the arbor adjoins the house, you can get some support from the house side. You can arrange the posts alongside the patio or deck, preferably where there is adjoining soil in which the vines can grow. It is possible to grow things in tubs, but these obviously restrict roots and you cannot expect to grow long-lasting and large plants in that way. Tubs might suit your annual and biannual growths.

A house-side arbor over a deck or patio can be made in a similar way to the large arbor (Figs. 10-4,5), but there will have to be a few structural differences. As it is closer to the living area, you might want to relieve its severity by decorating in some way. It is primarily a support, however, and most decoration will come from the foliage and flowers.

1. At the side of the house or other structure, it will be best to fit a rail the same depth as the cross members and notch them fully into it (Fig. 10-10A). This rail will have to take increasing weights as branches grow. Therefore, securely fasten it to the house side. Some of the load could be taken by two or more uprights to the ground or floor.

2. You can bevel the outer ends of the cross members below, but a molded cut is more decorative (Fig. 10-10B).

3. The stringers and posts can be the same as in the large arbor, but you will have to arrange post spacings to suit steps or other features already there. You can also decorate the stringers in this way or you can cut their ends square, depending on the situation.

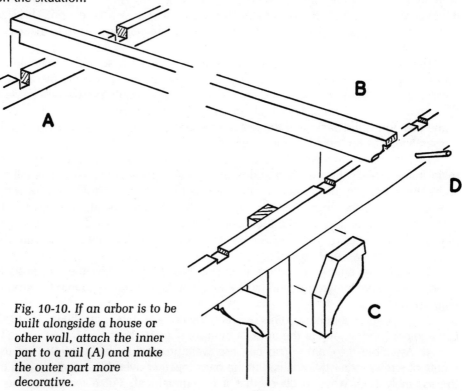

Fig. 10-10. If an arbor is to be built alongside a house or other wall, attach the inner part to a rail (A) and make the outer part more decorative.

4. You can carry the decorative theme further by putting brackets between the stringers and posts, and you can have matching moldings (Fig. 10-10C). The brackets are not intended to provide strength; you can nail or screw them in position.

5. There could be a rail at a suitable height between the posts to enclose a deck. You can put hooks under the stringers to take hanging plants or pots. Wood pegs or dowels (Fig. 10-10D) would serve the same purpose.

## PERGOLA

Arbor, bower, and pergola are names for things that are so similar that it is difficult to separate them. For the purpose of this book, a pergola is an enclosed type of arbor. It has an open-topped support around which a vine or tree provides a covering, while the sides are open or might be enclosed with latticework. A pergola can be round, square, or many-sided. Structural problems exist in making a truly round pergola. A square pergola can be easier to build, but one with more than four sides has an attractive appearance and is not much more difficult to make.

Although the number of sides could be any total, advantages exist in choosing six sides. This style makes a good-looking structure. In setting out six equal sides, you can use the fact that the radius of a circle can be stepped off six times around the circumference. In this assembly, all the cuts that are not square will be at 30 degrees or 60 degrees. The project has six posts equally spaced and a roof sloping at 30 degrees along the rafters to a central point (Fig. 10-11). The suggested size is 8 feet across the posts and most of the parts are 2-inch × 4-inch section. This size will be strong enough unless you are planning a much larger structure. In that case, increase wood sections.

The design shown in Fig. 10-12 has a full hexagonal base and is suitable for positioning where you can view all round it. It could make a centerpiece for a lawn or a focal point for paths. Of course, it is large enough for several chairs. If the pergola is to be at one side of a garden, it could be made as a half. The main frame then forms the back, and the rest of one side of the design is made in exactly the same way as for the complete assembly.

1. The size of the pergola is decided by a main frame (Fig. 10-12A). This main frame crosses the hexagon and is built of two posts with two rafters (all attached with halving joints). Set out the roof part and (a short distance down) the full-size posts on the floor. The slope of the rafters is not crucial, so long as both sides are the same. If you make the slope 30 degrees (Fig. 10-12B), that will simplify marking angles (if you are using a fence on a circular saw). Make sure the drawing has the two posts parallel.

2. Mark two rafters from the setting out (Fig. 10-12C). Cut the two posts to stand 7 feet above the ground and have enough at the bottom to go into the ground (Fig. 10-12D).

3. Mark and cut halving joints between the posts and the rafters (Fig. 10-13A). Cut another halving joint at the apex of the roof (Fig. 10-13B).

4. Assemble the frame. You can use waterproof glue in the joints, but use plenty of screws rather than nails. Put the parts together over the setting out and try the assembly both ways to check that it is symmetrical. Put a temporary piece

Fig. 10-11. This pergola has
six posts and a top taken to a
point.

across (Fig. 10-13C) to hold it in shape until it is brought together with the other parts.

5. The other four frames are like half of the frame just made, except for where they meet it at the apex. The posts and their joints to the rafters are the same. At the apex, cut back each rafter vertically (reduced by half the thickness of the main frame). Also cut there to 60 degrees (Fig. 10-13D) to make the two at each side into a pair (Fig. 10-13E).

6. The corners of the frames at the tops of the posts will fit the eave pieces closely if you bevel them 60 degrees each side of the center (Fig. 10-13F). You can cut that after you mount the posts in the ground, but it might be easier to do at this stage.

7. Set out the ground where the post holes have to come by using an impro-

**Table 10-4. Materials List for Pergola.**

| | |
|---|---|
| 6 posts | 102 × 4 × 2 |
| 6 rafters | 60 × 4 × 2 |
| 6 eaves | 52 × 4 × 2 |
| 6 purlins | 44 × 2 × 2 |
| 6 purlins | 30 × 2 × 2 |
| 6 purlins | 18 × 2 × 2 |

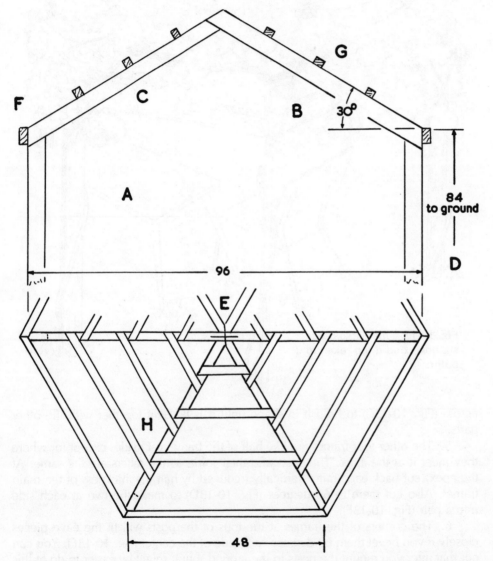

Fig. 10-12. The pergola is built with a central assembly and other parts brought up to it.

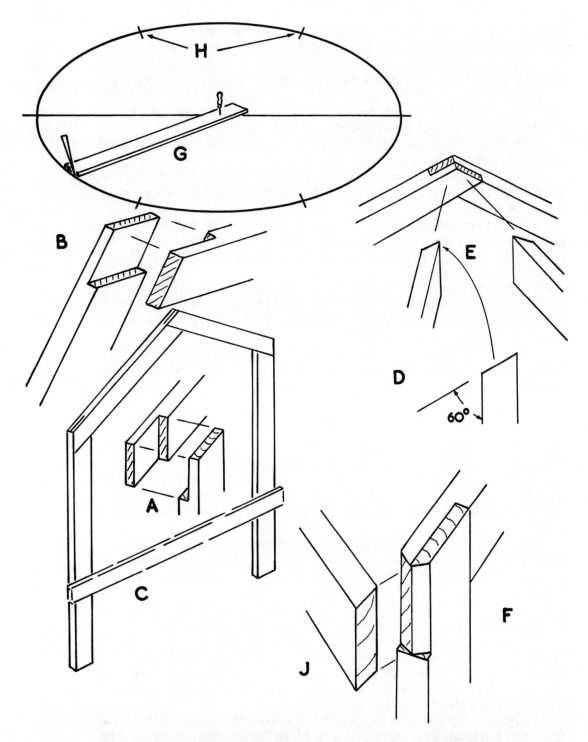

Fig. 10-13. Post positions are found with a circular layout. Half and nail joints.

vised compass. Use any piece of wood and put a spike through a hole 48 inches from the end. Push the spike into the ground at what will be the center of the pergola and use a sharp piece of wood against the end to scratch a circle on the ground (Fig. 10-13G). Mark across the centerline in the direction you want the main frame to be, and then measure 48 inches from these points on the circumference to the positions of the other posts on the circumference (Fig. 10-13H). Check that the distances between these positions is also 48 inches.

8. Erect the main frame. See that it is plumb in all directions and that a board temporarily clamped across the eave's corners is level.

9. Erect the other posts and bring the rafters to the center of the main frame and nail them there (Fig. 10-12E). Check distances apart around the eave's corners and adjust as necessary.

10. The eave's pieces (Fig. 10-12F), that go around and link the tops of the six posts, meet at the corners and will look best if cut to 60 degrees so they miter together (Fig. 10-13J). Nevertheless, you can nail them satisfactorily even if their ends do not meet closely.

11. Arrange the number of purlins on each slope to suit the type of climbing tree or vine, but a spacing of about 12 inches should be satisfactory (Fig. 10-12G). Put these strips first on three alternate sides of the roof, and then put the others on so they come against them (Fig. 10-12H).

12. The linked parts should provide mutual support and the pergola will be standing rigidly. Clean off any raggedness in the woodwork and finish it with preservative.

## BEAN POLES

Beans, peas, and other vegetables that need something to climb on as they grow often are supported by a collection of sticks and poles that do not match. Often they are tied together in such a way that the assembly is insecure and might collapse before the crop is ready for harvesting. If these are crops you grow every year, it is worthwhile making something that can do the job properly and be suitable for taking down and storing out of the growing season.

How many supports and how high you take them depends on what you grow, but a height of 6 feet or 8 feet is probable. For rows of beans, you want poles 12 inches or more apart. The length of the row will tell you how many poles to make. A fault with many improvised assemblies is their tendency to sway. This assembly has diagonal braces to prevent this (Fig. 10-14). The poles are shown pushed into the ground, but you can bolt them to lengthwise pieces at ground level.

The wood chosen should be straight-grained and free from knots. Much spruce, fir, and pine can satisfy these requirements. The wood need only be 1 inch square. If you have to use wood that does not have such a straight grain, increase the section slightly to provide strength. Surfaces could be left as sawn—which is better than being planed—for the vines to grip.

1. Prepare all the uprights (Fig. 10-15A) with pointed ends, but do not go to fine points that would soon crumble or split. About 7 inches from the top, drill for

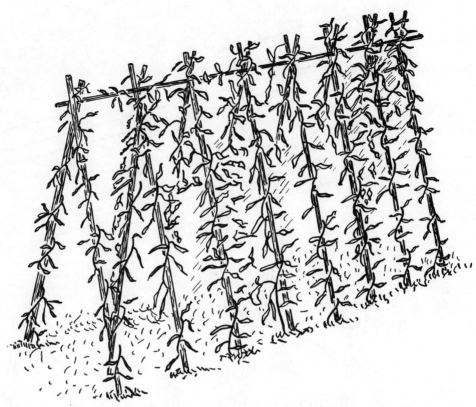

*Fig. 10-14. You can take these bean poles apart and use them for several years.*

**Table 10-5. Materials List for
Bean Poles.**

All parts 96 × 1 × 1
(quantity according to needs)

pivot bolts (³⁄₁₆-inch-stove bolts are suitable) and 2 inches below them, drill similar holes the other way for the horizontal bar (Fig. 10-15B).

2. Make the horizontal bar (Fig. 10-15C). For a long row, you will have to use more than one bar. It will be convenient to change sides where they overlap. Drill for bolts at the spacing you want.

3. Assemble two sets of hinged uprights and erect them temporarily, using the horizontal bar as a guide to get them spaced correctly at top and bottom. From this assembly, get the length of a diagonal (Fig. 20-15D). To allow for variations when you erect each year, drill a few extra bolt holes (Fig. 10-15E).

4. Grease the nuts and bolts when you erect the poles each year, to reduce rust and allow them to be released easily at the end of the season.

5. If you do not wish to push all the poles into the ground, there could be an-

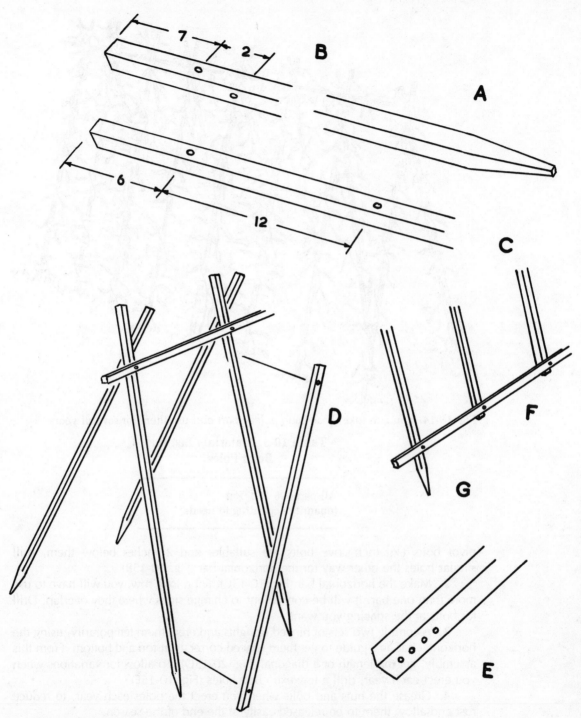

Fig. 10-15. The bean pole parts are square and drilled for bolts.

other horizontal bar near ground level each side (Fig. 10-15F), bolted in the same way as the top one. This bar might be lashed down to stakes, or you can let the end poles continue with points into the ground (Fig. 10-15G). It would be unwise to expect end securing only to hold a long length, so there should be poles or stakes into the ground at least every 8 feet.

## TOMATO POLES

Tomato and cucumber plants need something on which they can climb and spread. There could be poles with strings between, but it is better to have wooden-horizontal pieces so that there is more for the vines and tendrils to grip. Construction could be with 1-inch square, straight-grained strips, held together with bolts, as in the previous project. Alternatively, you can take nails through and you can clench them so that the parts could pivot on each other for compactness in storage. Sizes depend on the plants you grow, but poles 60 inches or more should be satisfactory.

1. A single pole with crosspieces (Fig. 10-16A) will do if your crop is just confined to a corner of the plot. Make the pole with a point and holes for the bolts holding the crosspieces (Fig. 10-17A).

2. The crosspieces could all be the same length or you could taper them slightly (Fig. 10-17B). Drill centrally for bolts.

3. When assembled for use, it might be sufficient to rely on tightening the bolts to hold the crosspieces square. To be more certain they will not move later, you can make shallow grooves in them (Fig. 10-17C). For storage, slacken the bolts and turn the parts as far into line as they will go (Fig. 10-17D).

4. There could be two uprights with the strips across them (Fig. 10-16B). The assembly is similar to the single pole, but you can provide a greater spread (Fig. 10-17E) and the pair of poles into the ground should be more rigid. The parts will fold for storage, but they will make a rather long package.

5. An alternative to upright poles is to arrange them sloping (Fig. 10-16C). The arrangement could stand independently or you could slope a pair toward each other. With the tops interlocked, there would be mutual support and a very rigid assembly.

6. Make a pair of poles with pivot bolts as for bean poles. Spread them to about 24 inches, and then mark where the crosspieces will come at even intervals (Fig. 10-17F). There should be no need to cut notches as the two bolts in each strip and the triangular shape of the assembly will provide rigidity.

7. If you do not want to fold the parts for storage, you can nail them. If you want to fold, you can take the bolts out of one pole so the crosspieces can swing almost in line on the other.

8. You can build any of the assemblies into groups so that the pattern has three, four, or more sides. You can link the sides, and this would strengthen them and allow for a greater spread for the crop. On the other hand, the inside will be sheltered and will not get as much sunlight. Fruit or vegetables there might not be as good as those on independently-standing poles.

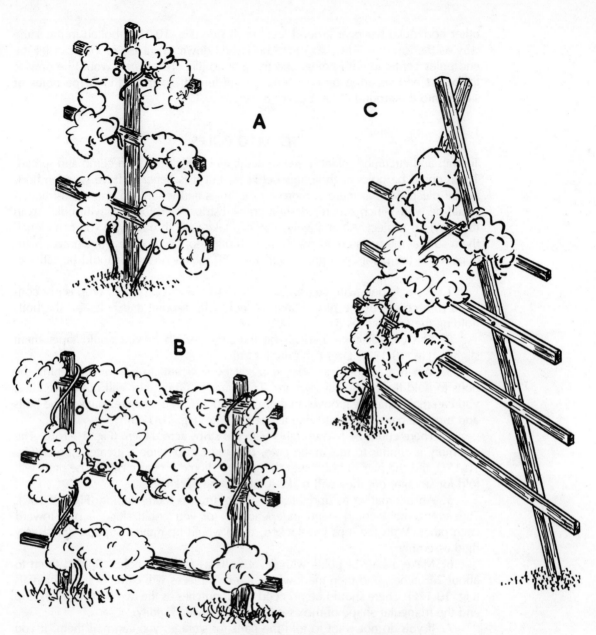

Fig. 10-16. Arrange tomato and cucumber poles on single or double uprights.

**Table 10-6. Materials List for
Tomato Poles.**

All parts 1 × 1 (quantity according to needs)

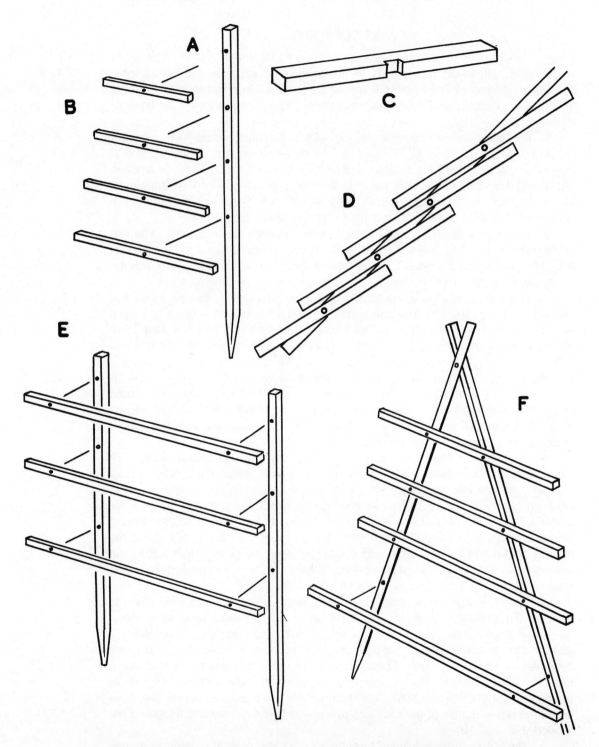

Fig. 10-17. If you bolt the parts, they can be taken apart or folded for storage.

# WIRE SUPPORTS

You can support some climbing plants with cords or wires instead of strips of wood. They will climb hairy ropes or intertwine through wire netting. In some cases, such as grapevines, they will spread along wires in preference to anything thicker. The constructional problems are then in arranging supports for the wires or ropes.

1. For beans and other vegetables that climb, the ropes could go to a central bar on uprights (Fig. 10-18A). The posts could be 2-inch-square pieces, pointed at the bottom, and drilled for a length of metal tube or rod (Fig. 10-19A), or wooden rods could drop into a slot at the top (Fig. 10-19B) and slip into loosely-fitting mortises if they are also to come down lower (Fig. 10-19C). The lower bars might not be needed, but they allow shorter cords to be arranged intermediately.

2. How you arrange the cords at the bottom depends on your needs. You can secure them to notched stakes (Fig. 10-19D). You can stake down a rod at the ends (Fig. 10-19E) and tie the cords to it. Whatever method you choose, make sure the cords cannot come away or slacken and damage plants climbing on them.

3. In some cases, it is better to spread the top supports by putting a crossbar on each post (Fig. 10-18B). You can bolt it on, and it could have a notch to keep it square (Fig. 10-19F). Drill the crossbars to take wires stretched between them (usually two, but there could be four). With the strain of the stretched wires, it is advisable to tie the ends down to stakes (Fig. 10-19G) or to very securely let the posts into the ground. You can use this arrangement at a lower position. Suppose the instructions on a packet of seeds says the supports should be 6 feet high. You could make this arrangement not more than 4 feet and the beans will climb first and go along the horizontal wires. This design makes picking easier, and with the upright cords to the outer wires, the insides get more sunlight and air.

4. Peas do not need high supports. Light trimmings of natural wood with many twigs and branches are ideal supports (if you have them). For another type of support, you can use wire mesh with large squares, such as turkey and pig wire, between posts (Fig. 10-18C). This style support is erected best before the peas are planted. The lower part of the wire mesh can have cut ends pushed into the ground or small stakes used there. The top need not be more than 36 inches above the ground, and it can be held level with a wire between the posts (Fig. 10-20A). An alternative is to use a piece of bamboo or a light lath that you push through the wire mesh and then nail it to the posts (Fig. 10-20B).

5. If you want to grow grapevines, they need a steady, tight wire fence to train on (Fig. 10-18D). A shaky and loose arrangement would be unsatisfactory. The usual height above the ground is about 5 feet. The posts should be nearly 7 feet long to allow for sinking in the ground. The distance between the posts might be 8 feet (or not much more). Because the fence needs to stand for several years, use a durable wood for the posts. Put preservative on the posts and erect them truly in line and upright (Fig. 10-21A). Drill the posts for two horizontal wires. The wires go within a few inches of the tops and just above halfway between there and the ground (Fig. 10-21B).

6. The wire can be galvanized steel wire rope about ⅛ of an inch in diame-

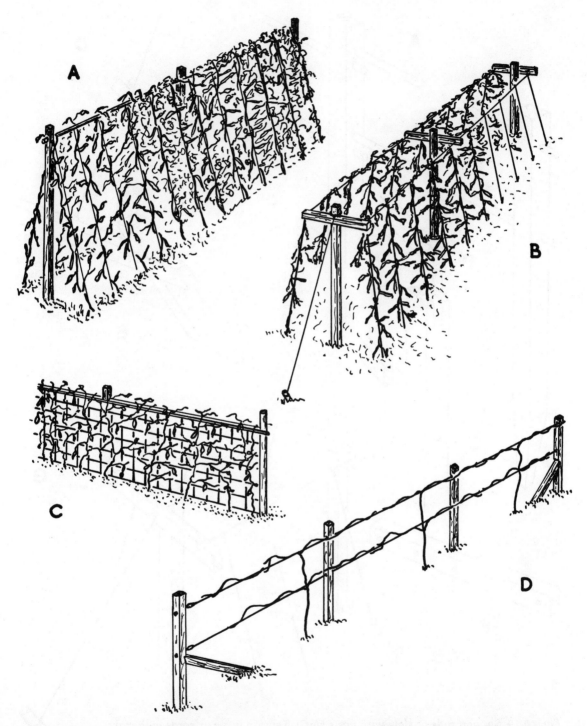

Fig. 10-18. *Several crops will climb on wire. You can support the wire in several different ways.*

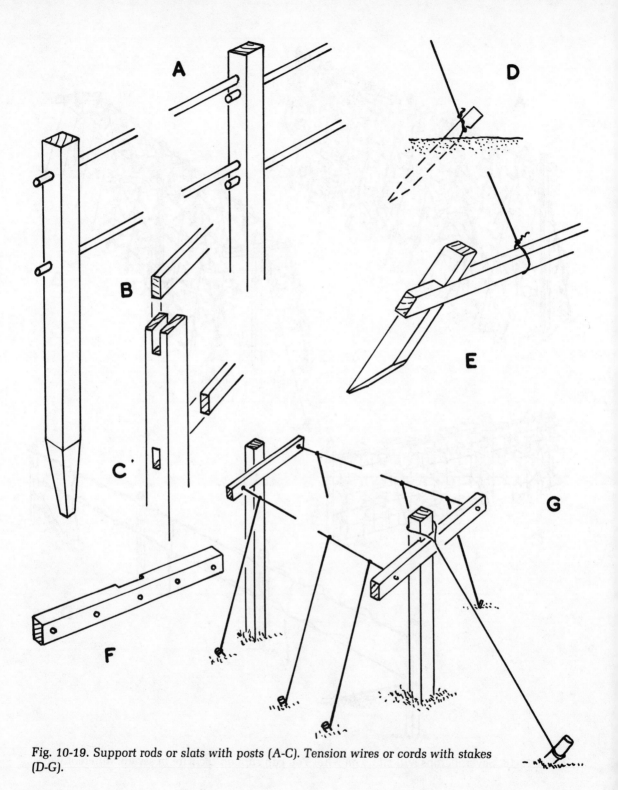

Fig. 10-19. Support rods or slats with posts (A-C). Tension wires or cords with stakes (D-G).

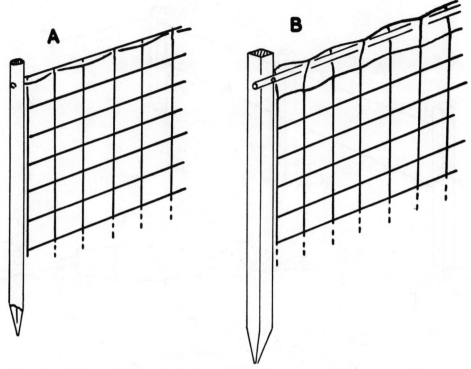

*Fig. 10-20. You can hold turkey wire mesh between posts with wire or a rod.*

ter. Drill the intermediate posts to allow the wire to slide through easily. At the ends there have to be either ¼-inch-diameter or ⁵⁄₁₆-inch-diameter eyebolts. If you can get a type with a very long, threaded portion or if you can cut the thread further yourself, the eyebolts might provide all you need to tension the wire rope (Fig. 10-21C). If not, you should include turnbuckles at one end of each wire (Fig. 10-21D) or at both ends if it is a very long assembly. Attach the wires to the eyebolts or turnbuckles with two wire rope clips (Fig. 10-21E).

7. It is unlikely that the end posts will be sufficiently rigid to withstand the pull of the tensioned wires. Therefore, you must stiffen them. One way is to put a strut inside (Fig. 10-21F). Notch it to the post (Fig. 10-21G). At the bottom, prevent it from being thrust deeper into the soil. One way is to dig down and put a board there (Fig. 10-21H).

8. If digging is impractical, you could drive in a stake and bolt the strut to it (Fig. 10-21J). Another method of support to resist the strain of the wires under tension is to arrange a stay at each end (Fig. 10-21K). If there is space, the longer this stay is the better because it gives a pull nearer horizontal. Ideally, it should come at an angle flatter than 45 degrees to the ground. Then you should drive the stake only slightly more upright than square to the line of the wire stay. Loop the wire

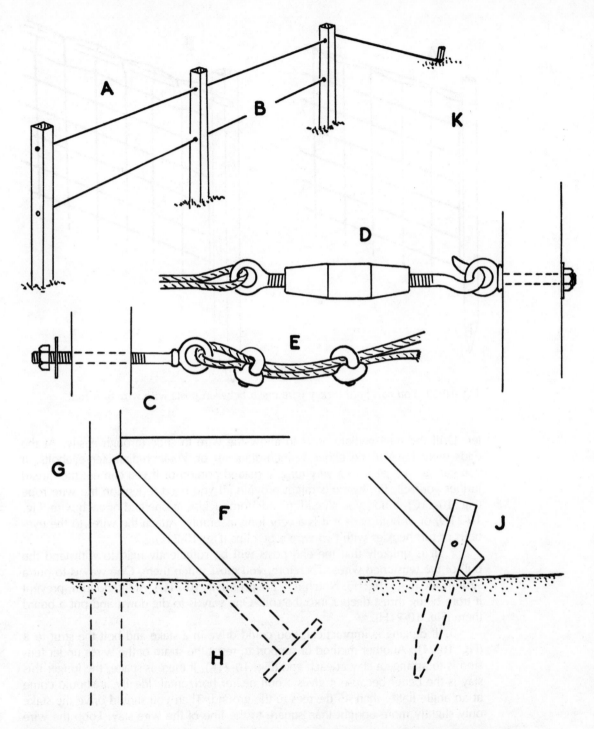

Fig. 10-21. Grape vines need tight wire that you must stretch between posts and held taut.

around a notch in the stake or use a ring bolt through it. At the top of the post, use a ring bolt and a turnbuckle in the same way as at the ends of the horizontal wires. Try to get the assembly tight so that the horizontal wires are reasonably rigid. There should be some adjustment left on the ringbolt nuts or the turnbuckle to take up later if necessary.

# 11

# Carts

SOME MEANS OF TRANSPORTING THINGS IS NEEDED IN ALMOST EVERY GARDEN and yard. You could carry some items in a basket or box, but it is often better to have something on wheels. It need not be big or have a large capacity, but it gets tools and plants to where you want them and allows you to take away trash or produce. How it is made and its size and shape depends on your needs and the layout of the garden. If there are broad tracks or paths, the cart can be quite large. You could even have a trailer to go behind a mini-tractor. If the routes about the garden are narrow, you have to make something more compact.

The traditional garden-size transport has been a barrow with one wheel. The attraction is that is can go anywhere wide enough to walk. It lowers onto two legs and is then quite stable, but when you are using it, your arms take at least half the load. Some older barrows were made of such heavy wood that it took quite an effort to manage the barrow without anything loaded into it. There are much lighter versions, but stability depends on your skill. Not everyone is happy with a wheelbarrow.

Two-wheel barrows and others use a wide roller instead of the one wheel. Both are more stable, but you still have to take much of the weight on your arms. If the two wheels are brought back to come on each side of the load, the wheels take nearly all the weight You need be concerned only with steadying and pushing or pulling.

The next step is to use four wheels to take all the weight and which are steady, but one pair has to be steerable. With any cart having wheels at the side, you must have wide enough paths. You cannot take this sort of cart everywhere that a barrow would go. The ultimate in effortlessness is a trailer behind a tractor, but that needs even more space. Places in the garden might exist that you cannot reach.

You have to weigh up your needs and facilities against what you would like to have. The following projects are examples of the various types that you can build or adapt to your land.

## GARDEN TROLLEY

A lightweight means of carrying tools, transporting plants, or gathering weeds is useful in a flower garden or a small vegetable plot where you cannot justify a larger barrow or cart. The trolley shown in Fig. 11-1 has a pair of wheels and two handles. It has space for long and short tools, and there is a bin where you could fit a

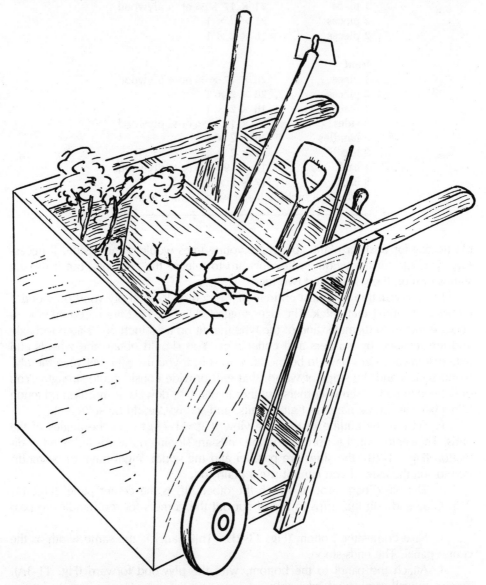

Fig. 11-1. A garden trolley will transport tools, plants, and other equipment.

### Table 11-1. Materials List for
### Garden Trolley.

**middle panel**

| | |
|---|---|
| 1 piece | 25 × 17 × ¼ or ½ plywood |
| 2 pieces | 25 × 2 × 1 |
| 2 pieces | 14 × 2 × 1 |

**bottom**

| | |
|---|---|
| 1 piece | 21 × 17 × ¼ or ½ plywood |
| 2 pieces | 21 × 2 × 1 |
| 2 pieces | 16 × 2 × 1 |

**front**

| | |
|---|---|
| 1 piece | 28 × 17 × ¼ or ½ plywood |
| 2 pieces | 26 × 2 × 1 |
| 1 piece | 16 × 2 × 1 |
| 2 sides | 27 × 17 × ¼ or ½ plywood |
| 2 handles | 36 × 2 × 1 |
| 2 legs | 31 × 2 × 1 |
| 1 back | 17 × 9 × ¼ or ½ plywood |
| 3 backs | 17 × 2 × 1 |
| 2 wheels 8 inch diameter with 25 inch axle | |

plastic bag for trash or plants, or where young trees would stand inside. If necessary, you can tilt the whole trolley forward to release the contents, but it usually stands firm on the wheels and two legs.

The construction is almost entirely of ¼-inch or ½-inch plywood on wood 2 inches wide and 1 inch thick. The sizes suggested in Fig. 17-2 are based on wheels about 8 inches in diameter and of the type that fit on a ⅜-inch or ½-inch rod axle and are retained by washers and cotter pins. You should obtain the wheels and axle first in case sizes have to be modified to suit. If you use glue between the plywood panels and the strips of wood, that will provide considerable strength. You only need to nail or screw corners or other joints. Use dowels or mortise and tenon joints between some parts, but glue, nails, and screws should be sufficient.

1. Set out the outline of the side view (Fig. 11-2A) to get the angles of the ends. The center panel is upright and the ends are sloping outward. In the other direction (Fig. 11-2B), the sides are parallel and the width might have to be modified to suit the axle, if you cannot use a plain rod.

2. The basic part, around which the others fit, is the center panel (Fig. 11-2C). Glue and nail the strips to it and cut out the corners for the handles to pass through.

3. Next comes the bottom (Fig. 11-2D). This panel is the same width as the center panel. The ends slope.

4. Attach the panel to the bottom, with the plywood forward (Fig. 11-3A). Screws as well as glue are advisable.

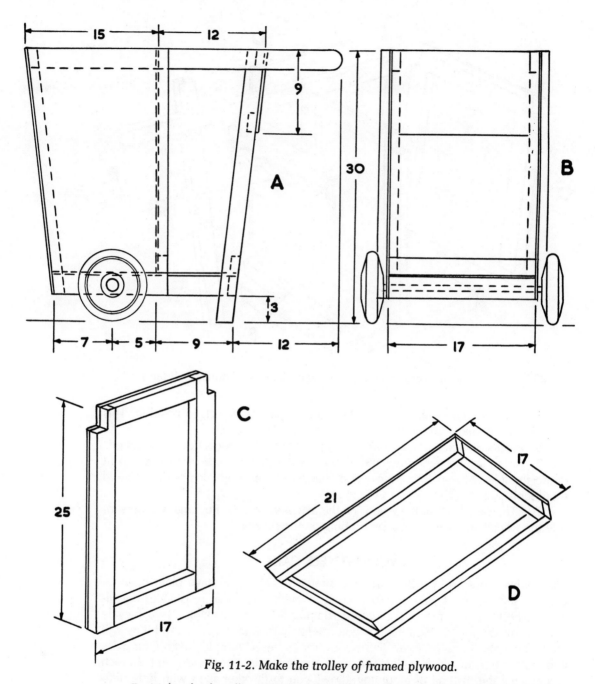

*Fig. 11-2. Make the trolley of framed plywood.*

5. Make the handles (Fig. 11-3B) and use them parallel with the bottom to check the height of the front panel. Make and frame that panel (Fig. 11-3C). Glue and nail it to the bottom and glue and screw the handles to both panels.

6. Make the plywood sides (Fig. 11-3D) and glue and nail them to the other parts to complete the bin.

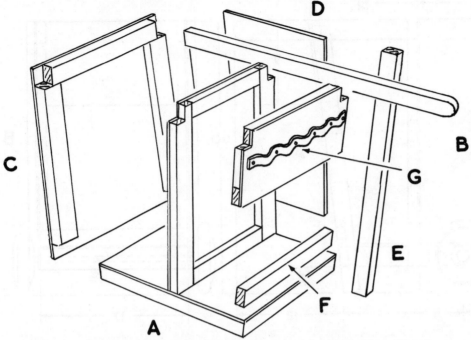

Fig. 11-3. *The trolley parts assemble over the base. Loops will hold small tools.*

7. Drill through for the axle and temporarily put the wheels in position. This positioning will allow you to make and fit the legs (Fig. 11-3E).

8. Put a strip across the bottom (Fig. 11-3F) to prevent tools from slipping off.

9. At the top between the handles and legs, stiffen a piece of plywood to fit inside the legs. After painting the wood, put a strap in loops across this to hold small tools (Fig. 11-3G).

10. Thoroughly paint the wood. Fit the axle and wheels. Put large washers inside the wheels to prevent wear by rubbing on the plywood.

## CYCLE WHEELS CART

Many wheels used on garden carts and similar load carriers have plain bearings and are stiff. Some of your energy is used in overcoming that resistance, but bicycle wheels have some of the easiest running bearings available. Two bicycle wheels will support as big a load as you are likely to want to push. And they will make it easy to push. They can be back or front wheels, complete with their axles and nuts, from an old bicycle. The sizes suggested in this project suit 26-inch wheels, but the method of mounting allows you to fit other sizes with little difficulty.

This cart is intended to be pushed or pulled with a pair of handles, but you can adapt it to suit towing behind a mini-tractor (see next project). It will stand level on its wheels and single leg, but its shape allows it to be tipped forward to empty a load of soil, sand, or stones. If you use wheels of another size, arrange them so the forward edge of the tread is at or forward of the bottom corner of the sloping front. The cart then will tip to bring the front almost flat on the ground (Fig. 11-4).

The main parts are made of plywood framed around with solid wood, but they could be made of solid boards assembled edge-to-edge. If you glue and nail all joints between plywood and solid strips, there should be ample strength with corners glued and screwed.

1. This side view (Fig. 11-5A) is the key shape that governs certain other sizes. The back is upright and the front slopes forward at about 30 degrees. Mark out one side on a piece of plywood, but do not cut it to shape yet. You can use it as a working drawing when making other parts.

2. Make the wheel assemblies first (Fig. 11-6A). These are strip-mild steel. If you have the means of bending it, use sections about 2 inches wide and ¼ inch thick. For easier working, you can come down to ³⁄₁₆ of an inch or even less. Make the width to fit over the axles and the top high enough to clear the tires.

3. Drill the inner sides for bolts that will go through the cart sides (Fig. 11-6B). When you have mounted the wheels, hollow the pads to clear the inner nuts (Fig. 11-6C).

4. Decide on the width you want the cart to be. It can be anything reasonable. Figure 11-5B shows a 25-inch width that is convenient for handling.

5. The assembly is based on framed ends over a bottom (Fig. 11-7). Make the upright end first (Fig. 11-7A), with strips glued and nailed to the outside.

6. Make the sloping end next, in the same way (Fig. 11-7B), using the layout on plywood as a guide to size and angles.

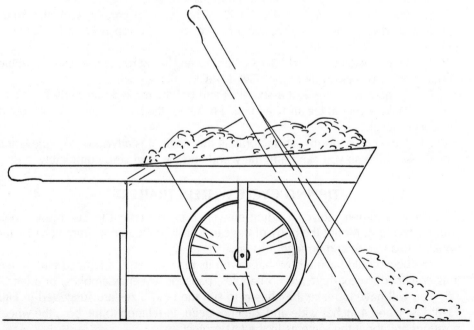

*Fig. 11-4. You can tip a cycle wheel cart to shed its load.*

**Table 11-2. Materials List for
Cycle Wheels Cart.**

**back**

| | | |
|---|---|---|
| 1 piece | 25 × 21 × ½ plywood | |
| 4 pieces | 21 × 2 × 1 | |

**front**

| | | |
|---|---|---|
| 1 piece | 31 × 25 × ½ plywood | |
| 2 pieces | 31 × 2 × 1 | |
| 2 pieces | 21 × 2 × 1 | |

**bottom**

| | | |
|---|---|---|
| 1 piece | 36 × 25 × ½ plywood | |
| 2 pieces | 36 × 2 × 1 | |
| 2 sides | 51 × 36 × ½ plywood | |
| 2 cappings | 54 × 2 × ¾ | |
| 2 cappings | 26 × 1½ × ¾ | |
| 2 handles | 76 × 3 × 1½ | |
| 2 packings | 51 × 5 × 1½ | |
| 1 leg | 18 × 3 × 1½ | |
| 1 leg pad | 9 × 3 × 1 | |
| 2 wheel pads | 18 × 4 × 1 | |
| 2 pieces steel | 48 × 2 × ¼ or ³⁄₁₆ | |

7. Cut the bottom piece of plywood and put stiffeners under its sides (Fig. 11-7C). Its ends will be stiffened by joining front and back.

8. Join the ends to the bottom and add the two sides (Fig. 11-7D).

9. Make the two handles (Fig. 11-7E). They will be parallel with the floor. You will need other pieces above them to strengthen the top plywood edge (Fig. 11-7F).

10. Unprotected plywood edges would suffer during rough use. It is advisable to put capping pieces on all round (Fig. 11-5C).

11. Fit pads for the wheel assemblies and bolt them on temporarily.

12. Make a central leg and pad (Fig. 11-7G) for the back of the cart to support the bottom level.

13. If the cart performs satisfactorily at this stage, it is advisable to remove the wheel assemblies so you can paint the wood and the steel strip completely.

## TIPPING CYCLE WHEELS TRAILER

If you have a mini-tractor or a riding mower, it is convenient to be able to hook your cart on to it. Mount the body of the cart just described on a simple chassis for hooking to a tractor and arrange it to tip.

The body could have a box shape with its top sloping to a tapered end. Make it as described except there are no handles, pads for wheel assemblies, or a leg.

You will have to make the chassis to suit the box. Sizes are suggested in Fig. 11-8. Use wood 4 inches wide and 2 inches deep. In relation to the box, the wheel positions are about the same as in the last project.

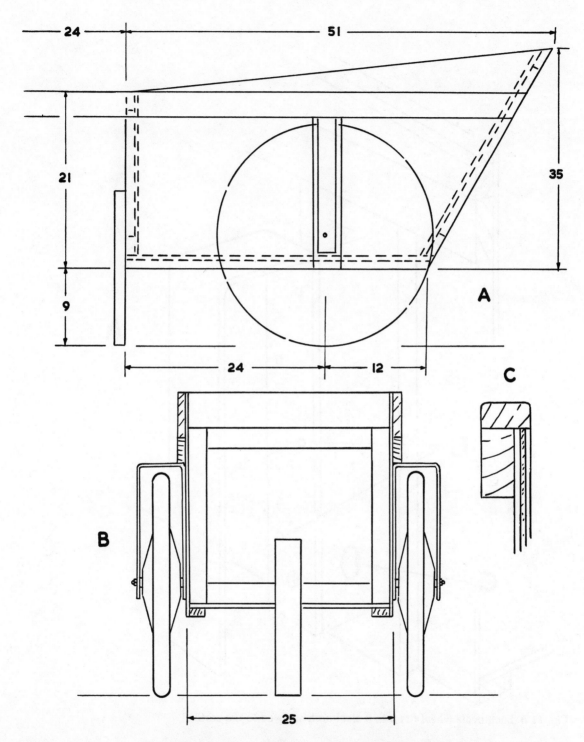

Fig. 11-5. Adjust the cart sizes to suit available wheels.

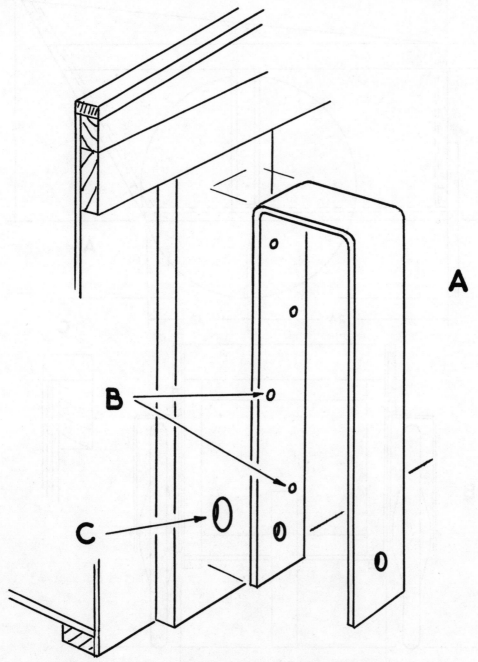

**A**

**B**

**C**

Fig. 11-6. Each cycle wheel fits into a steel arch screwed to the cart.

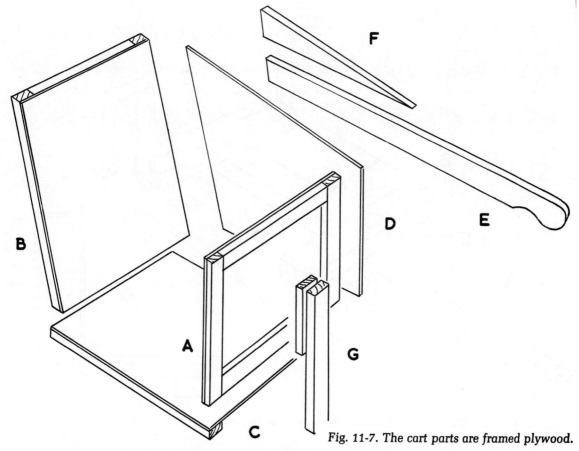

Fig. 11-7. The cart parts are framed plywood.

1. Make the box complete. With that as a guide, mark out the central piece of the chassis (Fig. 11-8A). The end crossbar comes with its center at the wheel position, and the other one (Fig. 11-8B) supports the upright end of the box (with its edge level with it). Bolt these parts securely and squarely together, without projections on top.

2. Place it under the box. A 4-inch-wide strip goes across to come level with the lengthwise strips and locate it over the end chassis members.

3. Fit strong hinges to the chassis (Fig. 11-8C) and to the piece under the box.

4. The wheel assemblies are similar to those on the cart. An exception is that you must extend them under the chassis crossbar (Fig. 11-8D) to which you have

**Table 11-3. Materials List for
Tipping Cycle Wheels Trailer.**

| | |
|---|---|
| Box as in previous project | |
| 1 piece | 58 × 4 × 2 |
| 2 pieces | 27 × 4 × 2 |

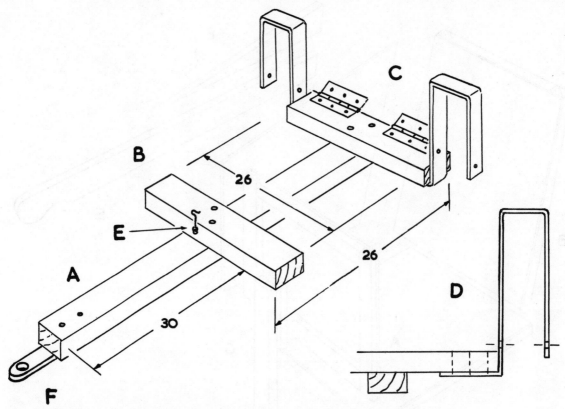

*Fig. 11-8. You can adapt the cycle wheel cart body to mount on this chassis so that you can tow it by a mini-tractor and can tip it.*

bolted them. Keep the bend close to the end of the wood in order to gain stiffness from it. The steel used must be stiff enough because it does not gain strength from the box sides in this case.

5. The box will keep level, due to gravity, but to prevent inadvertent tipping, use a hook and eye (Fig. 11-8E).

6. At the forward end, there must be an attachment to the tractor, and you will have to arrange this to suit. A bar with a hole for a pin is shown in Fig. 11-8F. Crank the bar up or down to suit the level of the tractor attachment.

## WHEELBARROW

A traditional wheelbarrow is the sort of equipment that is almost essential in a yard or garden—from the tiny backyard to property of several acres—even if you have other means of transporting things about. With its single wheel, it will go almost anywhere.

The early wheelbarrow was a very heavy assembly of wood. You can buy light metal alternatives, but they would be difficult to make with the usual home-crafts-man equipment. You can make a barrow with a framed plywood box on a light wood framework.

The important part is the wheel and its axle. It should be a free-running wheel with a 12-inch overall diameter. Many types are possible, and you might be able to buy or recycle something suitable. A tread breadth of about 3 inches will prevent the wheel from sinking in the soil too much. That size wheel will have a hub broad enough to withstand the rocking loads that are sometimes imposed. A wheel with a solid rubber tire is ideal. There could be an iron rim. You could make a solid wooden wheel with several thicknesses laid across each other and glued and screwed together. However, get the wheel and an axle at least 10 inches long before planning the other parts.

Flare the box in all directions. This procedure is complicated by the tapered width of the bottom, to suit the supporting handles, while the rim should be rectangular or nearly so (Fig. 11-9).This design results in outlines of box parts that are odd shapes and different angles. One way of getting over this problem is to make the bottom with parallel sides and have the box sides upright, but that removes some of the advantages of the traditional shape. It is not difficult to make a box with a flare all round (Fig. 11-10) if you work in steps. This shape allows the contents to be tipped forward or sideways without difficulty.

Figure 11-10 shows sizes that will give a reasonable proportion for a light wheelbarrow that should suit the average home garden. Deepen the box if most of your loads are bulky rather than heavy, and increase all sizes if you want to deal with really heavy loads. The drawing is based on a 12-inch wheel.

1. Start with the box; it is made of ½-inch plywood. Work from centerlines to get the bottom and ends symmetrical. Cut the bottom plywood to size (Fig. 11-11A). Frame it around with 1-inch-thick wood, 2 inches wide against the

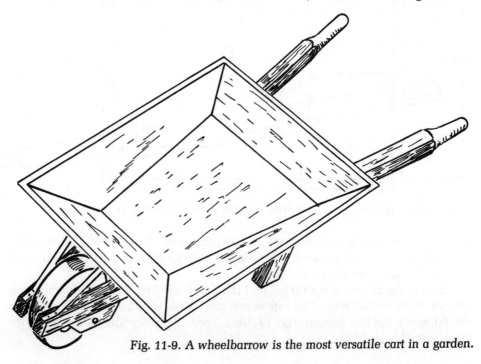

Fig. 11-9. A wheelbarrow is the most versatile cart in a garden.

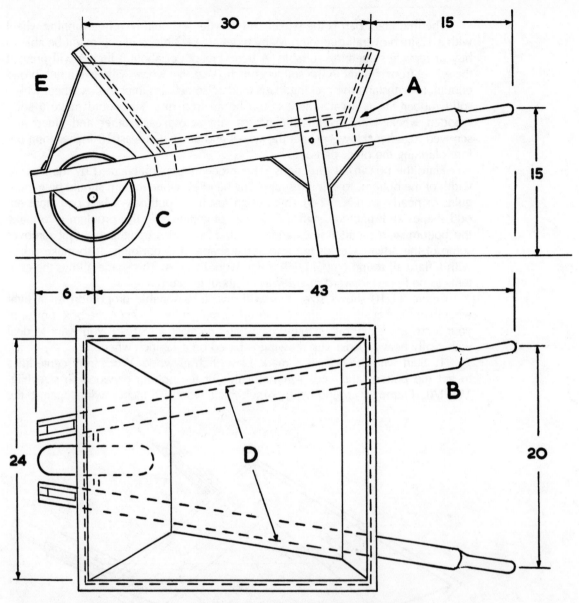

Fig. 11-10. Suggested sizes for a wheelbarrow with a framed plywood body.

plywood. Use nails and waterproof glue. At the ends, bevel at 60 degrees (Fig. 11-11B). Leave the sides square, but keep the nails far enough back from the edge to allow for some beveling there later.

2. Cut the plywood front (Fig. 11-11C) and back (Fig. 11-11D). Frame them around in the same way. The top edges will finish square. The bottom edges should match the box bottom (Fig. 11-10A). Leave the sides square, but allow for them being beveled later.

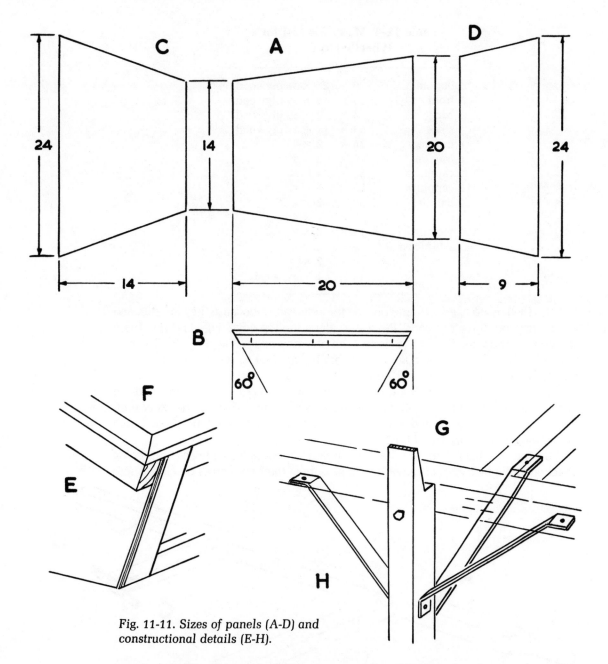

Fig. 11-11. Sizes of panels (A-D) and constructional details (E-H).

3. Join the ends to the bottom temporarily with one screw near each corner. Hold a piece of plywood for one side against this assembly and mark its outline. Check that the other side matches. Cut both pieces of plywood. If you hold a side against the other parts, you can see by their edges, what bevels you need. Plane the bevels. When you have a satisfactory fit, join all the box parts with glue and screws. Plain nails might not be strong enough, but you can use annular ring nails.

### Table 11-4. Materials List for Wheelbarrow.

| | | |
|---|---|---|
| 1 bottom | 20 × 20 × ½ plywood | |
| 1 front | 20 × 14 × ½ plywood | |
| 1 back | 24 × 9 × ½ plywood | |
| 2 sides | 33 × 17 × ½ plywood | |
| 6 framing | 25 × 2 × 1 | |
| 6 framing | 16 × 2 × 1 | |
| 2 cappings | 33 × 1½ × ¾ | |
| 2 cappings | 25 × 1½ × ¾ | |
| 2 handles | 56 × 2 × 2 | |
| 1 bracing | 20 × 2 × 2 | |
| 1 bracing | 14 × 2 × 2 | |
| 2 axle blocks | 9 × 2 × 2 | |
| 2 legs | 18 × 2 × 2 | |
| 8 struts | 14 × 1 × ³/₁₆ steel | |

4.  There is no need to frame outside the side panels because they are stiffened where they join the other parts. Put a strip along the top edge (Fig. 11-11E). There should be a capping all round to protect the plywood edges (Fig. 11-11F). The bottom plywood will be stiff enough as it is, but if you want to reinforce it, there can be another strip across, under its center.

5.  Make the two handles (Figs. 11-10B and 11-12A). Reduce the ends to comfortable round grips; a 1⅛-inch diameter is a suitable size. At the other end, thicken with blocks glued and screwed on to take the axle that will be about 1 inch below the handle strip (Fig. 11-12B).

6.  For very light work, the handles should get enough steadiness from being attached to the box, but it is advisable to give them their own cross bracing. These

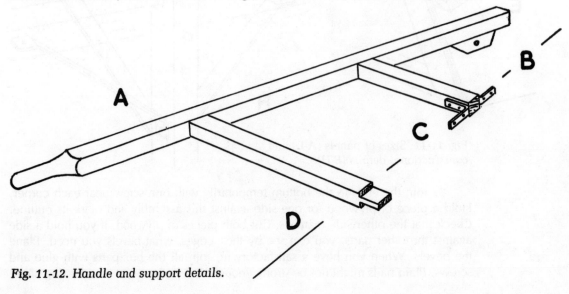

Fig. 11-12. Handle and support details.

are 2-inch-square pieces between the handles and under the ends of the box. You can lay out their lengths and angles by using the box. Invert the box and put the handles in position on it. They should come less than 1 inch in from the sides of the box bottom (Fig. 11-10D).

7. The pieces across could fit between the handle parts and be held with brackets (Fig. 11-12C), but this is a place where mortise and tenon joints are preferable (Fig. 11-12D). If you want to give a traditional appearance, let the tenons project so you can shape their ends.

8. If the axle is a rod through, you can assemble the under frame to the box now and leave it until later. If the axle is part of the hub assembly, drill to suit and fit the wheel now. Attach the box with screws down through the stiffening framing into the handles.

9. Bolt the legs to the handles and extend them up the sides (Fig. 11-11G). Bolting alone will not resist the many loads liable to come on the legs. They should have struts along the handles and to the cross bracing (Fig. 11-11H). Cold strip steel about 1 inch wide and $3/16$ of an inch thick is bent easily in a vise. It should be strong enough.

10. Similar struts can be put between the ends of the wood on each side of the wheel and the top front framing (Fig. 11-10E), but that is not so important. Check the stiffness of the front wood assembly.

11. Trimming the bottoms of the legs to length can be left until you have assembled everything. Then you cut them to get the barrow to the angle you want and the handles to a comfortable height.

12. Finish the wheelbarrow with paint. If you have made all the box joints with waterproof glue, it should be capable of carrying water or any liquid mixtures.

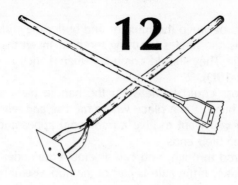

# 12

# Buildings

Y OU CAN STORE TOOLS AND EQUIPMENT IN LOCKERS OR OTHER SMALL CONTAINERS, but in many gardens there is a need for a small building for storage or for use as a greenhouse. It might be possible to build a shed on the side of a house or against a fence, but in many cases, it will have to be a freestanding structure. Building such a shed or greenhouse need not be very complicated, and you do not have all the restrictions that come with building a house. The structure can range from a simple shelter made from available material to a well-finished structure that looks like a smaller counterpart of your house.

Construction is usually of wood, but walls could be partially or completely made of bricks or precast blocks with wood above. It is not usually necessary to include insulation in walls or roof. Many sheds have nothing in the walls except the sheathing that is visible outside. You can treat roofs in a similar way, but they can include two or more layers to ensure weatherproofing.

A fairly large building will have to be built in position, but for sheds of a size often needed in a garden, you can bolt prefabricated panels together on the site. This procedure means you can make the parts in your shop or elsewhere (perhaps when the weather is unsuitable for work outside). It also allows you to take a building apart and move it to another position with minimum trouble.

Several ways are acceptable for covering shed walls. Simplest is to use sheets of exterior plywood or exterior-grade particleboard. This product has a plain appearance (Fig. 12-1A), and contributes more strength to the structure than any type of boarding made up of strips.

Boards laid vertically with battens over the joints (Fig. 12-1B) are more appropriate to barns. You can lay boards so they overlap (Fig. 12-1C) and fit better if they taper in thickness. Shiplap boarding makes a tight, attractive covering (Fig. 12-1D). You can lay tongued-and-grooved boards horizontally or vertically (Fig.

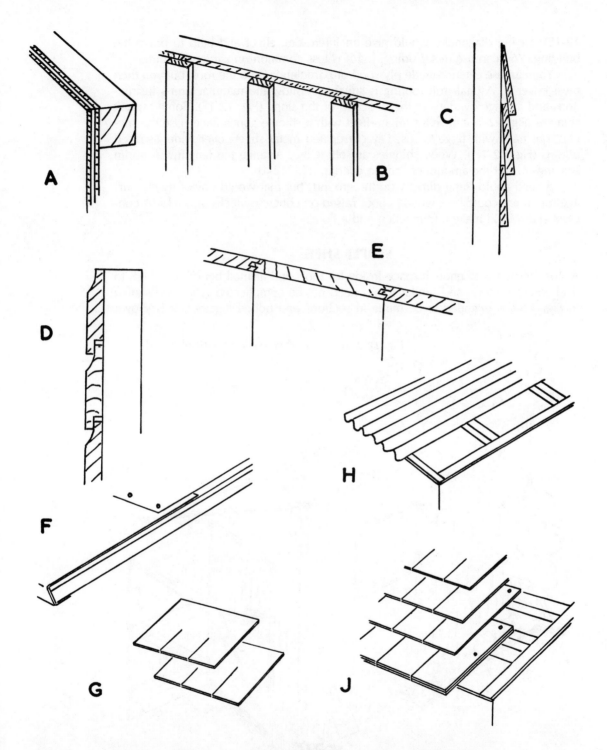

Fig. 12-1. Methods of covering the sides and roofs of garden buildings.

12-1E). Laying diagonally would give an interesting effect and help to brace the building. You can use metal siding, but it is less common on garden buildings.

You can use exterior-grade plywood or particleboard on the roof, but you then must cover it. Asphalt roll roofing is suitable. Follow the manufacturer's instructions and arrange overlaps in the direction of the slope (Fig. 12-1F). Some asphalt shingles (Fig. 12-1G) have a similar effect with a shingle appearance. Use the special roof nails with large heads. Lay corrugated metal sheets over widely-spaced purlins (Fig. 12-1H). Wood shingles are attractive. Arrange the lengthwise purlin spacings to suit the amount of shingle overlap (Fig. 12-1J).

A shed could stand directly on the ground, but that would obviously encourage rot. There could be a wooden floor raised on concrete blocks or bricks. A concrete slab would make a foundation and a floor.

## SIMPLE SHED

A storage shed with enough space inside for tools and a small bench on which to deal with seed trays and similar things need not be complicated. The shed shown in Fig. 12-2 is intended to be made in sections and bolted together. It is shown

Fig. 12-2. A simple shed covered with plywood.

covered with plywood, but you can use any of the other methods of sheathing. There is a wooden floor, but a concrete one would be just as suitable.

1. The sizes suggested in Fig. 12-3A allow you to make the plywood covering with the minimum of joints. You can use the same method for a shed of other sizes adapted to suit your available space. Although this is a freestanding shed, you can make it as a lean-to against an existing wall.

2. Several ways exist for dealing with frame corners. Bridle, or open mortise and tenon, joints might appeal to a craftsman (Fig. 12-4A), but with plywood providing some strength, simple nailing will do (Fig. 12-4B). For that or other covering, you could include a block to give extra nailing surface (Fig. 12-4C). Another way of strengthening for any covering is to nail on triangles of galvanized sheet steel or aluminum (Fig. 12-4D). In general, let uprights overlap horizontal and sloping members.

3. The ends provide the key shapes. Make the back first (Fig. 12-3B). Trim the covering level at the edges. If there is to be a wooden floor, let the plywood extend below the edges, enough to at least partially cover it. If you are using shiplap

### Table 12-1. Materials List for Simple Shed.

| | | | |
|---|---|---|---|
| 2 roof frames | 96 = | 2 × 2 | |
| 4 roof frames | 48 = | 2 × 2 | |
| 6 end frames | 44 = | 2 × 2 | |
| 2 end frames | 84 = | 2 × 2 | |
| 2 end frames | 78 = | 2 × 2 | |
| 4 side frames | 90 = | 2 × 2 | |
| 4 low side frames | 78 = | 2 × 2 | |
| 3 high side frames | 84 = | 2 × 2 | |
| 3 window frames | 28 = | 2 × 2 | |
| 4 window frames | 28 = | 2 × ⅝ | |
| 4 window frames | 28 = | 1 × ⅝ | |
| 2 door frames | 72 = | 3½ × ⅝ | |
| 1 door frame | 31 = | 3½ × ⅝ | |
| 2 door frames | 90 = | 4 × 2 | |
| 4 floor frames | 40 = | 4 × 2 | |
| 6 door boards | 72 = | 5 × ¾ | |
| 3 door ledgers | 30 = | 5 × ¾ | |
| 2 door braces | 48 = | 5 × ¾ | |
| | | | |
| ½ inch plywood: | | | |
| 2 ends | 84 = | 42 | |
| 3 low sides | 78 = | 30 | |
| 1 high side | 84 = | 48 | |
| 1 high side | 84 = | 42 | |
| 1 floor | 86 = | 38 | |
| 1 roof | 96 = | 48 | |

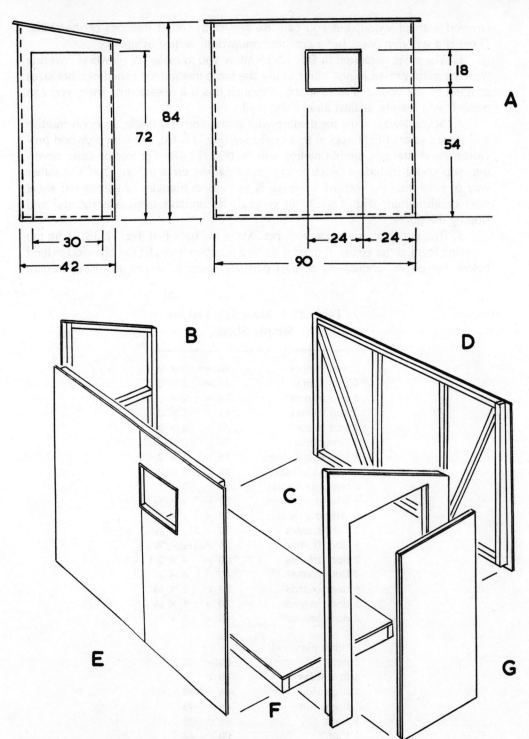

Fig. 12-3. Sizes and assembly of the simple shed.

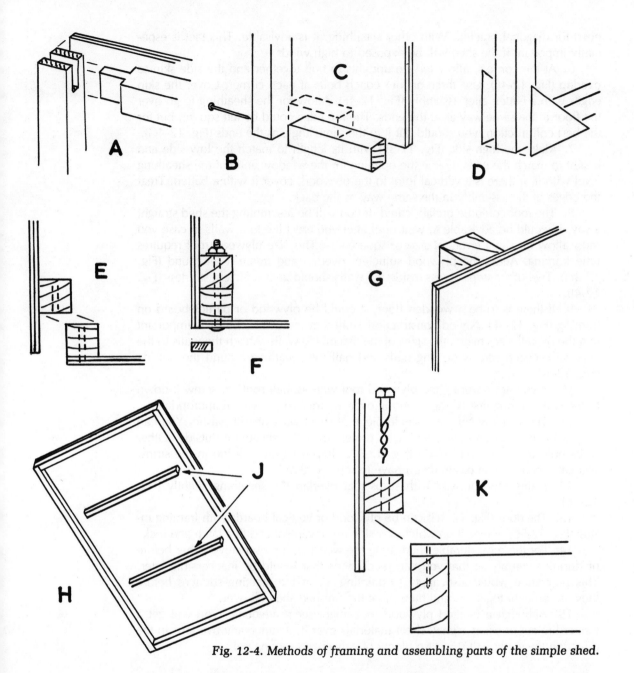

Fig. 12-4. Methods of framing and assembling parts of the simple shed.

boards, allow for the bottom one to go over the edge of the floor, but you do not need to fit it yet.

4. Assemble the other end over the back so that it makes a pair (Fig. 12-3C). Include the framing for the door and check this opening for squareness as you join the strips.

5. Make the low side (Fig. 12-3D). With a plywood skin, there is probably no

need for diagonal bracing. With other sheathing, it is advisable. This fact is especially important if the shed will be exposed to high winds.

6. At the corners, allow for the uprights to bolt together and the side skin to overlap (Fig. 12-4E). Use three or four coach bolts at each corner. Cover the skin edges with a batten after assembly (Fig. 12-4F). Allow for the sheathing to go over the floor in the same way as at the ends. The top edge could be left square, but for the best construction, you should cut it to the same angle as the ends (Fig. 12-4G).

7. Make the high side (Fig. 12-3E) with its length to match the low side and height to match the ends. Frame the opening for the window and cut the sheathing level with it. If there is a vertical joint in the plywood, cover it with a batten. Treat the edges of the assembly in the same way as the back.

8. The roof could be prefabricated. If you will be assembling the shed straight away, it would be advisable to wait until after you erect the four walls in case you must allow for slight errors of size or squareness. This size plywood roof requires little framing. Allow the plywood sufficient overlap and frame it all round (Fig. 12-4H). Two other strips across inside the walls should give sufficient stiffness (Fig. 12-4J).

9. If there is to be a wooden floor, it could be plywood or particleboard on framing (Fig. 12-3F). Nailed construction is all that is needed, but it is important that the overall sizes match the sizes of the assembled walls. Attach the walls to the floor with coach screws or long nails and nail the sheathing around the outside (Fig. 12-4K).

10. If you are covering the plywood roof with asphalt roofing, screw it down to the wall framing first. Wrap covering over the roof edges, where appropriate.

11. The window can be a single piece of sheet glass or stiff plastic. You can fit it with strips around the opening to project over the sheathing outside. Other strips hold the glass from inside (Fig. 12-5A). If you lightly nail the inside strips, you can remove them easily if you have to replace glass.

12. Frame the doorway with strips that overlap the sheathing slightly (Fig. 12-5B).

13. The door (Fig. 12-3G) can be plywood or vertical boards with framing inside (Fig. 12-5C). Hinge it on whichever side is convenient and fit a latch and lock.

14. For the most durable shed, treat the wood with preservative either before or during assembly so that you can reach parts that would be inaccessible later. This procedure would also apply to painting. Paint the meeting surfaces before they are brought together, and then paint the finished shed all over.

15. Although a painted plywood roof might seem adequate, you will get a longer life out of using asphalt sheet materials over it. Arrange any overlaps in the direction the water will run. Use plenty of galvanized roofing nails.

## PLAYHOUSE/SHED

If you have space to build a playhouse, your children will get a lot of satisfaction out of using it, but children grow up and you can reach a stage where a building that is just a playhouse has no further use. If it is a scaled-down size, there is not much you can do with it. If there is space, it is better to start with a building that

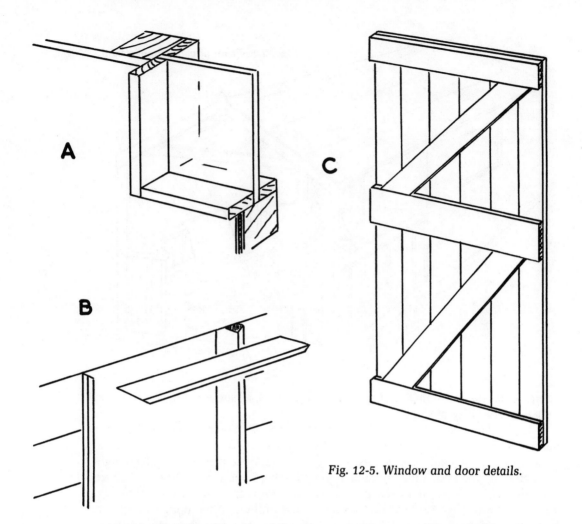

C

B

Fig. 12-5. Window and door details.

can have other uses. That means it should be large enough for adult use. Children will play quite happily in it.

This building shown in Fig. 12-6 has an enclosed part large enough for most adults to stand in and a porch area large enough for them to sit in. The whole thing gives plenty of scope for several children to use. The back is a large, lift-out door. Quite large garden equipment can be put inside for storage, and you can use that end for access even when children are playing at the other end.

The suggested sizes (Fig. 12-7A) allow for cutting plywood sheets with the minimum waste, but covering could be with wood siding or any other means suggested at the beginning of the chapter. The enclosed area is about 7 feet × 8 feet. This area gets natural light through windows at one or both sides and in the front door. The porch extends 5 feet and can have fixed side benches or there is ample space for several chairs. A wooden floor is shown, but the building could go on a concrete slab.

Modifications are easy at the planning stage. Check on available space and

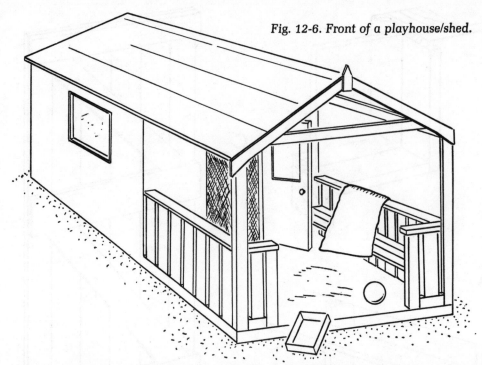

*Fig. 12-6. Front of a playhouse/shed.*

compare access and sitting arrangements to see that they are feasible if you intend to make very different sizes.

1. The key part is the central partition (Fig. 12-7B). You must match the other parts to it; make it first. Most of the wood is 2 inches × 4 inches. Check the actual dimensions; they could be undersized. Five lengthwise pieces should go right through from one end of the building to the other (without joints if possible). There is a ridge (Fig.12-7C) and two eaves (Fig. 12-7D), with other pieces at the side (Fig. 12-7E) and foot (Fig. 12-7F). You can notch them fully into the uprights, but it is better to cut a small amount (⅝ inch is suitable) out of the long piece and more out of the upright (Fig. 12-8A). At the ridge, nail the rafters against the lengthwise piece (Fig. 12-8B). Include a central upright piece over the door.

2. At the eaves, notch the lengthwise piece into the upright. Then arrange the rafter to fit over the upright (Fig. 12-8C). The piece above the door should have its underside level with the eaves (Fig. 12-8D). Nail it to the rafter.

3. With all the partition parts prepared, assemble them on two sheets of plywood that meet over the central upright. It is advisable to use plywood for this partition even if you are covering the outside with shiplap or other boarding. Assemble with glue and nails. Be careful to keep the doorway sides parallel. If the plywood needs stiffening, put pieces across the side panels at half door height. Use this assembly as a pattern for making other parts.

4. For the back of the shed, make an assembly to the same overall sizes as the partition. Alter the door opening to almost full width (Fig. 12-9A). Unless you absolutely need the maximum door width to get your equipment in, it is advisable to have a little width left on each side of the doorway for the sake of stiffness.

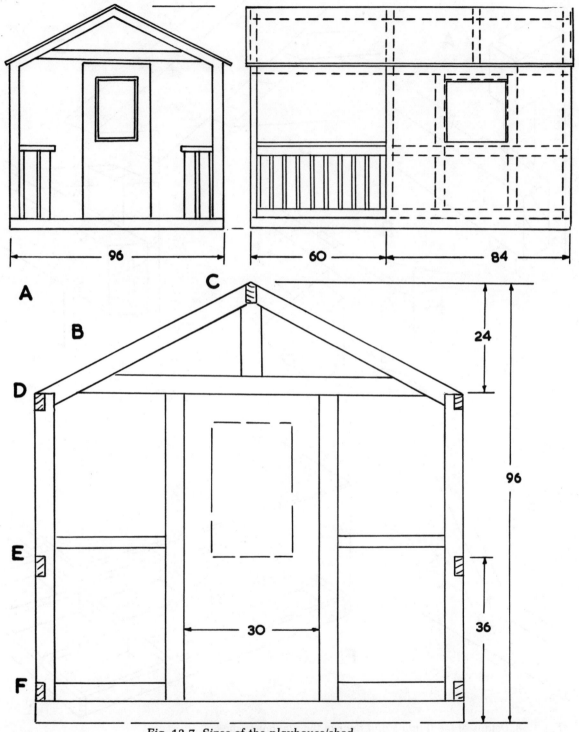

Fig. 12-7. Sizes of the playhouse/shed.

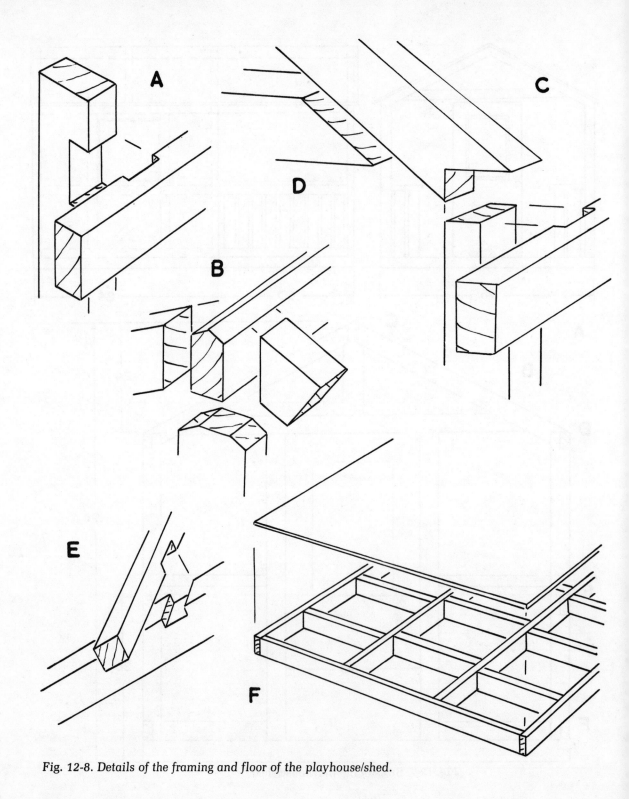

Fig. 12-8. Details of the framing and floor of the playhouse/shed.

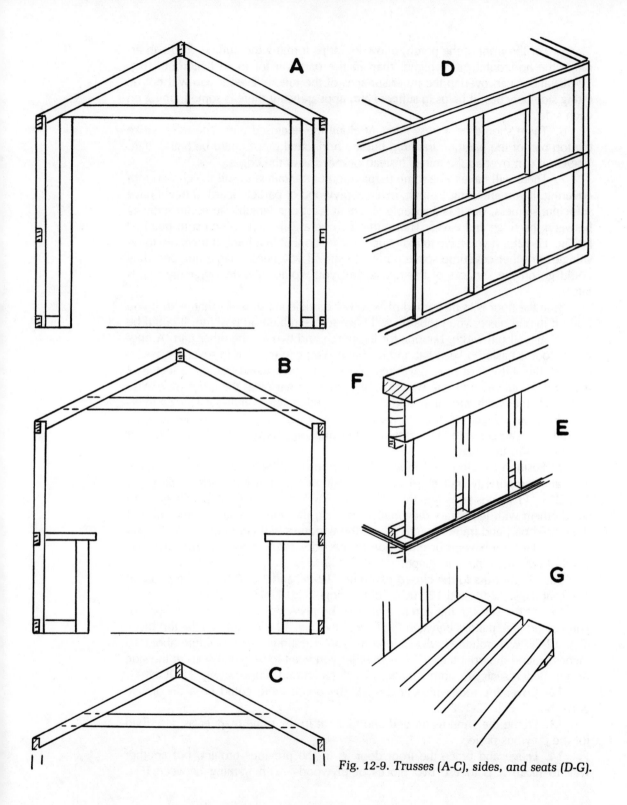

Fig. 12-9. Trusses (A-C), sides, and seats (D-G).

5. For the front of the porch, allow for strips forming the outline. You can arrange the horizontal piece higher than in the partition for more headroom (Fig. 12-9B) and it can overlap the inner surfaces of the rafters. Even if you will not be fitting side benches, it helps in stiffness and appearance if there is some framing on each side.

6. There should be a truss midway along the enclosed part. The truss is like the top part of the partition framing, but the horizontal piece could be higher (Fig. 12-9C). It can overlap the rafters instead of meeting at the edges.

7. There will have to be some preparation of the rafters to suit the chosen roof covering. If you are using ½-inch, exterior-plywood or particleboard, it might have sufficient stiffness, but it is advisable to use at least one lengthwise purlin midway between the ridge and eaves. That purlin can be a 2-inch- × -2-inch strip notched in (Fig. 12-12E). If you have to make up lengths, do that in a joint. If there are to be shingles or other covering, space purlins to suit. If you need a large number, they could go on the surfaces of the rafters, but you would have to cover their ends later.

8. If the floor is to be framed plywood or particleboard, make that next. If you build it in one piece, you probably will have to assemble it in position. It could be in sections, all full width, but one for the porch and two for the other part. A one-piece floor is easier to keep flat and in shape. You can frame it in several ways.

For the stiffness of most covering, you should not exceed framing 2 feet × 2 feet or the equivalent (if one way is longer, make it narrower the other way). You can divide the width into three, and then pieces fitted across at about 18 inch intervals. You can stagger meetings to make nailing easier (Fig. 12-8F). Make sure the overall width agrees with the partition and its matching parts, but you can allow for slight errors in the length.

9. Position the floor and mount the partition and back on it. Check squareness and temporarily nail these parts in position. Put the long side strips (Figs. 12-7D, E, F) in position. See that the main parts are upright. You will have to steady them with temporary diagonal struts. Add the other uprights to the sides of the closed part and frame around where the windows will come (Figs. 12-9D and 12-10A). Fit the plywood or other skin to the sides of the building. This plywood will hold the main parts in shape.

10. Fit the truss to the closed part (Figs. 12-9C and 12-10B) and the porch at the front (Figs. 12-9B and 12-10C). Put the ridge (Fig. 12-7C) in place.

11. At the sides of the porch, there can be plywood closing the lower part or you can arrange palings between the long strips (Fig. 12-9E). Arrange the top piece (Fig. 12-9F) with rounded edges along the rail. Continue this procedure about 18 inches around the front (Fig. 12-7A) whether you want to fit bench seats at the side or not. Bench seats are simply made with strips on end supports (Fig. 12-9G).

12. Cover the roof with shingles. At the porch there could be a decorative barge board (Fig. 12-10D).

13. Frame the window around and glaze it in the same manner as described for the previous project.

14. Ledge and brace the front door as in the previous project, but another way to make it is to use two pieces of plywood—with framing between (Fig.

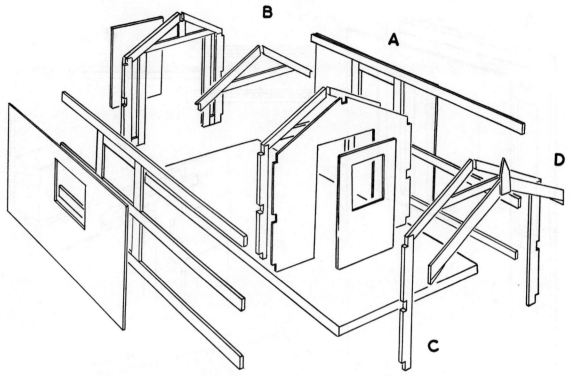

*Fig. 12-10. The subassemblies of the playhouse/shed.*

12-11A). Make sure there is solid wood where the hinges, lock, and window come. You can let the plywood edges be exposed or cover them with thin strips. Frame around for the window and hold the glass in with strips (Fig. 12-11B).

15. The back door could be a frame covered with plywood or shiplap boards and then hinged at one side, but it is rather wide and heavy for that support. You can make it as a pair of doors hinged at both sides and meeting at the middle. Another way is to make it like a single door (Fig. 12-11C), but arrange for it to lift out when you want to get large equipment in or out.

Projections on the bottom can fit into slots in the floor (Fig. 12-11D). Bolts and a stop inside the top will hold it up (Fig. 12-11E) and you cannot open from outside.

## GREENHOUSE

An enthusiastic gardener needs a greenhouse. It could be a small lean-to against a wall or a freestanding one of any size. The example shown in Fig. 12-12 is a project about as small as you could reasonably use. You can adapt the method of contruction for a freestanding greenhouse of almost any size. You can glaze it to the ground, but it is shown with shiplap boards to bench height. There is a door at one end, with a low ventilation flap, and another ventilator is high in the opposite end.

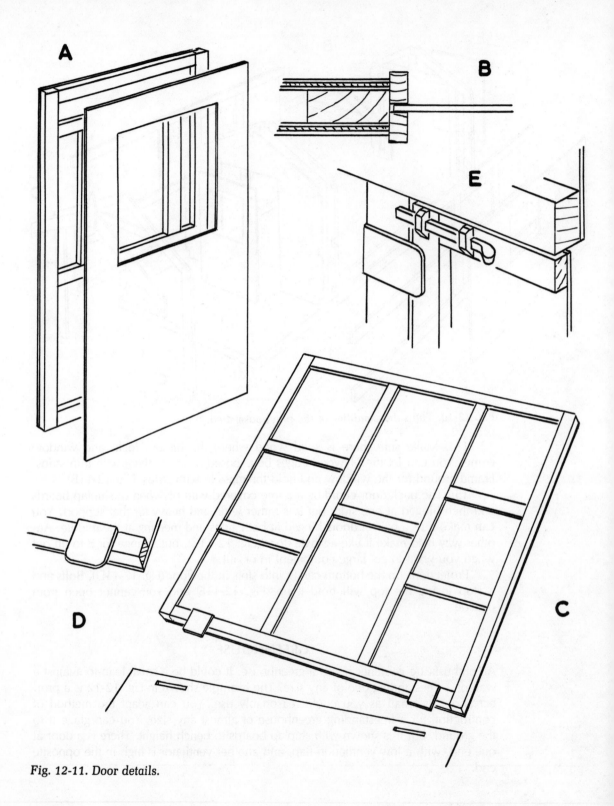

Fig. 12-11. Door details.

Fig. 12-12. A greenhouse with the lower part boarded.

Much of the structure is made from 2-inch-square wood, and with 2-inch-×-4-inch wood where you need extra strength. There is a sill all around, above the lower boarding. Putty in the glass. Some modern glazing compounds, however, are better than traditional putty. You can cut glass to approximate squares and overlap it as it is set in putty. The wood could have rabbets cut in it for the glass, but it is simple to nail on strips of about 1-inch-×-¾-inch section (Fig. 12-14A).

The main sizes (Fig. 12-13) allow a door with sufficient headroom and a roof sloping at about 30 degrees.

1. Using Fig. 12-13 as a guide, make the door end. The pieces on each side of the door and the strip above it should be 4 inches thick, but all other parts are 2 inches square. You can just nail corners and other joints, but notching in allows nailing both ways (Fig. 12-15A, B). Above the door, locate the strip with shallow grooves (Fig. 12-15C). At the sill level, notch the strip in to the door and corner posts (Fig. 12-15D). Leave at least 2 inches extra at the corner to be mitered or fitted to the side sills during assembly.

2. Assemble the door end (Fig. 12-16A) with the shiplap boards cut level.

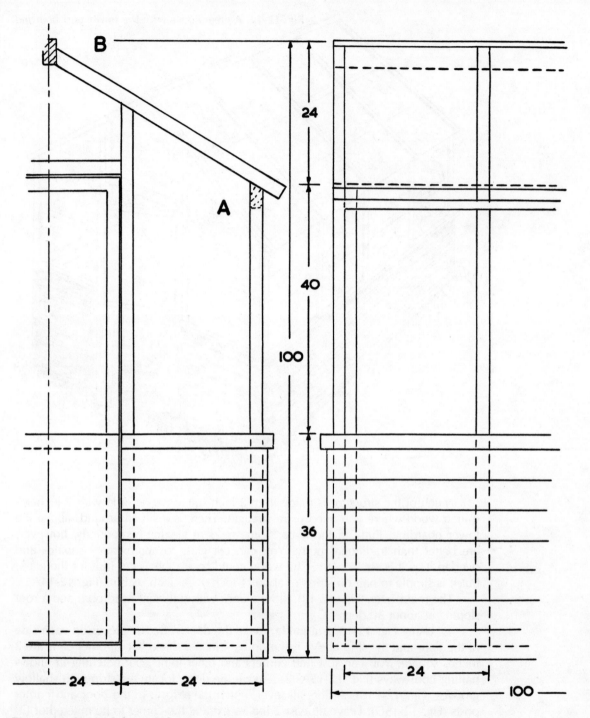

Fig. 12-13. Sizes of the greenhouse.

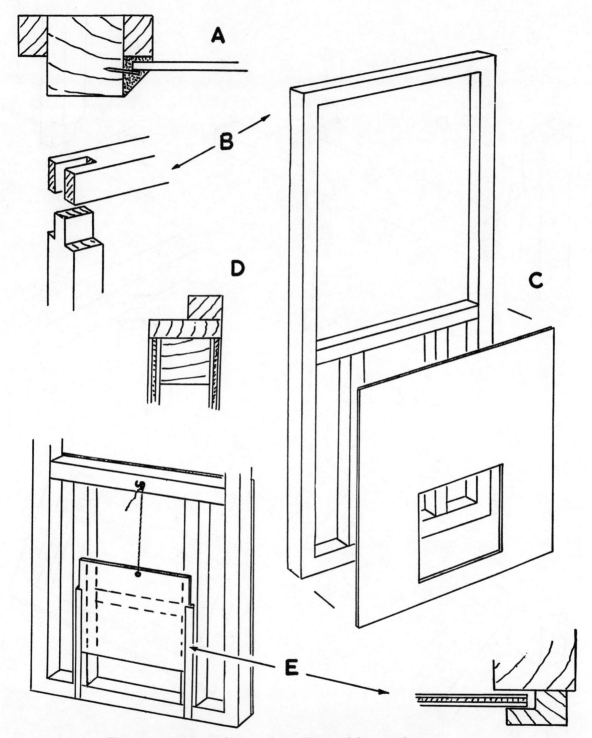

Fig. 12-14. Framing, door, and ventilators of the greenhouse.

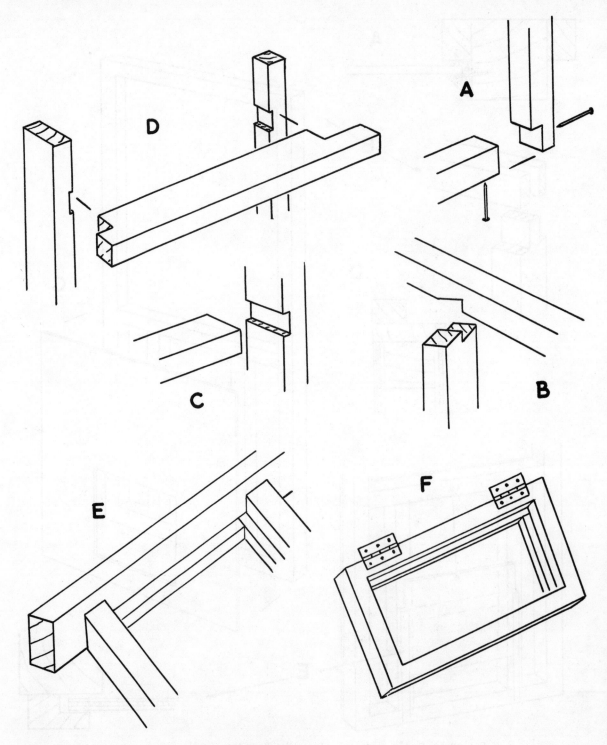

Fig. 12-15. Joints in the upper part of the greenhouse.

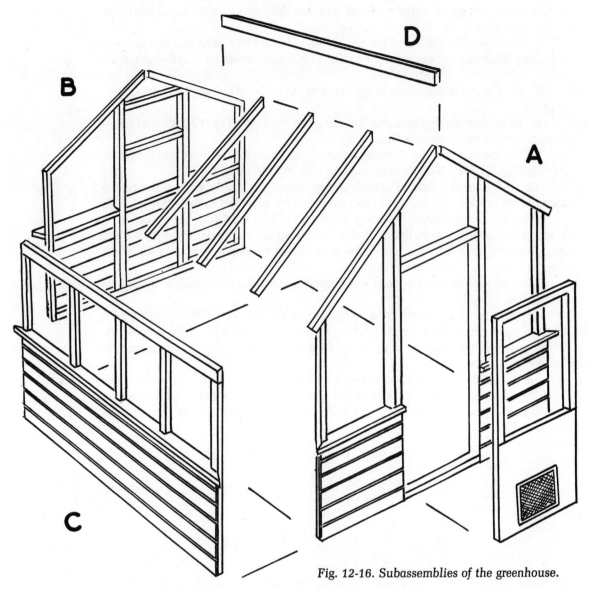

*Fig. 12-16. Subassemblies of the greenhouse.*

3. Use this end as a guide when making the opposite end (Fig. 12-16B). It all can be made with 2-inch-square wood. Put an extra piece at the top between the uprights to support the ventilator. At sill level, take one piece right across and do the same with the shiplap boards.

4. The sides are identical. At the eaves, prepare 4-inch pieces at an angle to suit the roof (Fig. 12-13A). All other parts, except the sills, are 2 inches square. Make up the two sides (Fig. 12-16C). Use corner joints as suggested for the ends. Fit the sills level with the inside surfaces of the uprights and with a little extra at each end.

5. There could be a wooden floor, as suggested for earlier projects, or the

greenhouse could go on a concrete slab. In some situations it could stand on bricks or rammed gravel.

6. Assemble the sides and ends with bolts through the ends that overlap the side uprights. Miter the corners of the sills. Check squareness by measuring diagonals.

7. Fit a 4-inch-deep ridge (Figs. 12-13B and 12-16D) into the tops of the ends.

8. Make roof glazing bars that are nailed to the ridge (Fig. 12-15E) and overhang the eaves by about 4 inches.

9. For the high ventilator, make a frame with strips for the glass and hinges at the top (Fig. 12-15F). It can swing outward and be held by a stay.

10. The door is made of 2-inch-square strips, preferably with glued bridle joints at the corners (Fig. 12-14B), and covered with plywood to the sill level (Fig. 12-14C). You can make a sill to cover the plywood (Fig. 12-14D), but do not let it extend because that would interfere with the house sill and prevent the door from swinging very far. When you mount the door, bevel the end of the sill beside it on the hinge side to allow more movement.

11. The ventilator in the door is an opening with wire mesh over it and a flap inside (Fig. 12-14E).

12. Nail on strips where the glazing is to come (Fig. 12-14A), including over the eaves and across the ridge. Except for the final coat, paint all of the woodwork before glazing. Nongloss paint in the rabbets will help the glazing compound to bond to the wood.

13. Glaze the sides and roof from the bottom up so that joints in the glass will have their overlaps downward. Locate the glass in the putty with fine pins or headless nails that you will putty over. Let the eaves glass overhang to the ends of the wooden bars.

# Glossary

The making of outdoor tools and equipment forms only part of the crafts of woodworking and metalworking. The selection of words that follows are some that are particularly appropriate to the subjects of this book, and might be helpful to readers unfamiliar with the language of craftwork.

**aggregate**—Stone, gravel, or sand used with cement to make concrete.
**alloy**—A substance composed of one or more chemical elements, at least one of which is metal. Brass is an alloy of copper and zinc.
**anchor bolt**—Bolt set in concrete with its threaded end projecting.
**annealing**—Softening metal. To anneal steel, it is heated to redness and cooled slowly.
**apex**—The top or peak of a roof.

**backfill**—Fill in excavation around a post or foundation.
**barrel bolt**—Sliding door fastener.
**batten**—Narrow strip of wood.
**beam**—A horizontal, load-bearing structural member.
**blind**—Not right through, such as a stopped hole.
**brass**—An alloy of copper and zinc.
**brazing**—Joining parts by flowing a thin layer of nonferrous filler metal in the space between them. This procedure is ordinarily done at temperatures above 800 degrees F. At lower temperatures the process is called soldering.
**bridging**—Wood fitted between joists to spread load.
**butt**—End to end.

**carriage bolt**—Bolt with shallow round head and a square neck.

**cast**—Pour metal or concrete into a mold. Twisting of a surface that should be flat.

**cement**—Fine powder, which is the active ingredient of concrete when mixed with sand and stones with water.

**check**—Split in wood in direction of grain.

**cleat**—Strip of wood used as a support or a brace across other wood.

**clench** (clinch)—Turning over the extending end of a nail.

**concrete**—Mixture of sand, cement, aggregate, and water.

**conversion**—The general term for cutting a log into boards and smaller pieces of wood for use.

**counterbore**—Let the head of a screw or bolt below surface.

**countersink**—Set the screw or bolt head level with the surface.

**course**—Row of stones, bricks, or shingles.

**dado**—Groove cut across the grain of a board.

**dead pin**—A wedge or dowel.

**drift**—Tapered punch used to drive through holes to bring them in line.

**eaves**—Overhang of roof over wall or an angle between them.

**feather edge**—Thinned edge of a piece of wood.

**ferrule**—Metal tube at end of handle to reduce risk of splitting when a tool tang is driven in.

**float**—Flat wooden tool for smoothing surface of concrete.

**footing**—Masonry or concrete form to support wall.

**foundation**—Support in ground for a structure.

**foxiness**—Sign of the first onset of wood rot.

**frost line**—Depth frost is expected to penetrate into soil.

**gable**—Vertical end of a building with inverted V end of roof.

**galvanized iron**—Iron or mild steel coated with zinc as protection against rust.

**girder**—Wood or metal beam.

**glazing**—Glass pane. Fitting a glass pane.

**glazing compound**—Sealing and glass-setting compound as alternative to traditional putty.

**grade**—A slope (gradient).

**grout**—Thin mortar to pour into cracks.

**gusset**—Wood or metal joint cover.

**haft**—Long handle of hammer or similar tool.

**handed**—Made as a pair.

**hardware cloth**—Woven steel mesh.

**jamb**—Side or head lining of window or door.

**joggle**—Offset double bend in a strip of metal.

**kerf**—Slot made by a saw.

**lag screw**—Large wooden screw with head for a wrench.
**laying out**—Setting out the details of design and construction.
**ledger**—Strip of wood fitted in position to support board ends.
**level** (spirit level)—Instrument to determine horizontal direction.
**lintel**—Support for a load over an opening.

**mild steel**—Iron with a small amount of carbon content.
**mortar**—Sand, cement, and water mixture used to bond bricks and stones.

**particleboard**—Board made by bonding wood chips with a synthetic resin.
**pegging**—Dowels or wooden pegs through joints.
**pier**—Masonry column.
**pilot hole**—A small hole used as the guide for a drill point when making a larger hole.
**pitch**—Slope of roof. Distance between tops of a screw thread.

**quartered** (quartered sawn)—Board cut radially from a log.

**rabbet** (rebate)—Angular notch in the side of a piece of wood, as letting in glass.
**rail**—A horizontal framing member.
**retaining wall**—Supporting wall subject to lateral pressure.
**riddle**—Sand or soil sifter.
**ridge**—Top or apex of roof where sloping sides meet.
**rive**—To split wood.
**roll roofing**—Roof covering consisting of felt impregnated with asphalt.
**run**—Lumber quantity can be described as so many feet run.

**sash**—Frame containing a pane of glass.
**screw**—A screw for wood has a tapered thread, but a bolt with its thread almost to the head is also a screw.
**seasoning**—Drying out wood to an acceptable low level of sap.
**shake**—Natural crack in wood that develops in the tree.
**shank**—Neck or part of a tool between the handle and the blade.
**sheathing**—A covering such as plywood over a frame.
**shiplap**—Boards rabeted to fit into each other.
**siding**—Covering for outside of a framed structure.
**sill**—Lowest member of a frame construction or of an opening.
**slat**—Narrow thin wood.
**span**—Distance between supports.
**splay**—To spread.
**spud**—Chisel-like tool for removing bark.
**square**—Besides an equal-sided rectangle, this also means corners at 90 degrees.

**steel**—Iron alloyed with carbon. With the correct proportions it can be hardened and tempered.

**stringer**—Support for cross members, as at the sides of stairs.

**stud**—Vertical support in a wall.

**tang**—The tapered end of a tool, such as a file or chisel, to fit into a handle.

**template** (templet)—Pattern to be used to check or mark pieces to be cut or drilled.

**tines**—Prongs, as in a fork.

**toe nailing**—Nailing diagonally where the end of one piece of wood meets another.

**tongue and groove**—Board edges meeting with a projection on one fitting a groove in the other.

**truss**—Structural members joined to provide strength and shape, as in a roof truss.

**vent**—Arrangement in a wall or roof to allow air to flow through.

**waney**—Edge of board showing shape of outside of log.

**warping**—Going out of shape as wood dries.

**winding**—Board twisting in its length.

# Index

**A**

adaptable hoe, 96
alloys, iron and steel, 15-16
aluminum, 22
annealing, iron and steel, 16-18
arbors
    center poles, 182
    large, 177
    rose, 179
    wall-supported, 184

**B**

bean poles, 190
bending metal (see conical developments)
bird protectors, 89
board tool box, 130
bolts, 9, 24
boxes and bins, 110-146
    handles for, 114
    joints and nailing for, 113
    window box, 125
brass, 20
brazing, 1, 20-21
buildings, 218-238
bulb planter, 102

**C**

carts, 202-217
center pole arbor, 182
chests, 130-133
climbing supports, 171-201
compost bin
    permanent, 143
    sectional, 74, 139
    stacking, 140
conical developments, metal, 24-27
containers, 3, 110
copper, 20
cotter pins, 24
cycle-wheel cart, 206

**D**

display equipment, 147-170
door detail, 225, 232
dowels, edge joints using, 12, 13
Dutch hoe, 58, 59

**E**

edge joints, 11-14
edger, turf, 93
edgings, 88
end supports, shelving, 151
expanding wood trellis, 172

**F**

fences, wire support-type, 196
ferrules, 33, 34
flat hand fork, 45
flooring, 228
forks
    flat hand, 45
    twisted tine, 48
formal raised trough, 163
framing, 223, 228
freestanding wall shelves, 151

**G**

garden trolley, 203
gilding metals, 21
glass and glazing, 231
glues, 5-6, 9, 11
grape arbor, 177
greenhouse, 231

**H**

hand hoe, reversible, 100
hand tools, special usage, 93-109
handles, 28-41
    boxes and bins, 114
    carved and shaped, 39
    ferrules for, 33, 34
    fitting to tools, 33-35
    metal, 35-37
    rounding end of, 32
    rounding square stock for, 30-32
    short, 37
    tangs for, 33, 34
    tapering, 30
    tubing for, 35
    turning, 33, 37, 39, 40
    wood, cutting, 29
hanging pot holders, 124, 126, 128
hard solder, 20

hardboard, 5
hardening, iron and steel, 16, 19
hardwoods, 4
high-carbon steel, 16
hoes
    adaptable, 96
    blade shapes for, 66-68
    Dutch, 59
    one-hand Dutch, 58
    onion, 54
    push-pull, 62
    reversible hand, 100
    simple, 52
    weeding, 63
hook tool, 100, 106

**I**

iron and steel, 15-19

**J**

joints, 9-14

**K**

kneeler, 83, 85
knife, paving stone weeder, 102

**L**

large arbor, 177
lathes, 1-2
lead, 21
line winders, 70, 72
locker, tool, 136
low-carbon steel, 16
lumber (see wood)

**M**

machine screws, 6
metal, 1, 15-27
    conical developments for, 24-27
    fasteners for, 24
    iron and steel, 15-19
    nonferrous, 20-22
    rivets for, 22-24
    tool handles of, 35-37
metal line winder, 72
metal-thread screws, 6

mild steel, 15-16
mortise-and-tenon joint, 9-11

## N
nailed plant pot container, 121
nails, 6-9
    edge joints using, 13-14
nonferrous metals, 20-22
nuts, 24-25

## O
one-hand Dutch hoe, 58
onion hoe, 54

## P
paling pot container, 165
paving stone hook and knife, 100, 102
pergola, 186
permanent compost bin, 143
planing, 30
planishing, copper, 20
plant pot container, 118, 121
plant stand, slatted, 157
planters
    formal raised trough, 163
    hanging pot holder, metal, 124
    hanging pot holder, plywood, 128
    hanging pot, wood, 126
    paling pot container, 165
    pot container, 118
    pot container, nailed, 121
    rustic trough, 160
    stacking seed boxes, 79
    take-down trough, 168
    wall box, 123
    window box, 115
playhouse/shed, 224
plywood, 5
plywood hanging pot holder, 128
plywood tool box, 133
push-pull hoe, 62

## R
raised rustic trough, 160
rakes
    simple, 56
    wood-and-nails, 107
reversible hand hoe, 100
ridger, 103

riveting, 1, 22-24
rod hanging pot holder, 124
roofing, 219
rose arbor, 179
row markers, 86
rust, 16
rustic trough planter, raised, 160

## S
screws, 6-9
    edge joints using, 13-14
    metal fastening, 24
seasoning wood, 4
secret slot screwing, 14
sectional compost bin, 74, 139
seed boxes, stacking, 79
seed drill tool, 69
set tool, rivets and, 22
shed, simple, 220
shelves
    end supports for, 151
    freestanding wall, 151
    slatted, 157
    step-type, 155
    wall-mounted, 148
siding, 219
silver solder, 21
simple equipment, 70-92
slatted plant stand, 157
slot screwing, 12-14
small hand tools, 42-69
socketed trowel, 45
softwoods, 4
solder, 20-21
special hand tools, 93
spelter, 20
square line, 75
stacking compost bin, 140
stainless steel, 16
step-type shelves, 155
supported arbor, 184

## T
take-down trough stand, 168
tangs, 33, 34
tapering, 30
tempering, iron and steel, 17-19
thistle hook, 106
tin, 21
tipping cart, 208
tomato poles, 193

tool box, 78
    board, 130
    plywood, 133
    vertical locker-type, 136
tool carrier, kneeler and, 85
tool steel, 16
trellis
    expanding wood, 172
    supports for, 175
    tomato, 193
    wire supports, 196
trolley, 203
troughs
    formal, 163
    paling, 165
    rustic, 160
    take-down, 168
trowel, 43
    socketed, 45
trusses, 229
tubing, handles from, 35
turf edger, 93
turnbuckles, 200
tusk tenons, 11
twisted tine fork, 48

## V
ventilator, greenhouse, 235
vertical tool locker, 136

## W
wall box, 123
wall shelves, 148
wall-supported arbor, 184
weeder, 50
weeding hoe, 63
welding, 1
wheelbarrow, 212
window box, 115, 125
window detail, 225
wire supports, 196
wood, 4-6
    joints for, 9-14
wood screws, 6
wood turning, 2
wood-and-nails rake, 107
wooden hanging pot holder, 126
wooden line winder, 70

## Z
zinc, 20